GUAM

HOW TO INVEST, START AND RUN PROFITABLE BUSINESS IN GUAM GUIDE

PRACTICAL INFORMATION, OPPORTUNITIES, CONTACTS

International Business Publications, USA
Washington DC, USA

GUAM

HOW TO INVEST, START AND RUN PROFITABLE BUSINESS IN GUAM GUIDE

PRACTICAL INFORMATION, OPPORTUNITIES, CONTACTS

UPDATED ANNUALLY

Cover Design: **International Business Publications, USA**

We express our sincere appreciation to all government agencies and international organizations which provided information and other materials for this guide

2015 Updated Reprint International Business Publications, USA
ISBN 978-14330-8348-8

This guide provides basic information for starting or/and conducting business in the country. The extraordinary volume of materials covering the topic, prevents us from placing all these materials in this guide. For more detailed information on issues related to any specific investment and business activity in the country, please contact Global Investment Center, USA
Please acquire the list of our business intelligence and marketing guides and other business publications. We constantly update and expand our business intelligence and marketing materials. Please contact the center for the updated list of guides on over 200 countries.

in the USA: **Global Investment Center, USA.**
P.O.Box 15343, Washington, DC 20003
Phone: (202) 546-2103, Fax: (202) 546-3275, E-mail: rusric@erols.com

For additional analytical, marketing and other information please contact Global Investment Center, USA

Printed in the USA

GUAM

HOW TO INVEST, START AND RUN PROFITABLE BUSINESS IN GUAM GUIDE

PRACTICAL INFORMATION, OPPORTUNITIES, CONTACTS

TABLE OF CONTENTS

STRATEGIC AND DEVELOPMENT PROFILES

STRATEGIC PROFILE

Capital		Hagåtña
Largest village		Dededo
Official languages		English Chamorro
Ethnic groups		37.1% Chamorro 26.3% Filipino 11.3% Pacific 9.8% Mixed 6.9% White 6.3% other Asian 2.3% other
Demonym		Guamanian
Government		Representative democracy
-	President	Barack Obama (D)
-	Governor	Eddie Calvo (R)
-	Lt. Governor	Raymond Tenorio (R)
-	Delegate	Madeleine Bordallo (D)
Legislature		Legislature of Guam
		Area
-	Total	541.3 km^2 (194th) 209 sq mi
-	Water (%)	negligible
		Population
-	2010 census	159,358
-	Density	320/km^2 (37th) 830/sq mi
GDP (PPP)		2010 estimate
-	Total	$4.6 billion
-	Per capita	$28,700
HDI (2008)		▲0.901 very high
Currency		United States dollar (USD)
Time zone		Chamorro Standard Time (UTC+10)
Calling code		+1-671
ISO 3166 code		GU
Internet TLD		.gu
		Website Guam.gov

Guam (/□□w□□m/ or /□□w□m/; Chamorro: *Guåhån*) is an organized, unincorporated territory of the United States in the western Pacific Ocean. It is one of five U.S. territories with an established civilian government. Guam is listed as one of seventeen Non-Self-Governing Territories by the Special Committee on Decolonization of the United Nations. The island's capital is Hagåtña (formerly rendered Agana). Guam is the largest and southernmost of the Mariana Islands.

The Chamorros, Guam's indigenous people, first populated the island approximately 4,000 years ago. The island has a long history of European colonialism, beginning with its discovery for Europe by Ferdinand Magellan during a Spanish expedition on March 6, 1521. The first colony was established in 1668 by Spain with the arrival of settlers including Padre San Vitores, a Catholic missionary. For more than two centuries Guam was an important stopover for the Spanish Manila Galleons that crossed the Pacific annually. The island was controlled by Spain until 1898, when it was surrendered to the United States during the Spanish–American War and later formally ceded as part of the Treaty of Paris.

Guam is the largest island in Micronesia and was the only U.S.-held island in the region before World War II. Guam was captured by the Japanese on December 8, 1941, just hours after the attack on Pearl Harbor, and was occupied for two and a half years. During the occupation, the people of Guam were subjected to acts that included forced labor, torture, beheadings, and rape, and were forced to adopt the Japanese culture. Guam was subject to fierce fighting when U.S. troops recaptured the island on July 21, 1944, a date commemorated every year as Liberation Day.

Today, Guam's economy is supported by its principal industry, tourism, which is composed primarily of visitors from Japan. Guam's second largest source of income is the United States Armed Forces.

Background:	Guam was ceded to the US by Spain in 1898. Captured by the Japanese in 1941, it was retaken by the US three years later. The military installation on the island is one of the most strategically important US bases in the Pacific.

GEOGRAPHY

Location:	Oceania, island in the North Pacific Ocean, about three-quarters of the way from Hawaii to the Philippines
Geographic coordinates:	13 28 N, 144 47 E
Map references:	Oceania
Area:	total: 549 sq km land: 549 sq km water: 0 sq km
Area - comparative:	three times the size of Washington, DC
Land boundaries:	0 km
Coastline:	125.5 km
Maritime claims:	exclusive economic zone: 200 NM territorial sea: 12 NM
Climate:	tropical marine; generally warm and humid, moderated by northeast trade winds; dry season from January to June, rainy season from July to December; little seasonal temperature variation

Terrain:	volcanic origin, surrounded by coral reefs; relatively flat coralline limestone plateau (source of most fresh water), with steep coastal cliffs and narrow coastal plains in north, low-rising hills in center, mountains in south
Elevation extremes:	lowest point: Pacific Ocean 0 m highest point: Mount Lamlam 406 m
Natural resources:	fishing (largely undeveloped), tourism (especially from Japan)

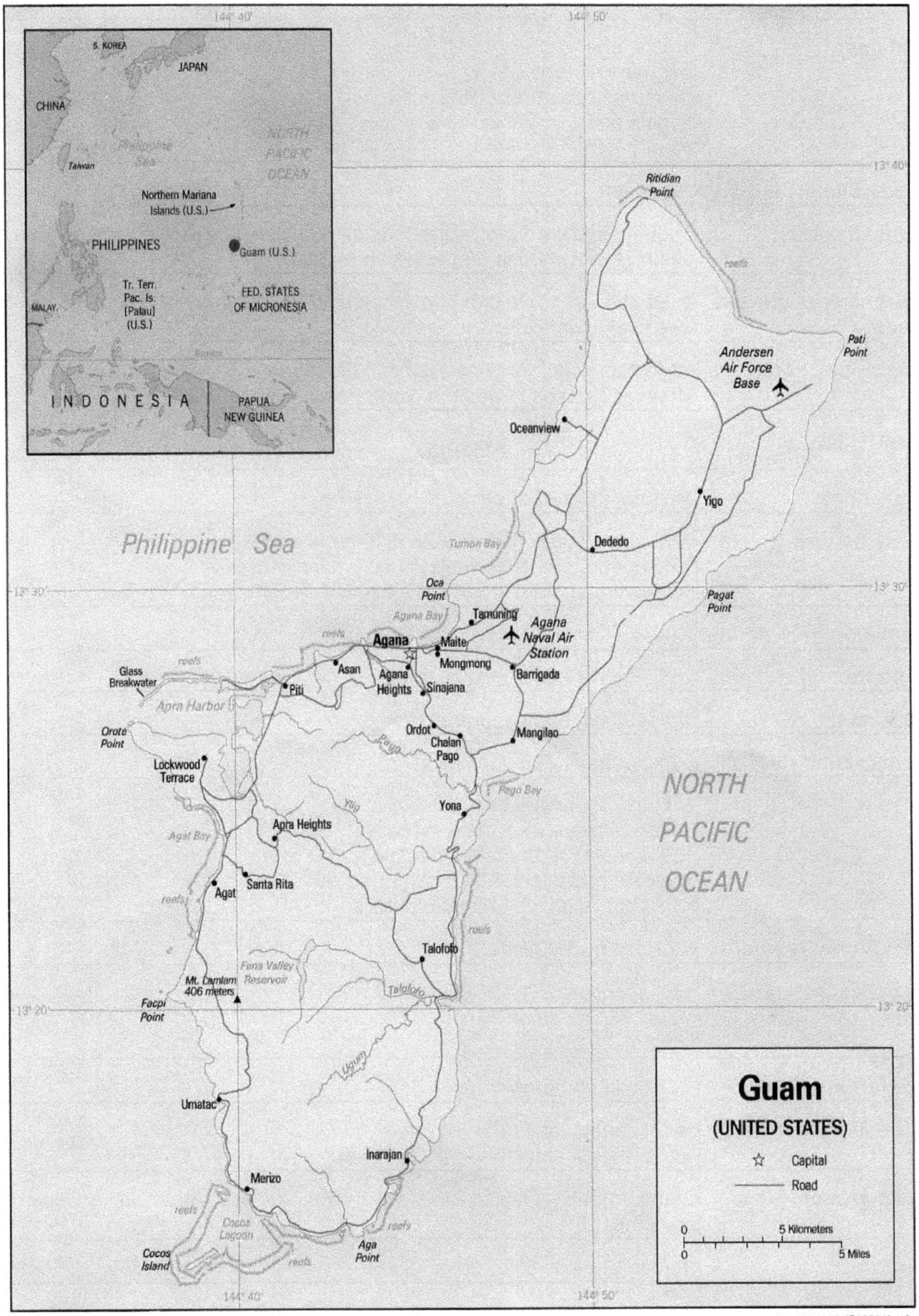
S. KOREA
JAPAN
CHINA
Taiwan
Philippine Sea
NORTH PACIFIC OCEAN
Northern Mariana Islands (U.S.)
PHILIPPINES
Guam (U.S.)
Tr. Terr. Pac. Is. [Palau] (U.S.)
FED. STATES OF MICRONESIA
MALAY.
INDONESIA
PAPUA NEW GUINEA
Philippine Sea
NORTH PACIFIC OCEAN
Ritidian Point
Pati Point
Andersen Air Force Base
Oceanview
Yigo
Dededo
Tumon Bay
Oca Point
Pagat Point
Tamuning
Agana Bay
Agana Naval Air Station
Agana
Maite
Mongmong
Barrigada
Glass Breakwater
Asan
Agana Heights
Sinajana
Piti
Apra Harbor
Orote Point
Ordot
Chalan Pago
Mangilao
Lockwood Terrace
Pago Bay
Yona
Apra Heights
Agat Bay
Santa Rita
Agat
Talofofo
Fena Valley Reservoir
Mt. Lamlam 406 meters
Facpi Point
Umatac
Inarajan
Merizo
Cocos Lagoon
Cocos Island
Aga Point
Guam
(UNITED STATES)
Capital
Road
5 Kilometers
5 Miles
Base 801622 (E00281) 1-91

Land use:	arable land: 11% permanent crops: 11% permanent pastures: 15% forests and woodland: 18% other: 45% (1993 est.)
Irrigated land:	NA sq km
Natural hazards:	frequent squalls during rainy season; relatively rare, but potentially very destructive typhoons (especially in August)
Environment - current issues:	extirpation of native bird population by the rapid proliferation of the brown tree snake, an exotic species
Geography - note:	largest and southernmost island in the Mariana Islands archipelago; strategic location in western North Pacific Ocean

PEOPLE

Population:	157,557 (July 2001 est.)
Age structure:	0-14 years: 35.07% (male 28,978; female 26,270) 15-64 years: 58.78% (male 48,704; female 43,902) 65 years and over: 6.15% (male 4,871; female 4,832)
Population growth rate:	2.09%
Birth rate:	25.07 births/1,000 population
Death rate:	4.2 deaths/1,000 population
Net migration rate:	0 migrant(s)/1,000 population
Sex ratio:	at birth: 1.14 male(s)/female under 15 years: 1.1 male(s)/female 15-64 years: 1.11 male(s)/female 65 years and over: 1.01 male(s)/female total population: 1.1 male(s)/female
Infant mortality rate:	6.71 deaths/1,000 live births
Life expectancy at birth:	total population: 77.94 years male: 75.66 years female: 80.55 years
Total fertility rate:	3.85 children born/woman
Nationality:	noun: Guamanian(s) adjective: Guamanian
Ethnic groups:	Chamorro 47%, Filipino 25%, white 10%, Chinese, Japanese, Korean, and other 18%
Religions:	Roman Catholic 85%, other 15%
Languages:	English, Chamorro, Japanese

Literacy:	definition: age 15 and over can read and write total population: 99% male: 99% female: 99%

GOVERNMENT

Country name:

conventional long form: Territory of Guam
conventional short form: Guam
local long form: Guahan
local short form: Guahan

Dependency status:

organized, unincorporated territory of the US with policy relations between Guam and the US under the jurisdiction of the Office of Insular Affairs, US Department of the Interior

Government type:

NA

Capital:

name: Hagatna (Agana)
geographic coordinates: 13 28 N, 144 44 E
time difference: UTC+10 (15 hours ahead of Washington, DC, during Standard Time)

Administrative divisions:

none (territory of the US)

Independence:

none (territory of the US)

National holiday:

Discovery Day, first Monday in March (1521)

Constitution:

effective 1 July 1950; amended many times, last in 2012 (2013)

Legal system:

common law modeled on US system; US federal laws apply

Suffrage:

18 years of age; universal; note - Guamanians are US citizens but do not vote in US presidential elections

Executive branch:

chief of state: President Barack H. OBAMA (since 20 January 2009); Vice President Joseph R. BIDEN (since 20 January 2009)
head of government: Governor Eddie CALVO (since 3 January 2011); Lieutenant Governor Ray TENORIO (since 3 January 2011)
cabinet: heads of executive departments; appointed by the governor with the consent of the Guam legislature
elections: under the US Constitution, residents of unincorporated territories, such as Guam, do not vote in elections for US president and vice president; however, they may vote in Democratic and Republican presidential primary elections; governor and lieutenant governor elected on the same ticket by popular vote for a four-year term (can serve two consecutive terms, then must wait a full term before running again); election last held on 2 November 2010 (next to be held in November 2014)
election results: Eddie CALVO elected governor with 50.6% percent of vote against 49.4% for Carl GUTIERREZ; Ray TENORIO elected lieutenant governor

Legislative branch:

unicameral Legislature (15 seats; members elected by popular vote to serve two-year terms)
elections: last held on 6 November 2012 (next to be held in November 2014)
election results: percent of vote by party - NA; seats by party - Democratic Party 9, Republican Party 6
note: Guam elects one nonvoting delegate to the US House of Representatives; election last held on 6 November 2012 (next to be held in November 2014); results - percent of vote by party - NA; seats by party - Democratic Party 1

Judicial branch:

highest court(s): Supreme Court of Guam (consists of 3 justices)
note - appeals beyond the Supreme Court of Guam are heard by the US Supreme Court
judge selection and term of office: justices appointed by the governor and confirmed by the Guam legislature; justices appointed for life subject to retention election every 10 years
subordinate courts: Superior Court of Guam - includes several divisions; US Federal District Court for the District of Guam (a US territorial court; appeals beyond this court are heard before the US Court of Appeals for the Ninth Circuit)

Political parties and leaders:

Democratic Party [Carlo BRANCH]
Republican Party [Mike BENITO]

Political pressure groups and leaders:

Guam Commission on Decolonization

Guam Federation of Teachers' Union
Guam Waterworks Authority Workers
We Are Guahan

International organization participation:

IOC, PIF (observer), SPC, UPU

Diplomatic representation in the US:

none (territory of the US)

Diplomatic representation from the US:

none (territory of the US)

Flag description:

territorial flag is dark blue with a narrow red border on all four sides; centered is a red-bordered, pointed, vertical ellipse containing a beach scene, a proa or outrigger canoe with sail, and a palm tree with the word GUAM superimposed in bold red letters; the proa is sailing in Agana Bay with the promontory of Punta Dos Amantes, near the capital, in the background; blue represents the sea and red the blood shed in the struggle against oppression
note: the US flag is the national flag

National symbol(s):

coconut tree

National anthem:

name: "Fanohge Chamoru" (Stand Ye Guamanians)
lyrics/music: Ramon Manalisay SABLAN [English], Lagrimas UNTALAN [Chamoru]/Ramon Manalisay SABLAN
note: adopted 1919; the local anthem is also known as "Guam Hymn"; as a territory of the United States, "The Star-Spangled Banner," which generally follows the playing of "Stand Ye Guamanians," is official (see United States)

ECONOMY

Economy - overview:

The economy depends largely on US national defense spending, tourism, other services. Total US grants, wages and salaries, and procurement outlays amounted to approximately $1.6 billion. Over the past 30 years, tourism has grown to become the largest income source following national defense.

GDP (purchasing power parity):

$4.6 billion
country comparison to the world: 173

GDP (official exchange rate):

$4.6 billion

GDP - real growth rate:

1.3%
country comparison to the world: 168

GDP - per capita (PPP):

$28,700
country comparison to the world: 54

Agriculture - products:

fruits, copra, vegetables; eggs, pork, poultry, beef

Industries:

national defense, tourism, construction, transshipment services, concrete products, printing and publishing, food processing, textiles

Labor force:

69,390
country comparison to the world: 186
note: this number is for the civilian labor force only

Labor force - by occupation:

agriculture: 0.3%
industry:
services: NA%

Unemployment rate:

8.2%
country comparison to the world: 92

Population below poverty line:

23%

Budget:

revenues: $942.6 million
expenditures: $1.082 billion

Taxes and other revenues:

20.5% of GDP
country comparison to the world: 160

Budget surplus (+) or deficit (-):

-3% of GDP
country comparison to the world: 122

Fiscal year:

1 October - 30 September

Inflation rate (consumer prices):

4%
country comparison to the world: 139

Exports:

$44 million
country comparison to the world: 198

Exports - commodities:

transshipments of refined petroleum products, construction materials, fish, food and beverage products

Imports:

$901 million
country comparison to the world: 180

Imports - commodities:

petroleum and petroleum products, food, manufactured goods

Exchange rates:

the US dollar is used

ENERGY

Electricity - production:

1.734 billion kWh
country comparison to the world: 140

Electricity - consumption:

1.635 billion kWh
country comparison to the world: 145

Electricity - exports:

0 kWh
country comparison to the world: 144

Electricity - imports:

0 kWh
country comparison to the world: 152

Electricity - installed generating capacity:

552,000 kW
country comparison to the world: 134

Electricity - from fossil fuels:

100% of total installed capacity
country comparison to the world: 16

Electricity - from nuclear fuels:

0% of total installed capacity
country comparison to the world: 98

Electricity - from hydroelectric plants:

0% of total installed capacity
country comparison to the world: 174

Electricity - from other renewable sources:

0% of total installed capacity
country comparison to the world: 180

Crude oil - production:

0 bbl/day

country comparison to the world: 176

Crude oil - exports:

0 bbl/day
country comparison to the world: 121

Crude oil - imports:

0 bbl/day
country comparison to the world: 194

Crude oil - proved reserves:

0 bbl
country comparison to the world: 139

Refined petroleum products - production:

0 bbl/day
country comparison to the world: 151

Refined petroleum products - consumption:

14,490 bbl/day
country comparison to the world: 145

Refined petroleum products - exports:

0 bbl/day
country comparison to the world: 182

Refined petroleum products - imports:

6,579 bbl/day
country comparison to the world: 138

Natural gas - production:

0 cu m
country comparison to the world: 138

Natural gas - consumption:

0 cu m
country comparison to the world: 152

Natural gas - exports:

0 cu m
country comparison to the world: 110

Natural gas - imports:

0 cu m
country comparison to the world: 200

Natural gas - proved reserves:

0 cu m
country comparison to the world: 145

Carbon dioxide emissions from consumption of energy:

1.103 million Mt

COMMUNICATIONS

Telephones - main lines in use:

67,000
country comparison to the world: 157

Telephones - mobile cellular:

98,000
country comparison to the world: 193

Telephone system:

general assessment: modern system, integrated with US facilities for direct dialing, including free use of 800 numbers
domestic: digital system, including mobile-cellular service and local access to the Internet
international: country code - 1-671; major landing point for submarine cables between Asia and the US (Guam is a transpacific communications hub for major carriers linking the US and Asia); satellite earth stations - 2 Intelsat (Pacific Ocean)

Broadcast media:

about a dozen TV channels, including digital channels; multi-channel cable TV services are available; roughly 20 radio stations

Internet country code:

.gu

Internet hosts:

23

country comparison to the world: 219

Internet users:

90,000
country comparison to the world: 163

TRANSPORTATION

Airports:

5
country comparison to the world: 182

Airports - with paved runways:

total: 4
over 3,047 m: 2
2,438 to 3,047 m: 1
914 to 1,523 m: 1

Airports - with unpaved runways:

total: 1
under 914 m:
1

Roadways:

total: 1,045 km
country comparison to the world: 185

Ports and terminals:

major seaport(s): Apra Harbor

MILITARY

Manpower fit for military service:

males age 16-49: 38,358
females age 16-49: 36,869

Manpower reaching militarily significant age annually:

male: 1,701
female: 1,608

Military - note:

defense is the responsibility of the US

TRANSNATIONAL ISSUES

Disputes - international:

none

IMPORTANT INFORMATION FOR UNDERSTANDING GUAM

Guam is the largest and southernmost island in the Northern Mariana Archipelago. It is approximately 24 miles long with an average width of 4 miles wide, encompassing 212 square miles. Short flights to all major markets in the Pacific Rim make Guam the best location in the Western Pacific to conveniently and affordably meet your international travel needs.

GOVERNMENT

***Local*:** The island of Guam is an incorporated area of the United States with effective self-government. The Organic Act of Guam adopted in 1950 provides for the protection of fundamental rights and freedoms of the individual; for the making of laws through a Legislative Branch; the Executive Branch led by an elected Governor; and the Judicial Branch as the administrator of the laws. These three (3) branches of government allow for an equal balance of power.

The Legislative Branch consists of a unicameral legislature with 15 members elected for two-year terms. These officials are responsible for creating laws to protect the community and promote its development.

Guam's judicial branch decides issues of local laws and interprets how these laws should be applied. The judiciary consists of two bodies - a Superior Court and the recently established Supreme Court of Guam.

Finally, the executive branch is managed by the island's highest elected officials - the governor and lieutenant governor of Guam. These officials implement Guam's laws through the departments, bureaus, committees and agencies that make up the Government of Guam.

Federal: The United States government also maintains a presence on the island. As set out in the Organic Act of Guam, the government of Guam shares, but in most instances defers, its authority and duties in certain areas of governing our island to the federal government. The existence of an elected government and the presence of the United States government create a secure and stable political climate.

ECONOMY

With a Gross Island Product of $3 billion plus annually, Guam boasts a stable and diverse economy. With more than 1.4 million visitors annually, tourism constitutes the island's number one industry. Other key industries include transshipment, telecommunications, fisheries, and financial services.

POPULATION

The current estimated population is 145,881, inclusive of active military personnel and dependents, who total 15,523. Guam's indigenous people, Chamorros, represent the largest ethnic group on the island at 43%. Filipinos account for 23%, Caucasians for 14% and the remainder includes Korean, Japanese, Chinese and other Pacific Islanders.

CLIMATE

Guam's tropical climate is pleasantly warm throughout the year with a mean annual temperature of 81 degrees Fahrenheit. For more information about Guam's weather forecast see the United States Weather Service Forecast Office and Chicken Little's Weather Page of Guam.

GUAM VISA WAVIER PROGRAM

This program allows residents of 16 nations to travel to Guam, as tourists or to conduct business, for a maximum stay of 14 days without having to obtain a visa. Countries currently covered by this program include: Japan, Korea, Taiwan, Australia, Brunei, Burma, Indonesia, Malaysia, Nauru, New Zealand, Papua New Guinea, Singapore, the Solomon Islands, United Kingdom (including Hong Kong), Vanuatu, and Western Samoa. All other visitors must conform to U.S. passport and visa requirements. Check the Guam Visitors Bureau web site for details.

BUSINESS INFRASTRUCTURE

Communication: Guam possesses the most advanced telecommunication infrastructure in this region. Fiber-optic cables that traverse the floor of the Pacific Ocean converge on Guam, making it a telecommunications hub for many international service providers, and regional headquarters for information telecommunications giants like MCI, AT&T and Sprint.

Financial Services: With more than 16 banks with affiliates from America, Asia, and Europe, all of the conveniences of modern banking are available to conduct financial transactions with virtually every corner of the globe. Other support services existing on Guam include major stock brokerage firms and expansive legal and accounting services.

Offshore Banking: The absence of federal income taxes, and the fact that interest earned by banks through the operation of an offshore lending facility in Guam is not treated as a Guam-source income for tax purposes are also powerful incentives for investment.

Postal Services: Private courier services are also available for off-island deliveries. The U.S. Postal Service is the main air and surface parcel carrier on island with numerous satellite offices.

WAY OF LIFE

Guam's small island community provides for a warm and friendly atmosphere. This island tradition, called the **"*Hafa A'dai spirit,*"** is found throughout. You will find it in our business services as well as our public sector. You will find our government representatives, including our Governor, accessible. This accessibility extends to regulators, government officials and throughout the business community.

LAND USE:

arable land: 11%
permanent crops: 11%
meadows and pastures: 15%
forest and woodland: 18%

other: 45%
Irrigated land: NA sq km

SOCIETY AND CULTURE

Perhaps one of the last real "melting pots" in the world, the cultural melange of Guam's many ethnic and social communities provide flavor and variety in every aspect of daily life.

From the charming local vendors at the picturesque Chamorro Village open market to international students at the University of Guam, the island is alive with a unique feeling created by many varied languages, customs, cuisine and cultures.

Predominant in Guam's cultural mix are:

Chamorros (the indigenous people of Guam - 40 %)
Filipino (20%)
Caucasian (10 %)
Japanese (5%)
Chinese (5%)

Local European, East Indian, Korean and Australian natives also brighten the island's cultural landscape.

An average day for anyone living on Guam provides many opportunities to dip into the nuances of foreign influence. Expansive marble hotel lobbies bustling with foreign visitors, locals and visitors sharing a seaside barbecue in a handmade hut, high-powered international negotiations in a boardroom overlooking the Philippine Sea... all happen each and every day on Guam.

Perhaps the most alluring gift Guam has to offer is the gentle spirit of her native people -- the Chamorros. As fierce warriors and hunters who lived in highly socialized villages in ancient times, the Chamorro people have built a proud heritage based on strong familial ties, a strong sense of sharing, commitment to hard work and religious faith that is still very much alive today.

EDUCATION

There are 36 public schools, 21 private schools, a community college and four-year accredited university on Guam which are patterned after school systems in the continental United States. Public schools are accredited by the Western Association of Schools and Colleges. Learn more about Guam's public school from the Guam Department of Education's web site: www.doe.edu.gu

Post Secondary Level Guam Community College (GCC):

Established in 1977 and accredited by the Western Association of Schools and Colleges, GCC offers more than 40 courses of study.

By recognizing its role in the economic prosperity of the community and staying abreast of business trends, the college responds to the predominant training needs of the region by developing new and innovative educational programs.

Programs at the college are intended to meet the many educational needs and interests of the community and include: accounting, supervision and management, information systems, computer science, construction trades, architectural engineering technology, civil engineering technology, criminal justice, electro-mechanical trades, horticulture, early childhood education, cosmetology, sign language interpreting, marketing, automotive technology, food and beverage operations, hotel operations, travel agency management, tour operations management, waterworks technology and the apprenticeship training program.

GCC also offers a variety of community service and special programs including English as a second language, adult basic education, general education development preparation and testing, and an adult high school diploma program. The college runs a comprehensive vocational high school program on its campus and offers vocational classes in all of Guam's public high schools.

University of Guam (UOG):

Founded as the Territorial College of Guam in 1952, this institution was granted its charter as the University of Guam in 1968. It is a land-grant institution accredited by the Western Association of Schools and Colleges.

The student body is made up of representatives from more than 40 countries in the Asia-Pacific Region and around the world. Enrollment in the five colleges, as well as those programs under the center for continuing education and outreach, is now more than 7,000 students and continues to grow.

The University's English Language Institute offers courses in English as a second language throughout the year, the primary purpose of which is to prepare non-English speakers to attend American universities.

There are four research units operating on campus. The Micronesian Area Research Center houses the island's best source of photographs and thousands of documents from the Spanish era, and other regional sources. The Marine Laboratory is recognized internationally and holds a collection of more than 20,000 specimens. UOG's Water and Energy Research Institute is considered by the U.S. government as one of the top five programs in the nation for work in this field. Finally, the Micronesian Language Institute is dedicated to the research, teaching and service on the indigenous languages of the region.

In addition, the university's spacious recreational complex (the University of Guam Fieldhouse) provides an excellent facility for indoor concerts, sports competitions, trade shows and other special events.

HEALTH CARE

Guam's health care system includes two major hospitals, a widespread clinic network, a broad selection of general and specializing physicians, and well-run medical evacuation operations to Hawaii, the U.S. mainland and the Philippines.

Guam's two hospital facilities are the Naval Regional Medical Center and the Guam Memorial Hospital. While the Naval hospital provides services to veterans, active-duty personnel and military dependents, Guam Memorial Hospital provides health care for the remainder of the general public. The Guam Memorial Hospital is a publicly-owned facility operated as part of the Government of Guam system.

The public hospital has a 192 bed capacity; 159 acute care beds and 33 long-term care beds. The hospital also has 16 newborn bassinets that accommodate more than 3,000 births per year.

All customary acute care services (adult and pediatric medical services, neonatal, pediatric and adult intensive care services) and skilled nursing care are provided. Guam Memorial Hospital is capable of providing for the basic and specialized health needs of our community and the region.

The hospital provides a host of diagnostic and therapeutic services to both inpatients and outpatients, including:

laboratory and blood bank services
dietary services
radiology; nuclear medicine and CT scan diagnostic services
pharmaceutical services
respiratory care and cardiopulmonary services
hemodialysis
physical, occupational, recreational and speech therapy
pastoral care services
social services
patient education

24-hour emergency operation Guam has seven speciality and emergency care clinic systems, more than 150 physicians, 28 dentists, 6 personal and family counselors and 11 optical centers. More than 20 pharmacies are availabe for perscription drug needs, and 9 insurance plans provide local residents with health-care coverage.

HOUSING

Guam offers a wide variety of housing options, from ocean view villas and executive homes with top-of-the-line ammenities to cozy condominiums, duplexes and homes well-suited for new and growing families.

Housing for purchase or lease on Guam is readily available. Construction costs range from $72 to $90 or more per square foot (depending on quality) giving an average three-bedroom house price of approximately $160,000. Mortgage loan funds are readily available from institutional lenders.

The rental market indices show two-bedroom units renting from $600 to $800 per month and three-bedroom units renting from $800 to $1,200 and up, depending on location and amenities.

GOVERNMENT AND POLITICAL SYSTEM

Guam is governed by a popularly elected governor and a unicameral 15-member legislature, whose members are known as senators. Guam elects one non-voting delegate, currently Democrat Madeleine Z. Bordallo, to the United States House of Representatives. U.S. citizens in Guam vote in a straw poll for their choice in the U.S. Presidential general election, but since Guam has no votes in the Electoral College, the poll has no real effect. However, in sending delegates to the Republican and Democratic national conventions, Guam does have influence in the national presidential race, though these convention delegates are elected by local party conventions rather than voters in primaries.

In the 1980s and early 1990s, there was a significant movement in favor of the territory becoming a commonwealth, which would give it a level of self-government similar to Puerto Rico and the Northern Mariana Islands. However, the federal government rejected the version of a commonwealth that the government of Guam proposed, due to it having clauses incompatible with the Territorial Clause (Art. IV, Sec. 3, cl. 2) of the U.S. Constitution. Contrasting movements are also in existence that advocate political independence from the United States, statehood, union with the Northern Mariana Islands as a single territory, or union with the current U.S. state of Hawaii.

ECONOMY AND ECONOMIC DEVELOPMENT

GENERAL ECONOMIC INDICATOR ANALYSIS

I. POPULATION

For the last several years, the Department of Commerce, in conjunction with the U.S. Bureau of the Census, has been planning and coordinating the 2000 Census of Population and Housing for Guam. The actual census will take place in April 2000. With the assistance of an Interagency Committee on Population, the questionnaire or instrument has been reviewed, revised and was finalized in early 1999.

The 2000 Census of Population and Housing will be the largest undertaking in the history of Guam's prior years' censuses. There are over 800 positions that will become available in early 2000. These positions will be on board anywhere from two weeks to three months.

The total population for 1990 was 133,152. Our projection shows that the total population will be 167,292 in 2000. Between 1990 and 2000 we are looking at reduced numbers for the military and their dependents, due to base closures starting in 1995. Military population has dramatically decreased, from 22,178 (active duty personnel and dependents) in 1992, to 12,739 in 1998. We are also looking at increased migration, especially of Micronesians, primarily due to the Compact of Free Association, which allows these people to travel freely to Guam and to be employed as U.S. citizens. Other events, namely Typhoon Omar in 1992, an 8.2 earthquake in 1993 and Typhoon Paka in 1997 are all major contributing factors to our population shifting up or down.

In a recent data analysis workshop sponsored by the Secretariat of the Pacific Community, we were able to estimate the mid-year population for 1995. In order to get this mid-year population we used the 1990 Census males plus the total male births (1990 to 1995), subtract total male deaths (1990 to 1995), to equal total males for 1995. This process is again applied to females. Take the 1990 Census females, add total female births (1990 to 1995), and subtract total female deaths (1990 to 1995) to equal total females for 1995.

The total mid-year population for 1995 was 148,104. Using the above information, plus a life expectancy rate, plus declining fertility rates we were able to high, medium and low projections for 2000, 2005 and 2010. The high, medium and low projections are 166,906, 165,687 and 163,936 respectively. the life expectancy rate was obtained by averaging the male deaths by age for 1993 to 1997, then dividing by the 1995 estimated male population by age. The result of this is the Age Specific Death Rate. This same process is applied to females. Using a "MORTPAK" software, the Age Specific Death Rate is entered and life tables are produced. The mortality rates are 73.4 for males and 76.0 for females. An earlier population projection using a constant growth rate and no in or out migration for 2000 was 167,292, which is just slightly higher than the high projection mentioned earlier.

In 1998, the Department of Commerce, through a Memorandum of Agreement with the U.S. Department of Commerce, Economics and Statistics Administration, U.S. Bureau of the Census, conducted the "1997 Economic Census of Outlying Areas" for Guam. The economic census is the major source of facts about the structure and functioning of the economy. Specific uses of economic census data include the following:

Policy-making agencies of the government use the data to monitor economic activity and to provide assistance to business;

Local governments use the data to assess business activities and tax bases within their jurisdiction;

Trade associations study events in their own and competing industries;

Individual businesses use the data to locate potential markets and to analyze their own production and sales performance relative to industry or area averages.

The economic census has been taken in Guam at 5-year intervals since 1958. In 1997 the total number of establishments with payroll was 2,707, compared to 1,955 establishments in 1992. Total sales and receipts for 1997 were $4.6 billion, up from $3.0 billion in 1992. There were a total of 42,477 paid employees in 1997 for the pay period including March 12th.

All results of the 1997 Economic Census are available on the U.S. Census Bureau's Website (www.census.gov), on Compact Discs (CD-ROM) for sale by the U.S. Census Bureau, and in printed form. For more information, see the Internet site, or write to the U.S. Census Bureau, Washington, D.C., 20233-8300.

II. EDUCATION

The educational needs of the territory are provided by an island-wide public school system (Guam Public School System) comprised of 5 high schools - grades 9 to 12; 6 middle schools - grades 6 to 8; and 24 elementary schools - grades 1 to 5, operated by the Government of Guam. The Catholic Archdiocese of Agana also operates a substantial school system with a total of 15 schools; 3 High Schools, 6 Middle Schools and 6 Elementary Schools. Several other religious denominations also operate schools in Guam. These include: Saint John's Episcopal School, Harvest Christian Academy, Guam Adventist Academy, Temple Baptist School and Trinity Christian School. Additionally, there are two Japanese Schools,one Chinese and one Korean. Total public school enrollment for academic year 1998-1999 is 31,860, total private school enrollment is 5,034 and military schools 2,511.

Vocational and technical education for students from high school through college is provided by the Guam Community College. The college has an average enrollment of 4,500. Students receive academic instructions as well as technical and professional instructions. There are 11 academic and professional degree programs available as well as 40 technical and vocational programs which award either an Associate Degree, Bachelor's Degree or Certificate of Completion. Journeyman Certificates are awarded in 22 vocations in the construction industry and 5 in the hotel and restaurant industry. The Guam Community College works in association with local high schools and the University of Guam and is fully accredited by the Western Association of Schools and Colleges (WASC).

The University of Guam offers degree programs within five different colleges, namely: CPBA-College of Business & Public Administration; CALS-College of Agriculture & Life Sciences; CAS-College of Arts & Sciences; COE-College of Education; and the College of Nursing & Health Sciences. Also available are five Baccalaureate programs (BA, BA ED, BBA, BS, and BSW) and five Masters programs (MBA, MED, MPA, MS and MA). Total fall enrollment for 1998-1999 was 3,748 and for 1999-2000 was 3,894.

III. HOUSING AND LAND

During FY 1993 the Guam Housing Corporation registered 1,151 applications for financial assistance. During this time fifty (50) applicants were approved for a total outlay of $5.1 million. Of the 50 approved, 26 were processed under the 6 percent financial assistance program, while the remaining were approved under the conventional loan program.

Affordable housing is still the number one priority of the Guam Housing Corporation. Land has been secured for the Lada Estates project but a funding source still needs to be located. Both Lada Estates and the Community Affordable Housing Action Trust programs were designed primarily to provide affordable housing for low and middle income families of Guam.

The Community Affordable Housing Action Trust (CAHAT) is a program designed to help both the homeowner and the private lending institution when it comes to purchasing a home. One of the benefits is that it enables potential homeowners to put a 5 percent down payment on a home rather than the usual 20 percent. There were 1,023 applicants for this program. So far 24 families were certified for the program for an amount of $960,000. Of those certified seven have actually closed, with the remaining seventeen are still pending.

The Guam Housing and Urban Renewal Authority (GHURA) was created in 1962 after the devastation of Typhoon Karen in November 1962, in recognition that only through urban redevelopment would villages be rebuilt. GHURA is charged with the responsibility of undertaking and pursuing an active urban renewal program to eliminate and to prevent the development and spread of slums and blighting influences on Guam.

Two of GHURA's first projects were the Yona and Sinajana Urban Renewal Projects. The Astumbo Subdivision project in Dededo provides for the development and improvement of 500 residential lots. Lots will be an affordable $2,500, enabling qualified families to build their homes.

One of GHURA's charters is to provide "decent, safe, and sanitary" housing for low income families. Some of their projects include: the "GHURA 500" project, which began in FY 1977; Low Income Public Housing under which there are approximately 833 units in various villages, with 82 units designed for elderly and/or handicapped persons; the Section 8 Housing Assistance Program, initiated in 1975, in which GHURA subsidizes rental payments for over 1,400 families; and the Guma Trankilidat, with 50 units designed for the elderly.

In 1997 there were 45,511 land parcels registered with the Department of Revenue and Taxation. A land parcel is any piece of registered land regardless of size. These parcels are located within 15 municipalities. A municipality is created by Executive Order.

The total appraised value of land for 1997 was $5.871 billion, down 2.8 percent from the $6.039 reported in 1996.

IV. EMPLOYMENT

The December 1998 Department of Labor's Current Employment Statistics Report shows total employees on payroll as 64,230 persons, a decrease of 3.8 percent from the December 1997 figure of 66,800 persons. Of the 64,230 employees, 44,780 are in the private sector and 19,450 persons are in the public sector.

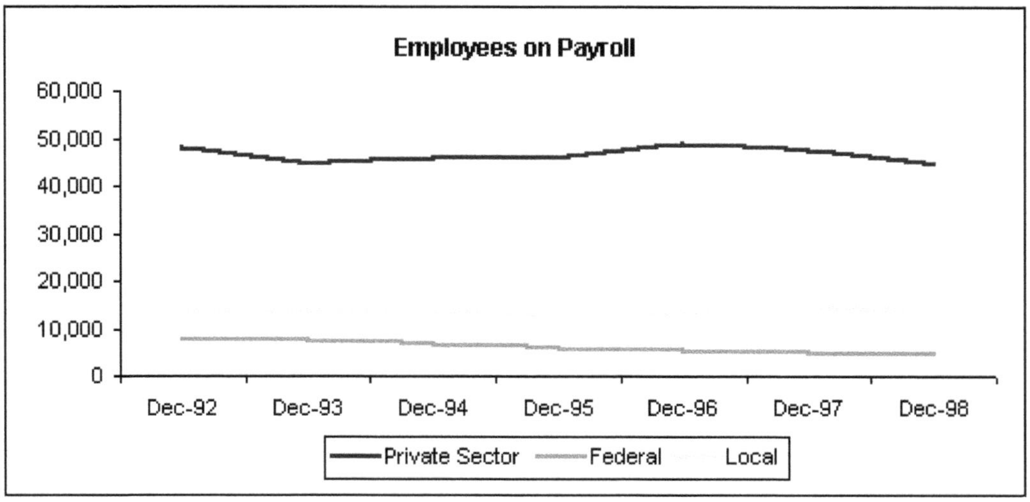

The number of Federal Government employees decreased 6.9 percent and the number of Territorial Government employees increased 5.3 percent.

The Manufacturing sector was the only private industry showing an increase of 7.9 percent in December 1998 over December 1997. All other sectors showed decreases with Agriculture, Wholesale and Services showing the greatest decreases at 14.7, 13.9 and 9.2 percent respectively.

The government performs functions in Guam not normally performed in the United States. The federal government employs 7.6 percent of the total work force while the Government of Guam employs 22.7 percent.

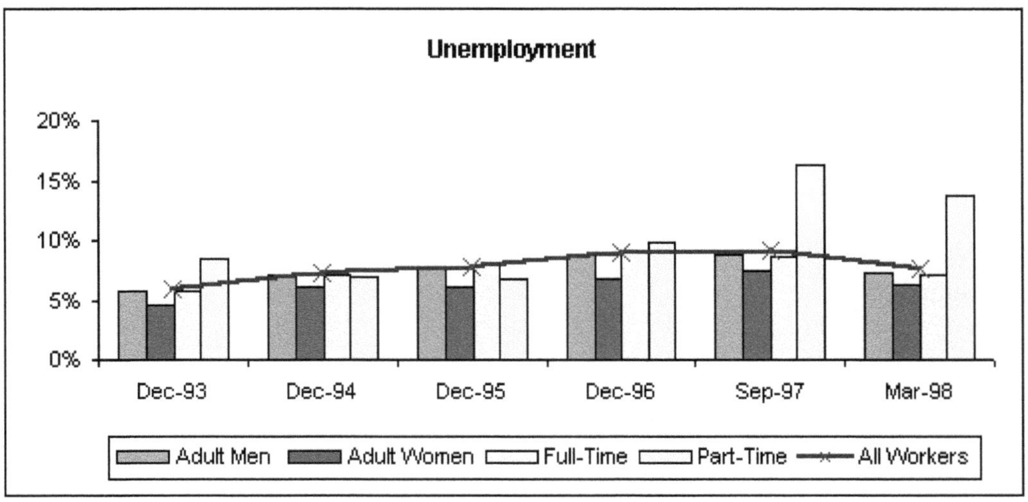

The Guam Department of Labor's "Annual Census of Business Establishments" shows that there were 2,533 business establishments in Guam as of March 1998, an increase of 4.5 percent from the 2,424 establishments in 1997. The number of establishments is broken down as follows:

PRIVATE	ESTABLISHMENTS	EMPLOYMENT
Agriculture	20	308
Construction	417	7,145
Manufacturing	66	1,782
Transportation & Public Utilities	188	5,616
Wholesale Trade	152	2,119
Retail Trade	757	12,621
Finance, Insurance & Real Estate	178	2,706
Services	754	14,768
Total Private	2,532	47,065
Federal Government	27	5,169
Foreign Governments	6	47
Local Government	59	16,432
Grand Total	2,624	68,713

V. TRADE INDICATORS

Guam is a duty-free port. It provides easy means for the movement of raw materials for manufacturing. Guam is a participant of two major trade programs which benefits export-oriented manufacturing. General Headnote 3(a) of the Harmonized Tariff Schedule of the United States (HTSUS) provides for the duty-free treatment of goods from U.S. insular possessions, provided the goods are: the growth or product of any such possession, or manufactured or produced in any such possession or of the customs territory of the U.S., or of both, which do not contain foreign materials to the value of more than 70 percent of their total value or more than 50 percent of their total value with respect to goods described in Section 213(b) of the Caribbean Basin Economic Recovery Act (CBERA), coming to the customs territory of the U.S. directly from any such possession.

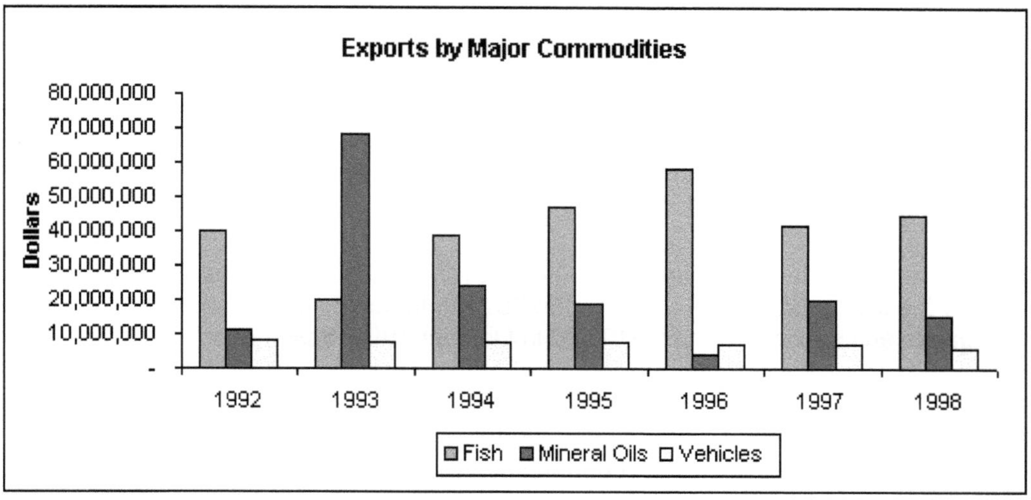

The Generalized System of Preferences (GSP) program, permits developing countries and territories greater access to markets of developed nations. Provisions may vary upon the nation allowing access to be an advantage. Guam in particular, is a beneficiary territory to the following countries: Japan, Australia, Canada, and the European Common Market.

Between January through December 1998, the Department of Commerce reported the total value of Guam exports at $86.4 million. Guam's major export commodities include: fish & crustaceans - $44.9 million; mineral fuels, mineral oils, mineral waxes - $15.2 million; tobacco and manufactured tobacco substitutes - $5.6 million; and Motor Cars for Transport of Persons - $3.1 million.

Total imports were valued at $52.1 million for January 1998, $42.8 million for April 1998, $58.3 million for July 1998 and $47.9 million for October 1998. Major imports include: meats, fish, iron & steel, paper, clothing, and leather goods.

VI. PRICE INDICATORS

The Department of Commerce has just started to use a new market basket for the Consumer Price Index (CPI) which is based on the Department's 1995 Consumer Expenditure Survey.

The Consumer Price Index (CPI) is one of the most widely used economic indicators. It is used as a measure of inflation and the effects of economic policy, as a deflator of other statistical series, and as an income or benefits escalator. Since consumers are constantly offered new items to include in their market basket, buying patterns change over time. In the U.S., the CPI market basket is updated approximately every 10 years. The implementation of a new CPI market basket is a big event for the local business community, government agencies and the people of Guam.

In Guam, the last revision of the CPI market basket of goods and services took place in 1978, which reflected 1978 buying patterns. Since 1978, consumer buying patterns in Guam have changed dramatically as a result of changes in prices, demographic characteristics, income and habits.

Using the results of the 1995 Household Expenditure Survey, the market basket of goods and services to be included in the CPI has been chosen with great care. Categories included are Housing, Apparel and Upkeep, Transportation, Medical Care, Entertainment, Food and Beverages and Other Goods & Services.

The Guam Consumer Price Index was officially released on June 1997. The 3rd quarter of 1996 is our base quarter and is therefore equal to 100. From this base quarter we worked backward to the 4th quarter of 1995 in order to obtain new index numbers based on the new market basket. Using the new weights we first calculated the percentage change of each quarter and compared them with previous quarters. The end result shows a 0.10 percent inflation rate for 1997 and a -1.28 percent inflation rate for 1998.

The All Items Index for the 3rd Quarter of 1999 is 101.27. This Index shows an increase of 0.49 percent over the 3rd Quarter 1998 Index of 100.78. The Index of 101.27 means that a market basket of goods and services costing $100.00 in October 1996 (base period), now cost $101.27

The Food and Beverages Index rose 0.49 percent in the 3rd Quarter 1999 over the same period a year ago. For this same time, Apparel & Upkeep, Medical Care and Entertainment showed decreases of 3.00 percent, 0.87 percent and 0.05 percent respectively. Further comparison shows that these decreases offset by a substantial increase in the Other Goods & Services category. This large increase may be attributed to higher prices recorded for personal and educational expenses, including school tuition, and also for higher prices recorded for tobacco products.

The Housing group and the Transportation group both rose moderately by 0.40 percent in 1998 over 1997.

VII. INCOME INDICATORS

In 1998, the estimated Gross Island Product decreased by 1.90 % to $3,020.5 million from the revised 1997 GIP of $3,079.0 million.

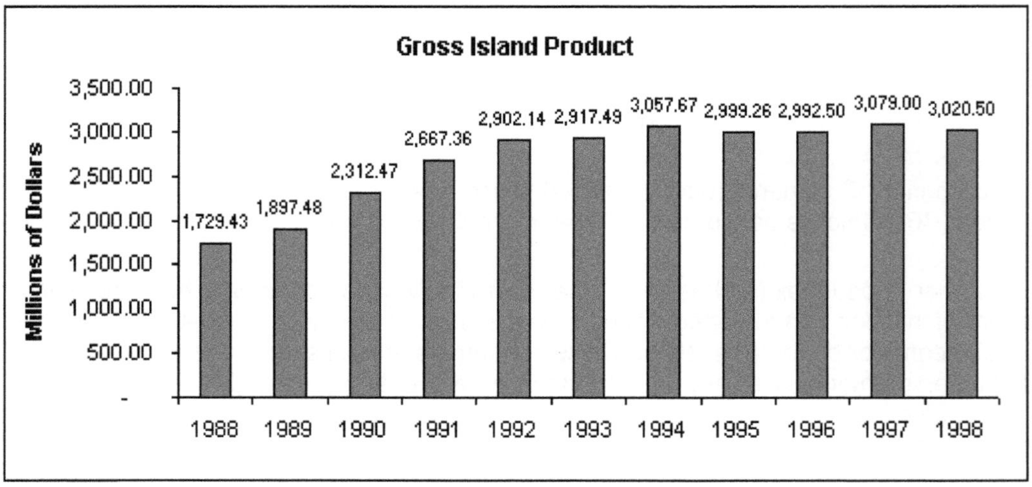

PHYSICAL INDICATOR ANALYSIS

I. WATER AND SEWER

The Guam Waterworks Authority (GWA) is tasked with the responsibility to manage water and wastewater services.

Water revenues for FY 1998 were $24.7 million. There were 43,841 water meters in service in FY 1998, and a total of 8.8 billion gallons of water was consumed in the respective time frame.

In Fiscal Year 1989, the Public Utility Agency of Guam (now GWA) installed a new Utility Billing System. This system had the capability of adjusting for previous billing errors and estimated consumption. The old system did not adjust for estimated and erroneous billing, therefore total reported consumption may not actually reflect cumulative consumption.

Several flood control projects were proposed for 1993 that are either still in the design stage or are currently in the construction stage. Among these projects are: Construction of River Bank at Aguada Bridge (Polaris) (cost $351,000); Dredging of Masso to remove Restriction at River Channel (cost $52,000); Replace Box Culvert at Fonte Bridge ($210,000); Construction of Roadway and Drainage System along Marata Street, Tumon ($600,000); Agana River Channel Improvements ($2.5 million); Ordot Landfill Improvements and Expansion of Ordot Landfill ($8.5 million); Drainage Cleaning in Maimai area ($70,500); and Reinforced Concrete Pipe and Inlet at Taigagao Road and Javier Avenue ($149,000).

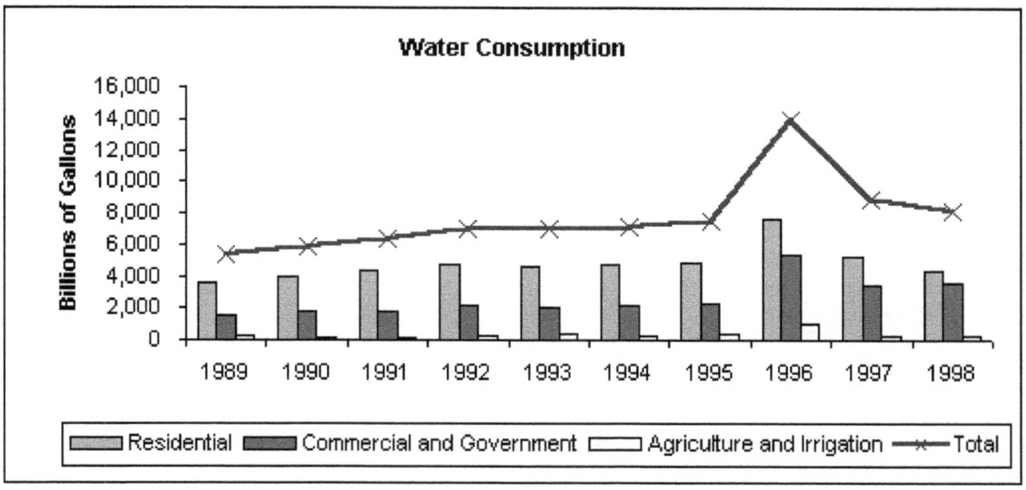

II. POWER

As of September 30, 1998, there were 44,269 power users, an increase of 0.3 percent over FY 1997. Power revenues totaled $178.1 million, down 8.3 percent from the $194.2 million total for Fiscal Year 1997. The $178.1 million includes $30.2 million from the U.S. Navy. The average residential power consumption per customer for FY 1998 was 13,333 kilowatt hours (KWH).

In December 1992, GPA raised $158 million in bond finance, part of a total authorization of $258 million. Phase 1 includes the purchase of 140 generators for the Public Utility Agency of Guam's water wells and pump sites. The second phase of bond issuance will enable GPA to purchase a

35-megawatt slow speed diesel baseload generator, the Supervisory Control and Data Assembly Upgrade, the Anigua Substation and the Cabras Switchyard Reconstruction III.

III. COMMUNICATIONS

Numerous communication companies provide telex, cable and facsimile services *and* international telephone, while courier services are available for off-island deliveries. Post Offices are open Monday through Friday with limited service on Saturday.

The Guam Telephone Authority's (GTA) system held up very well after the August 8, 1993 earthquake. There was virtually uninterrupted telephone service, primarily due to GTA's underground network.

The total number of primary telephone lines in FY 1998 was 84,134, a decrease of 1.8 percent from FY 1997. Telephone revenues increased 6.9 percent, from $35.3 million in FY 1997 to $37.8 million in FY 1998. Revenues from regulated and non-regulated services were identified and categorized in Fiscal Year 2004.

In 2004, the Guam Telephone Authority started the "Information Superhighway". Through a partnership with the Department of Education and Early Childhood Profession Development Network of South Carolina, GTA was able to beam head start development training from Guam to the islands of Majuro, Pohnpei, Kosrae, Chuuk, Palau, American Samoa, Rota, Tinian and Saipan. This was made possible by using MCI's earth station to up-link KGTF's production of an "interactive telecommunication broadcast" of the head start development training with SPRINT-GUAM paying for the long distance toll charges.

SOCIAL INDICATOR ANALYSIS

I. Food Stamps/Public Assistance

There was an average of 4,965 households or 16,399 persons who received public assistance of approximately $24.8 million in Food Stamps in Fiscal Year 1998. This was a decrease of 7.5 percent in the number of households and 3.6 percent in the value of food stamps. The following average number of persons qualified to receive public assistance in FY 1998: AFDC-Aid to Families with Dependent Children, 7,007 persons ($12,539,966); OAA-Old Age Assistance, 507 ($1,471,728); APTD-Aid to the Permanently and Totally Disabled, 96 ($268,692); AB-Aid to the Blind, 1 ($1,661); and GA-General Assistance, 1,612 persons ($3,078,534).

Total Public Assistance Expenditures, including $9.9 million for Medicaid, was $27.3 million, a decrease of 11.4 percent in FY 98 from FY 97.

II. JUSTICE

Guam's Judiciary system consists of one Federal District Court and a Superior Court of Guam.

The President of the United States, with the consent of the United States Senate, appoints the presiding judge of the Federal Court to an eight-year term. This Court has jurisdiction over cases involving federal issues.

The Superior Court of Guam has authority over all cases arising under the laws of Guam. This includes family matters, small claims, traffic, probate, civil and land registration.

The Superior Court has six judges. The Governor, with the consent of the Legislature, appoints a judge to an initial seven year term. In the subsequent election and every eight years for as long as the judge chooses to serve, the judge must receive a majority vote favoring retention.

The three-story courthouse contains eight courtrooms and offices for the Attorney General's Office.

In 1998 there was a total of 34,889 case filings. This includes: criminal cases-felony (946); criminal-misdemeanor (2,011); probate (153); civil cases (2,987); domestic cases (1,154); child support (810); and small claims (3,420). The number of offenses reported decreases substantially in 1998 over 1997.

For Part 1 Offenses which include murder, rape, robbery and theft, there were 7,781 offenses reported. This shows a decrease of 19.1 percent. Part 2 Offenses, or misdemeanors, had 9,390 offenses reported, which was 12.9 percent less than 1997.

PUBLIC SECTOR ANALYSIS

I. FEDERAL GOVERNMENT

The Federal government plays a leading role in the economic affairs of the Territory of Guam. Expenditures for the Federal government totaled $998 million in Fiscal Year 1998. Of the $998 million, $344 million was expended for wages and salaries, $266 million in grants awarded to the local government, $66 million in direct payment for individuals, $167 million for procurement, and $155 million for other programs. The U.S. Postal Service contributes $6.9 million in wages and salaries to the Guam economy.

The following is a list of Federal government agencies which maintain offices in Guam:

U.S. DEPARTMENT OF AGRICULTURE

-Farmers Home Administration
-U.S. Soil Conservation Service
-Animal Plant Health Inspection Service

U.S. DEPARTMENT OF DEFENSE

-U.S. Air Force
-U.S. Army
-U.S. Navy
-U.S. Marine Corps
-Corps of Engineers
-National Guard
-Selective Service

CONGRESS OF THE UNITED STATES

-U.S. House of Representative
The Honorable Robert Underwood

U.S. DISTRICT COURT OF THE TERRITORY OF GUAM

U.S. DEPARTMENT OF COMMERCE

-Bureau of the Census Field Office
-Weather Service Meteorological Laboratory
-National Marine Fisheries Service

FEDERAL AVIATION ADMINISTRATION

GENERAL SERVICES ADMINISTRATION

U.S. DEPARTMENT OF TRANSPORTATION

-U.S. Coast Guard

HOUSING & URBAN DEVELOPMENT /DEPARTMENT OF GUAM

U.S. DEPARTMENT OF INTERIOR

-War in the Pacific Park
-Office of the Inspector General
-Territorial and International Affairs
-U.S. Geological Survey

U.S. DEPARTMENT OF JUSTICE

-Federal Bureau of Investigation
-Drug Enforcement Administration
- Immigration and Naturalization Service
-U.S. Attorney
-U.S. Marshals
-Land and Natural Resources

U.S. DEPARTMENT OF LABOR

-Employment Standards Administration Wage and Hour

SOCIAL SECURITY ADMINISTRATION

SMALL BUSINESS ADMINISTRATION

U.S. POSTAL SERVICE

U.S. PROBATION SERVICE

U.S. DEPARTMENT OF VETERANS AFFAIRS

II. MILITARY

The Federal government allocated approximately $507 million for their military operation in Guam in Fiscal Year 1998, a 47% decrease from 1993's high of $748 million. Of this amount, $319 million was allocated for wages and salaries, and $160 million for military construction. Federal income taxes (Section 30 Funds) returned to the Government of Guam for FY 1997 was $36 million. The local base commissaries are now combined and called the Defense Commissary Agency (DECA).

In April 1995, the Naval Air Station (NAS), Agana, was officially closed, and control was transferred to the Government of Guam.

An interim lease has been signed pending resolution of base contamination and other issues prior to final transfer. Total active duty military personnel decreased 1.8 percent (114 personnel) in 1998 from 1997, from 6,265 to 6,379.

The American military has maintained bases on Guam of varying strength in both personnel and equipment since the turn of the century. After the end of World War II, Guam was the site of major naval and air force facilities to backstop U.S. defense commitments in the Asia-Pacific region.

Three Navy supply ships homeported in Guam; the San Jose, the White Plains, and the Niagara Falls, have been decommissioned and refitted as Military Sealift Command ships. When these ships return, it will be with a crew of about 100 merchant marine sailors and 40 Navy personnel as opposed to the 425 sailors and officers now on board.

However, the U.S. Naval presence was subject to the resolution of the Base Realignment and Closure Commission (BRACC) '95. BRACC '95 recommended closure of Naval Air Station (NAS), Naval Ship Repair Facility (SRF), the realignment (downsizing) of Naval Activities Guam, the "disestablishment" of the Fleet and Industrial Supply Center, and reassignment of naval air units formerly slated to be transferred from NAS to Andersen Air Force Base to locations outside of Guam.

The economic impact of these base closures, unit transfers and scaling back of defense activities have resulted in estimated job losses of about 4,800 (3,500 federal civilian jobs and 1,300 military positions). In terms of lost income, cumulative current dollar loss of Gross Island Product for the period 1996-1999 has been estimated at $942 million (Team Guam Report, The Way Forward... from Guam: Team Guam Report on DOD closure & Realignment Recommendations for BRAC '95, Draft Final Report, April 1995:46-54). In terms of job losses, more than 60 percent of the direct jobs were lost within the first two years, with the balance being lost in the subsequent two years.

Under the current implementation for closures and downsizing, total direct and indirect (those jobs lost to the multiplier effect of direct job income losses), jobs lost would be 6,807 (4,796 direct plus 2,011 indirect jobs). These are major job losses, considering that many of the jobs are high-paying skilled technical, professional and management positions; and that the cumulative number of jobs lost is equivalent to about 10 percent of Guam's total workforce.

While the impact on the economy in the short to medium term appears to be grim, particularly to those losing jobs and the the Government of Guam in terms of lost tax revenues, in the long run, military downsizing may turn out to be an economic shock which results in concrete actions needed to stimulate private sector development (e.g. income tax reform, privatization of selected government operations, increased public sector fiscal discipline coupled with upgrading of labor productivity while limiting growth of payrolls and number of public hires).

A factor which could greatly facilitate transition to an economy more reliant on private sector-led growth, is the favorable disposition of land and other assets now held by the military. Real property assets, which will become surplus to military needs are very substantial, and if made available for economic development purposes, could produce major benefits for Guam in the longer term. However, the present position of defense planners appears to be to retain control (or place major restrictions on use) of the bulk of military land and facilities which are scheduled to become inactive.

There are more than 4,000 acres of Navy land in Apra Harbor. The Naval Ship Repair Facility which is closed occupies 231 acres and encompasses 78 buildings with nearly 450,000 square feet of space, wharf footage of 4,900 feet with full utilities and 3 floating cranes, and two floating dry-docks. Within the complex there is an industrial laboratory, foundry and shop facilities for tool, sheet-metal boilermaking and ship vetting and other facilities. If land and facilities can be made available under lease on reasonable terms and conditions for private use, many of the constraints related to lack of facilities at the Port Authority of Guam (PAG) could be rectified, which would substantially improve the PAG's attractiveness to fishing fleets and other fleets now using the port.

Similar to the extensive land use planning that has been focused on NAS land, which have resulted in a base reuse master plan, basic agreement on joint-use or private use of designated areas needs to be worked out with the Navy and DOD, so that use of SRF assets can be incorporated into a new PAG master plan, or separate reuse plan addressing use of SRF.

With defense spending in Guam expected to decline as military facilities are closed, or downsized through consolidation, it is imperative that new initiatives be undertaken to achieve sustained growth through diversification of the economy.

As a major sector of Guam's economy, the presence of the U.S. military is expected to continue and its size will be stabilized after the downsizing.

III. LOCAL GOVERNMENT

Guam is an unincorporated territory of the U.S.A. which means that federal laws do not automatically apply to the island. For example, U.S. import tariff laws do not apply, and Guam is considered to be a duty free port. Federal banking and transportation laws and regulations apply to Guam, though some do not.

The Organic Act provides for three branches of government: executive, legislative and judicial.

The Governor heads the executive branch. Until 1970, the Governor of Guam was appointed by the President of the United States. Since the November 1970 election and the January 1971 inauguration, the Governor and the Lieutenant Governor have been elected for four year terms. In 2004, the Honorable Carl T. C. Gutierrez and the Honorable Madeleine Z. Bordallo (the first woman to ever hold this position) were elected Governor and Lieutenant Governor. The Governor is responsible for implementing all local and federal laws pertaining to Guam. He oversees the functions of the departments and agencies within the executive branch.

Guam has a unicameral legislature called the Senate. Fifteen senators are elected at large for two year terms. The Senate is responsible for appropriating from the general fund for government operations and other public purposes as well as making laws for the Territory.

The 25th Guam Legislature, elected in 1998, comprises 3 Democrats and 12 Republicans. Because of a plebiscite vote, the number of senators was reduced from 21 to 15. Incumbent delegate to the U.S. Congress, Democrat Dr. Robert A. Underwood, was re-elected unopposed.

Guam's delegate to the U.S. Congress has no vote on the floor, but he does have a vote in the committees and subcommittees of which he is a member. Congressman Underwood is a member of the Committee on Resources and the Committee on National Security. He is also a member of various subcommittees (of each of the above committees) among which are: Military Installations and Facilities, Native American and Insular Affairs, National Parks, Forests and Lands, Research and Development, and Morale, Welfare and Recreation Panel. The Congressman is also affiliated with the following Caucuses: Asian-Pacific American, Congressional Arts, Congressional Hispanic and the Travel and Tourism Caucus.

The Judiciary consists of one Federal District Court and a Superior Court of Guam. The President of the United States with the consent of the United States Senate appoints the presiding judge of the Federal Court to an eight-year term. This court has jurisdiction over cases involving federal issues.

The Superior Court of Guam has authority over all cases arising under the laws of Guam. This includes family matters, small claims, traffic, probate, civil and land registration. The Superior Court has six judges. The Governor with the consent of the Legislature appoints a judge to an initial seven year term. In the subsequent election and every eight years for as long as the judge chooses to serve, the judge must receive a majority vote favoring retention.

The Guam Organic Act provides for Guam income taxes to "mirror" federal income taxes. "Mirror" means that whenever the federal law refers to the federal tax jurisdiction, Guam law refers to Guam, and whenever federal law refers to Guam, Guam law refers to the federal jurisdiction. The Guam income tax law is the federal law with the revenue going to the Government of Guam.

Guam is free to pass other tax laws. The major taxes include a four percent tax on Gross Business Receipts. This applies to all business sales except for wholesale sales. There are also excise taxes on liquor, cigarettes and liquid fuels.

As required by Section 30 of the Guam Organic Act, the federal income taxes collected from military personnel and other federal government employees on Guam revert to the Government of Guam.

The United States Tax Reform Act of 1986 included a provision for Guam to develop its own income tax code. The code must have protection against double taxation, fraud and tax avoidance and evasion. The Guam Tax Code Commission was established in May 1990 to formulate a new tax system for Guam, and succeeded by the Guam Finance Commission in 2004.

The combined revenues and sources of funds for the Government of Guam General Fund for Fiscal Year 1998 was $738.0 million, compared with combined expenditures and uses of funds (including transfers) of $501.9 million, which left a surplus of $236.1 million for the year. The Government of Guam has been in deficit-spending mode for the past four years, moving from a surplus of $52.6 million at end of FY1990 to a deficit of $93.5 million at the end of FY1995. This deficit has been financed by borrowing from revenues in future years, borrowing internally from special funds and government agencies, a bond issue and delayed payments to vendors.

The new administration is committed to fiscal responsibility, and implemented plans to enable the budget deficit to be eliminated by FY 97.

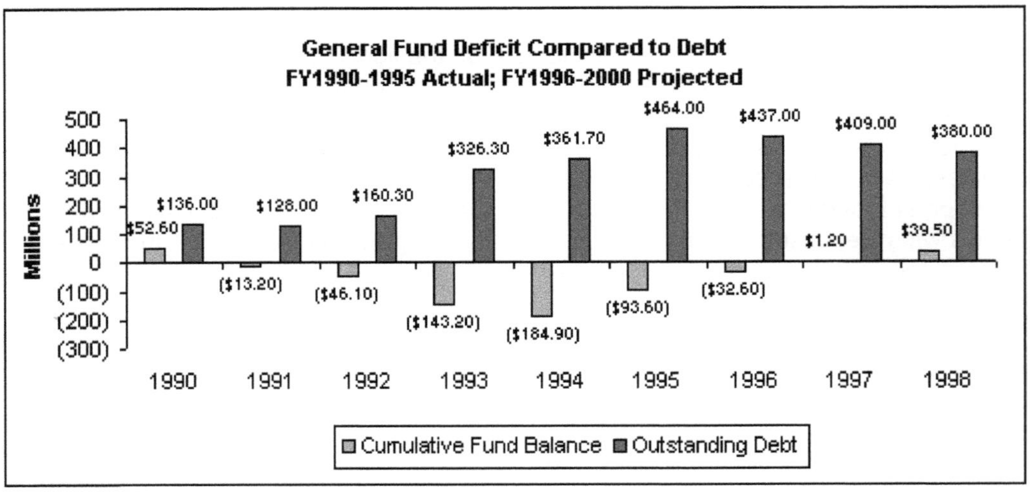

PRIVATE SECTOR ANALYSIS

I. AGRICULTURE, AQUACULTURE AND FISHERIES

1. *Agriculture*

Agriculture is Guam's smallest sector. It employs 290 persons out of a workforce of 64,230 as of December 1998. These persons earn an annual average salary of $17,372.

The Agricultural Development Services (ADS) division of the Guam Department of Agriculture is tasked with providing most farm services to the farmers. Some services provided include: processing of loans, under the Farmer's and Fisherman's Small Loan Revolving Fund, spraying services, agricultural water rate, vegetable and fruit seedlings, and equipment rental when available. Public Law 15-18 authorizing the Department of Agriculture to administer the Agricultural Land Lease Program, has been repealed in its entirety by the implementation of the Chamorro Land Trust Act. There are currently 57 leases comprising 574 acres being used by local farmers. These 57 signed leases are not affected by the Chamorro Land Trust Act. The Farmer's and Fisherman's Small Loan Revolving Fund provided 2 loans in FY 1993. There were 42 existing loans at the start of the fiscal year. Approximately five hundred thousand dollars ($500,000) has been disbursed since the inception of the program. Public Law 15-107 provides a subsidy to farmers who would lease certain farm equipment from private vendors for agricultural purposes such as bulldozing, plowing, tilling, mowing, etc. Seven vendors are presently licensed by the Department to provide these farm services as needed. Also, during FY 1993, there were 21 applications filed with the department with the majority of these for bulldozing services. There were approximately 125 acres of farmland that was prepared for farming activities such as field crops, livestock farming or fruit orchards.

A nine member Agricultural Board of Commissioners was created by Public Law 20-176. This Board has powers of review and recommendations regarding zoning, pest control, and the preparation of an agricultural development plan, looking into agricultural loans, and related matters. One major objective of the board is the eradication of the melon fly in Guam. The eradication of this pest will eliminate farm products trade restrictions with other countries. Other major plans include: funding for a pig slaughterhouse, upgrading the Artificial Insemination Program and seeking solutions for the land-lease farmers. The Board hopes to introduce a unified approach to agricultural development for everyone involved in the agricultural industry.

ADS has prepared a farm directory to provide information for clients who want to know where to go for farm equipment and supplies. An ornamental Plant Nursery listing was also compiled. Currently, there are 24 registered nurseries with the Department.

At present there are three Hydroponic farms in operation on the island. These Hydroponic farms introduce modern technology of growing vegetables on nutrient enriched water and under controlled conditions. These farms have the potential to supply the island with fresh vegetables such as tomatoes, cucumbers, lettuce, and other selected vegetables on a year round basis.

Through coordination with the U.S. Department of Agriculture (USDA) and the Plant and Quarantine Section of Guam's Department of Agriculture, Guam's Customs and Quarantine Agency is responsible for protecting the island's fruit, vegetable and ornamental plant industry from imported pests and disease infestation. Contraband is also intercepted and seized at the ports of entry.

Under the direction of the Department of Commerce, the Government of Guam has built a new Public Market now called the Chamorro Village or "Y Sengsong Chamorro". Its overall design reflects the Chamorro/Spanish heritage. It is situated in Agana and large enough to provide activities for both tourists and the local community. The main objective of the "Y Sengsong Chamorro" is to provide a unique, attractive, centrally-located retail complex where individual vendors congregate to sell locally produced goods. It also functions as a tourist attraction.

2. *AQUACULTURE*

Aquaculture represents a part of the economy that still has great untapped potential as a major sector within Guam's economy. The aquaculture industry is relatively new to Guam. The first experimental and demonstration farm was established in 1973, followed by the first commercial operation in 1975. Since that time the industry has grown significantly despite numerous obstacles. Today, there are over 100 acres of ponds constructed. The species currently under cultivation include tilapia, milkfish, mullet, freshwater giant prawn, marine shrimp, Chinese carp, and catfish.

At that time, the main limiting factor to the development of the aquaculture industry on Guam was the lack of an on-island hatchery facility. The Guam Aquaculture Development and Training Center (GADTC), administered by the Department of Commerce, fills that void and provides the needed postlarvae and fry to the commercial aquaculture farmers on a reliable and more economical basis. It also provides training and research services to help further development of the industry. GADTC serves the Western Pacific Region, and has established itself as a world recognized aquaculture facility. Products of GADTC have been shipped on a regular basis to commercial farms in Hawaii, and recently to CNMI with occasional shipments to the Continental U.S. Requests for products of GADTC have been received from locations as far away as Central America, South America and Israel.

A) INDUSTRY PRODUCTION

Aquaculture production by private farms on Guam concentrated on tilapia and milkfish over the past five years. Commercial farming of shrimp was re-established in 1991, as a result of the initiation of postlarvae production at the Guam Aquaculture Development and Training Center (GADTC). Skyrocketing shrimp production totals offset declines in milkfish and catfish production between 1991 and 1993. Marine shrimp production has increased from $13,300 in 1991 to $355,600 in 2004. Shrimp production in 1995 fell to $40,000, but tilapia production reached $264,000 and milkfish production totaled $1.2 million.

Another major transition in production occurred in 1995, when the largest aquaculture farm on Guam changed ownership, and production was converted from marine shrimp to milkfish for live bait. At the same time, another farm converted some of its ponds to milkfish bait production. As a result of this shift in production, marine shrimp production decreased to $40,000 in 1995, while milkfish production for live bait totaled over 1.2 million.

This shift in production reflected the development of a new market on Guam for milkfish fingerlings (5 to 6 inch size) as a live bait for the tuna longline fishery. Tuna longline vessels prefer to use live milkfish as bait because it is significantly more effective than other baits. Milkfish have been shown to be 3 to 5 times more effective in catch rate than dead bait. Milkfish is also preferred over other live baits because it tolerates handling and long term holding in bait wells and usually remains alive on the longline for extended periods. To avoid a lengthy down time in fishing, Taiwanese vessels fishing in the Western Pacific region prefer to purchase bait on Guam, rather than return to Taiwan to obtain more bait. This has provided the opportunity for substantial foreign investment in milkfish bait culture on Guam and significant expansion of the local aquaculture industry. One new bait fish farm was under construction at the end of 1995, as a result of a partnership between Taiwanese investors and a local landowner. Other Taiwanese companies have shown strong interest in establishing aquaculture farms on Guam to supply their fleets with live bait.

Guam's commercial aquaculture plant is comprised of five active farms with approximately 100 acres currently under production. Activity in the commercial sector of aquaculture has increased during the past five years. This includes the diversification of production and the increased level of interest by entrepreneurs. This has resulted from the higher profile GADTC has taken in the past two years through media (TV, radio, and newsprint) and market promotions after the establishment of the production capability of the facility and the staff was completed. New farms have been established or are nearing establishment (clearing the permit process). There has also been an increase in "backyard" or small-scale farms.

The estimated value of Guam's commercial aquaculture production in 1996 totaled $1.44 million. With the operation of the GADTC, the value of production from the commercial aquaculture farms on Guam is expected to exceed the value of total domestic fishery (subsistence and commercial) within a three to four year period, and has already exceeded the commercial sector of the domestic fishery, further emphasizing the potential role and importance of aquaculture in Guam's economy. Additionally, the island imports over $10 million worth of fisheries products annually. Production from the aquaculture industry can replace a significant portion of these imports. Thus import substitution on a competitive basis is a major objective in Guam's aquaculture program.

Guam currently exports aquaculture products to the region and Hawaii on a regular basis. This export market offers opportunity for substantial expansion. Expansion of the local market for aquaculture products was carried out from the traditional weekend Flea Market to the tourism industry serving the up-scale hotels and restaurants. Marine shrimp served as this initial entrant; however, since this has increased the general awareness of aquaculture products and their superior quality, some of the other aquaculture products are beginning to gain access.

Diversification of products produced has been a key area of need by the industry. This has been addressed with the marine shrimp. Mullet have developed into a commercially cultured product with the establishment of the hatchery technology at GADTC. In addition, work has been initiated to develop grouper culture to further diversify the product mix. To further diversify the commercial opportunities in aquaculture, the examination of marine aquarium fish was initiated. The international aquarium trade is over a billion dollars annually.

B) DEVELOPMENT ASSISTANCE MEASURES

To facilitate the development of the commercial sector, government has the responsibility to assure the uproots coordination of government agencies in meeting the needs identified by the private sectors. Therefore, the Director of Commerce established the Aquaculture Industry Advisory Committee (AIAC) in April 1991 to facilitate identification of the needs of the commercial aquaculture industry on Guam, and the Governor established the Aquaculture Coordinating Committee (ACC) in April 1991 for inter-government agency coordination in the development of the aquaculture industry.

Industry members of the AIAC identified the regulatory process as the major current constraint to the further development of the aquaculture industry on Guam. This regulatory process serves as a major entry barrier to the industry for new farms. This is not unique to Guam. In the report by the Joint Subcommittee on Aquaculture (June 1993) entitled "Aquaculture in the United States: Status, Opportunities, and Recommendations" it identifies the regulatory constraints as the major impediment to the development of the aquaculture industry in the U.S.

The National Association of State Aquaculture Coordinators (Guam is a member) is compiling a status report on the regulatory process applied by each state. Guam has participated in this program and has provided detailed information on each of the regulatory steps involved in starting an aquaculture business on Guam.

To address this problem in Guam, the Department of Commerce has compiled a review of the regulatory process, and is also working to develop a one stop permit application process. Interest in starting new ventures has been high, especially since the establishment of the Guam Aquaculture Development and Training Center, but no new large aquaculture farms have been started. The difficulty of obtaining permits continues to be one of the constraints that have limited the start-up of new ventures. From the perspective of the entrepreneur, the permitting process is too complex, redundant, time consuming, and costly.

The Governor's Forum on Aquaculture held in June 2004, focused on this problem with commitment of political leaders to resolve the issue. Under Public Law No. 23-05, the Department of Commerce worked with other government agencies to evaluate the existing aquaculture permitting process and develop a procedure for a one stop aquaculture permit process. This work resulted in the development of a Master Aquaculture Permit Application and supporting documents, which were submitted to the Guam Legislature in 1995. The one stop permit process is presently awaiting approval by the Legislature.

3. FISHERIES

SMALL SCALE FISHERIES REPORT

Commercial opportunities in the area of small scale fisheries fall primarily into two categories: (1) troll fisheries and (2) charter boat fishing operations.

Catch rates for troll fisheries have historically accounted for most of the island's recorded fisheries harvest. There are an estimated 300 boats which participate in the fishery. During Fiscal Year 1998, catches from trolling, totaling 377.7 metric tons comprised the bulk of of the 529.2 mt recorded for the offshore harvest. Five major pelagic species accounted for 96 percent of the troll catch by weight, and are broken down as follows: mahi mahi (Coryphaena hippurus), 29 percent, bonita (Katsuwonus pelamis), 23 percent, wahoo (Acanthocybium solandri), 20 percent; Pacific blue marlin, (Makaira mazara), 6 percent; and yellowfin tuna (Thunnus albacares), 18 percent.

Guam's charter boat fishing industry is fortunate to have in place all of the requirements for a successful and economically feasible business activity, these being: a dependable and seasonably abundant stock of game fish; satisfactory capital infrastructure support; and community and government support. In 1998, over 1.1 million visitors to Guam were recorded. Of this total, an estimated 2.6 percent participated in charter boat fishing as an optional tour. It is estimated that these tourists make direct expenditures of $2.3 million to the charter boat fleet. In addition, most of the fish caught on charter boats are sold in local markets, with proceeds accruing to the vessels and crew. Charter boat fishing represents a profitable enterprise, and is a valued component of the overall tourism economy.

Fisheries related incentives provided by the Government of Guam include a liquid fuel tax exemption for vessels engaged in commercial fisheries of $0.14 per gallon for diesel fuel and $0.15 per gallon for gasoline. Full time commercial fishermen can request a full waiver of the four percent gross receipts tax.

The Guam Fishermen's Cooperative, a nonprofit organization established over 20 years ago to aid fishermen in promoting and marketing their catch, has a 50 year government lease for one acre of land adjacent to the Hagåtña Boat Basin. The annual fee for the lease is one dollar.

In general, Guam's offshore fisheries activities are functionally limited to the resources within an approximate 50 mile radius due to limitations in vessel size and equipment. A previous constraint faced by small scale fishermen wishing to expand their operations was the difficulty in securing loans for the purchase of larger fishing vessels that would substantially increase vessel range and increase accessibility to fishing grounds for small scale local fishermen. The Guam Economic Development Authority now offers loans for fish harvesting activities under the Agriculture Development Fund. The level of funding is made available to fishermen under the loan program, which has an interest rate of four percent, is contingent on the availability of funds and the applicant's collateral.

LARGE SCALE FISHERIES REPORT

Guam presently serves as a major transshipment and port of call for large scale fishing fleets operating in the Western Pacific. Two primary types of fishing vessels, purse seiners and longliners, utilize Guam for a variety of operations. Direct and indirect fishing vessel activities include, but are not limited: Fueling; Provisioning; Unloading; Air and Sea Transshipment; Net and Vessel Repairs; Crew Repatriation; and Medical and Warehousing purposes.

The 1998 longline tuna transshipment total of 12,742 metric tons, posted a 75 percent increase over the 1997 figure of 5,027 metric tons. Longline tuna is fresh tuna that is offloaded from longline vessels at Guam's Commercial Port for air transshipment to Japan for the lucrative sashimi markets. In 1998, the species breakdown was primarily bigeye and yellowfin tuna making up the bulk of the transshipments and accounting for 40% and 48% respectively. Transshipment was conducted almost exclusively by Taiwanese and Japanese vessels. Port of calls by longliners for 1998 numbered 845. Most of the port of calls were made by Taiwanese vessels (474).

Publications Available

The Secretariat of the Pacific Community (formerly South Pacific Commission) has prepared the "Marianas Islands 1998 Pelagic Fisheries Assessment, Oceanic Fisheries Programme Country Report No. 12". Compiled at the request of Guam Governor Carl Gutierrez and Commonwealth of the Northern Marianas Governor Pedro Tenorio, the report contains a review of the biology and stock assessment of the four species of commercial importance to the Marianas Islands - Skipjack, Yellowfin, Bigeye and Blue Marlin. A review of oceanography from waters surrounding the Marianas Archipelago and its possible effect on pelagic fisheries is followed by an analysis of available fisheries statistics for both Guam and the CNMI. Regional fisheries information forms the basis of an assessment of the status of tuna and blue marlin stocks.

Infrastructure Projects

The Division of Aquatic and Wildlife Resources of the Department of Agriculture is implementing several projects to enhance fisheries opportunities for local residents. An environmental impact assessment was developed for plans to construct a small boat ramp in the village in Inarajan. The Inarajan ramp would provide small boats with direct fishing access to the east side of Guam. Presently, all public boat ramps are located on the island's western and southern coasts. This new location would also provide greater response capabilities for search and rescue operations, and an additional safe harbor for stormy conditions and emergencies. Plans call for a double boat ramp, paved parking, lighting, restrooms and rinse station.

Repairs and upgrades at the Merizo ramp were completed. The existing facility has suffered deterioration from increased use and exposure to the elements. Upgrades and additions include a double boat ramp, a boat wash area and more lighting.

A total of nine Fish Aggregating Devices are now operational for Guam's boaters. Existing sites are offshore from the following areas: Ritidian; Urunao; Adelup; Facpi; Umatac; and Cocos. Future plans call for FAD deployment for east coast waters at Pati, Fadian and Asiga. The FAD project is funded under the Dingle-Johnson Sport Fishing grant fund.

Fisheries Management Activities

Guam is a participant in the Western Pacific Fisheries Information Network (WPacFIN), operated through the National Marine Fisheries Service in coordination with the Fisheries Data Coordinating Committee under the Western Pacific Regional Fishery Management Council. The purpose of the network is to collect and compile data from offshore and inshore fisheries to assist in monitoring and managing the fisheries industry. The Division of Aquatic and Wildlife Resources, for the past 20 years, has been conducting monthly surveys among various boat launching locations along Guam's shoreline to assess fisheries participation, effort and harvest. WPacFin funding also supports data collection and analyses of the impact on the quantity and size of yellowfin tuna and other prevalent longline species on Guam. The project is conducted by the Guam Department of Commerce.

As a result of the Magnuson Fishery Conservation and Management Act of 1976, a law which established exclusive U.S. jurisdiction over all fisheries resources in the federal waters of the Fishery Conservation Zone (FZC) extending 200 nautical miles outward from the territorial sea, Guam participates in the Western Pacific Regional Fishery Management Council (WesPac).

Fourteen members from American Samoa, Commonwealth of the Northern Marianas, Guam and Hawaii, represent the fishery community, government bodies and the scientific community. The council's main task is to manage the fisheries within the FCZs to prevent over-fishing while encouraging economic development.

II. CONSTRUCTION

Construction has been a major economic sector in Guam although this sector experienced lots of ups and downs during three decades.

The construction industry accounted for a significant share of the island's economic boom in the early 1970s. Construction receipts accounted for approximately one-quarter of Guam's gross business receipts. Following the economic recession in the mid-1970s, construction receipts fell 40 percent from $109 million in 1974 to $64 million in 1976. Hotel occupancy rates dwindled and there was no further demand for hotel construction. High vacancy rates in office space appeared while many higher-priced residential units built during the boom years remained unsold.

Construction was once again on the upswing during 1977 and 1978 following Super Typhoon Pamela in May 1976. Over $200 million in federal funds were authorized for typhoon relief and reconstruction of damaged military, civilian and government facilities within this period. Over $70 million worth of defense construction projects were completed during fiscal year 1978 as compared with approximately $48 million during the previous two-year period. Construction receipts rose to an estimated $75 million in calendar year 1977 and $111 million in 1978. Construction employment increased from 3,300 in March 1977, or a gain of 21 percent. However, nearly three quarters of those employed in the construction industry were non-immigrant aliens.

There were a couple of construction booms in the 1980s and 1990s. An example can be taken for 1993 – Guam's building sector grew with the opening of several establishments including: the 448 room Hyatt Regency Hotel ($150 million); 291 room Holiday Inn ($60 million); 381 room Leo Palace Hotel; and the 200 room Leo Palace Resort ($600 million). Later on, several hotel projects started construction, including: DanDan Estates & Country Club ($160 million); Johyo Sangyo Resort ($160 million); Asahi Beer Hotel Inc. ($240 million); S & R Guam ($18 million) and the Tumon Crown Hotel (156 units).

In 1995, the Department of Defense offered more than $124 million in United States Naval construction projects. Over 300 family housing units were scheduled to be built at Apra Heights at an estimated cost of $56 million. Other projects include: the $29 million hanger apron at Andersen Air Force Base (AAFB); a hazardous material storage facility ($14.8 million); a Tomahawk mill magazine ($8.2 million); a child development center at AAFB ($2.9 million); and a storage facility ($5.2 million).

As of December 1993 there were 2-27 hole and 5-18 hole public golf courses on Guam. One 27 hole, 10-18 hole and 1-9 hole course developments have been approved, some of which had been completed in the next four years.

After two decades, the construction scale was much larger than before. Total construction permits issued during 1998 was 2,775, compared with 1,548 in 1997, an increase of 79.3 percent. The total value of these permits was $321.9 million, compared with $307.8 million in 1997, a 4.6 percent increase.

There were about 6,110 persons employed in the construction industry in December 1998, a decrease of 4.7 percent from 1997. Additionally, there were about 300 alien construction workers employed in 1998.

Foreign-owned companies dominate the construction industry. Foreign-owned contractors enjoy favorable currency exchange rates and minimal enforcement of employment-regulation laws.

Until 1997, wages in the construction sector have been depressed mainly because of cheap alien labor brought into Guam under the temporary alien labor employment program (H-2 program). The H-2 program allows nonimmigrant workers with job skills not available locally to be employed temporarily. In 1997, the U.S. Department of Labor initiated a series of increases in the minimum wage to be paid to H-2 workers in the construction trades which doubled the 1976 wage rates by 1979.

While intended to encourage local labor participation in the construction trades, this move is expected to increase construction costs by as much as 40 percent over and above other increases stemming from rising prices for construction materials. Problems in Guam's labor market have been discussed in the last few years.

The construction industry will probably stabilize, with private projects such as condominiums replacing defense-related construction. Government of Guam infrastructure-related projects are expected to continue at about the same level. With the expected expansion of tourism in the near future, new hotels and other tourist facilities will be needed.

III. TRANSPORTATION

AIRLINES

There are currently nine international airlines and three commuter airlines serving the Guam International Air Terminal. These airlines are: Air Nauru, All Nippon Airways, China Airlines, Continental Micronesia, Inc., Japan Airlines, Japan Asia Airways, Korean Airlines, Northwest Airlines and United Airlines. The commuter airlines include: Freedom Air, Micronesian Aviation Systems and Pacific Island Aviation. Progress was also made in the expansion area. Local government and Naval officials have agreed on the transfer of over 125 acres for the construction of aircraft parking aprons, maintenance hangars and other support facilities. The $260 million expansion of the existing airport is currently underway, and will nearly triple the size to accommodate the growth that Guam is expected to experience in the coming years.

In Fiscal Year 1997, total passenger movements (arrivals + departures) were up 5.6 percent over FY 1996 passenger movements, from 3,134,180 to 3,308,400. This solid increase demonstrates the island's ability to recoup and accommodate its visitors despite our natural disasters.

GUAM MASS TRANSIT AUTHORITY

The Guam Mass Transit Authority (GMTA) was created in 1980 to provide land based passenger transportation for Guam. From 1982 to 1984 it operated the I'Bus system which provided an average of 80 trips per day. Since October 15, 1985, it has operated the Guam Public Transit System.

PORT AUTHORITY OF GUAM

Guam's Commercial Port was established in March 1950 as a division of the Department of Commerce within the Government of Guam. It was originally located on 24.5 acres of U.S. Navy property in the Inner Apra Harbor region. In 1966, the Commercial Port was established as a separate department of the Government of Guam. On October 1975, the Commercial Port was renamed the Port Authority of Guam and reestablished as a public corporation and autonomous agency of the Government of Guam.

Guam's port is a major transshipment center of the Western Pacific. It is equipped to move containerized breakbulk and tuna cargo. Presently, ten shipping lines serve the Port Authority, providing services to Hawaii and the U.S. mainland, the Far East, and Micronesian ports. However, the "Jones Act" restricts shipping between Guam and other U.S. ports to U.S. registered ships. Currently, only Matson Navigation and CSX Lines (formerly Sea-Land) service U.S. ports from Guam. This is widely believed to be an impediment to trade within the region, and the government is seeking an exemption to the Jones Act from the U.S. Congress. The number of vessels calling at the Port in FY 1997 was 2,752, an 11 percent decrease over the number calling in FY 1996. Although the vessel calls had dropped slightly overall, the port had been servicing larger vessels carrying more containers.

IV. RETAIL AND WHOLESALE SECTOR

Guam's retail and wholesale sectors are major sectors, which are heavily influenced by tourism growth. They can respond quicker than other sectors to changes in income, consumer preferences, and population changes and import prices.

In the last two decades, these sectors have developed remarkably. In 1998, these sectors employed 14,860 persons out of a total employment of 64,230.

Retailing and wholesaling are generally not regarded as leading sectors, but as sectors which respond to growth in basic industries. Retailing on Guam plays as important a role as the tourism industry.

Relatively high visitor expenditures on gifts and souvenirs may in part reflect the cultural habits of Japanese visitors but also reflect Guam's low prices for many brand name goods. Guam is a duty free port and there are no special "luxury" taxes on consumer goods unlike in many other jurisdictions such as the U.S. and Japan.

About 25% - 40% of retail sales were generated by the tourist industry, with each tourist spending on average about $560 on shopping. Based on the Guam Department of Commerce's survey, a typical Japanese tourist in 1995 spent $129.55 per day locally. Japanese normally stayed 4.3 days and spent 51% of their expenditures on shopping. Purchases by visitors contribute to high retail and wholesale receipts.

The military population also contributes substantially to retail sales. It is believed that many of Guam's numerous temporary residents, resulting from the military presence and from the use of contract labor from Asia or from the United States, purchase a significant portion of their lifetime purchases on durables while on Guam.

There has been a big expansion in the number of shops and outlets in recent years. Most small shops have opened in rural areas.

There is evidence of a change in the character of the retail trade, indicating changes in consumer habits along with changes in land use patterns and in the local economy. Small stores in separate buildings are closing or moving into shopping centers and stores are opening in shopping centers. A major shopping center opened in Agana in November 1978. This 30 shop center includes a supermarket and a department store. A grocery department store complex in Tamuning, which already had two restaurants and small shops, added a mall with 8 shops to form another large shopping center.

A new warehouse club concept is now on Guam. On May 1992, a new 24,000 square-foot store opened in Harmon. In 2004 a second store was opened in Tamuning. In 1995 another warehouse type discount store opened in Harmon/Barrigada Heights. Selling in volume has enabled discount operators to keep prices lower than the competitors, selling everything from clothing to groceries to electronics. Consumers on Guam have evidently taken a liking to this type of shopping.

Liberty House and the new DFS facility in Tumon are trading well. In addition, a number of other retail developments projects have come on-line (Cost-U-Less and K-Mart opened in the first half of 1995). These major retail developments will give far greater depth to the Guam retail economy.

As a sector complementing the tourist industry and responding to a generally rising standard of living, this sector is expected to play an important role in the coming years. However, it cannot be relied upon as a major, dynamic income generating sector. Furthermore, Guam's price level and structure will continue to be determined by external factors such as mainland prices, exchange rate fluctuations, etc.

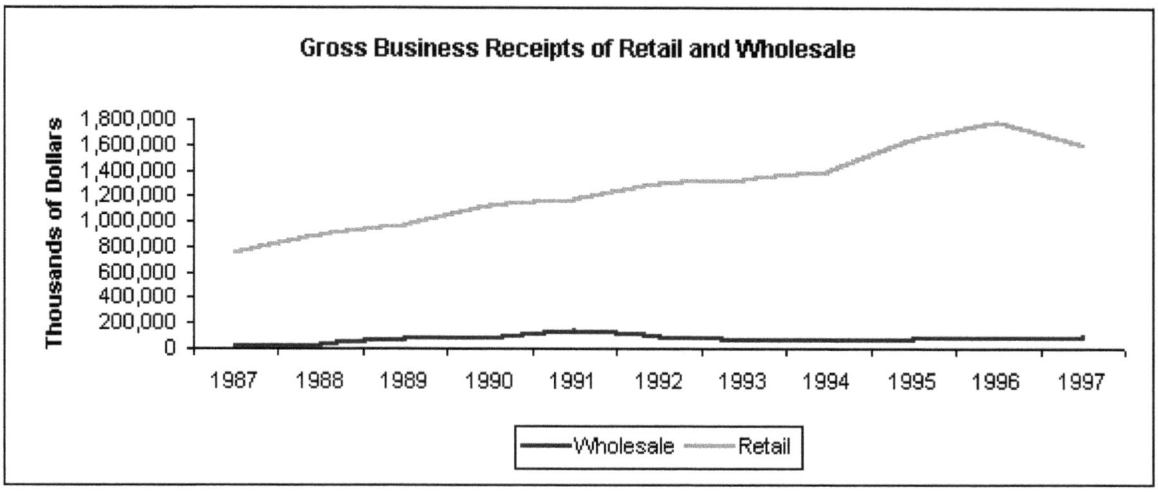

V. FINANCIAL INSTITUTIONS & INCENTIVES

The Sixteenth Annual Report of the Banking Commissioner (latest available) has listed the following licensed financial institutions for 1998: two (2) National Banks; three (3) State Banks; two (2) Territorial Banks; five (5) Foreign Banks; two (2) Savings and Loans Associations; three (3) Off-Shore Lending Facilities and twenty four (24) Finance Companies.

The combined total assets of all financial institutions domiciled on Guam as of December 31, 1998 was $3.8 billion, a 9 percent decrease over the previous year ($4.1 billion).

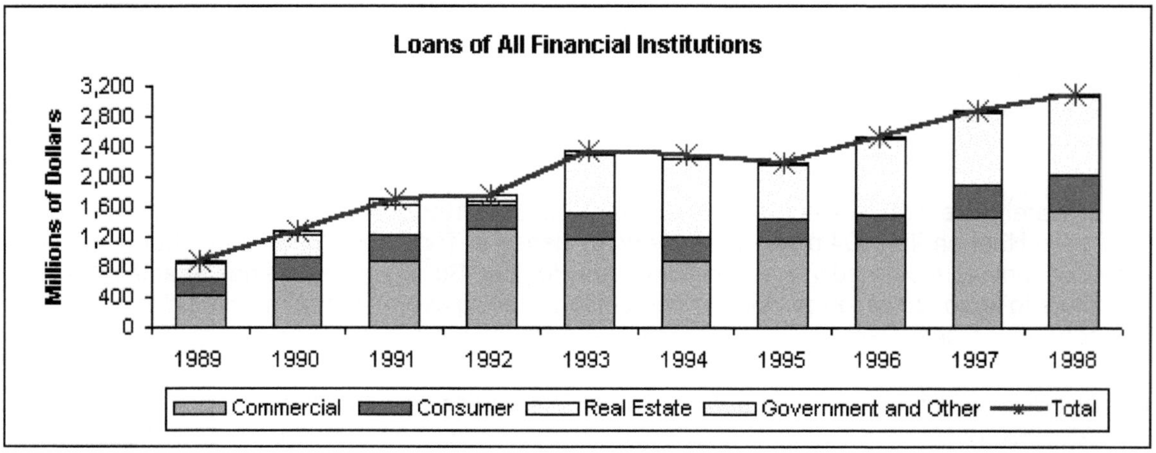

The System of State and Federal banking regulations is known as the dual banking system. This system allows both State (Territorial) and Federal Governments to charter and regulate banks.

Federal regulators include the Federal Reserve, which regulates banks and bank holding companies, and the office of the Comptroller of the Currency which charters and regulates National Banks. In addition, the Federal Deposit Insurance Corporation (FDIC) serves as insurers of both National and State-Chartered Banks. National Banks are automatically members of the Federal Reserve and must be insured by the FDIC as are the two Territorial Banks.

Total deposits for all financial institutions was $1,472.6 million as of December 1998, which was down 9.5 percent from December 1997. Total loans for the same period was $3,086.5 million, an increase of 6.8 percent from December 1997's figure of $2,890.3 million.

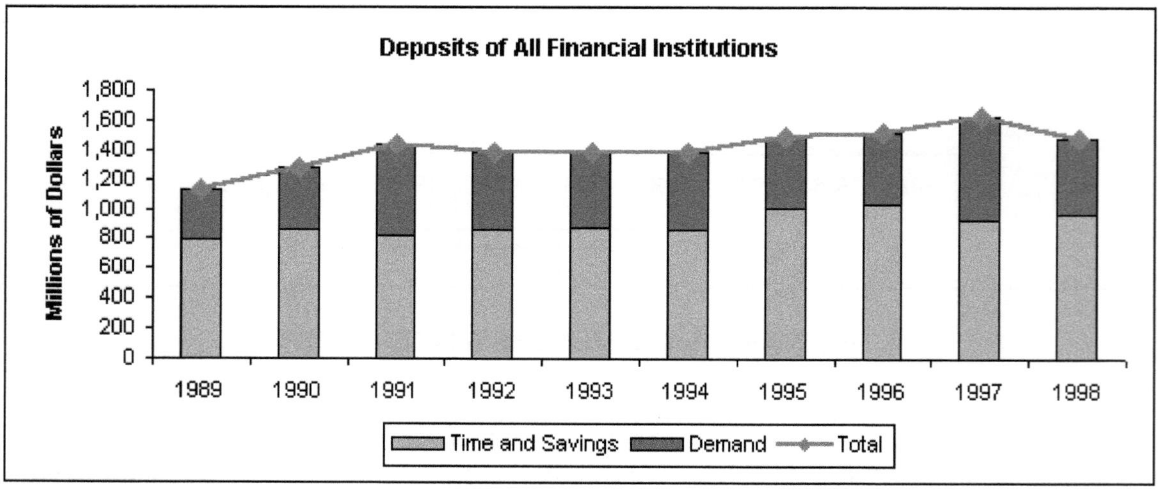

INSURANCE

The Thirty-Ninth Annual Report of the Insurance Commissioner shows 134 insurers transacting insurance business on Guam in 1997. Among the 134 insurers, 113 are foreign companies, 17 are alien companies, and 4 are domestic companies.

GUAM ECONOMIC DEVELOPMENT AUTHORITY

The Guam Economic Development Authority (GEDA) was created August 1965 with the passage of Public Law 8-80. GEDA's main objective is to stimulate the economic growth and development of the Territory, specifically in the areas of commerce, agriculture, industry and tourism.

One program that was designed to enhance economic development is the Qualifying Certificate Program. GEDA is authorized to allow tax rebates and abatements to qualified investors in the form of Qualifying Certificates.

Qualified individuals and companies may be granted a maximum of 75% income tax rebates for up to 20 years; 100% abatement on real property taxes for up to 10 years; and abatement on gross receipts taxes on petroleum and alcoholic beverages made in Guam up to ten years.

As of December 1991 there were 19 Qualifying Certificate recipients who have invested more than $1.9 billion in Guam.

VI. TOURISM

VISITOR ARRIVALS

Total visitor arrivals came to 1,137,026 for CY1998. There were significant decreases in visitor air arrivals for all quarters of 1998 as compared to 1997. The most notable decreases were in the second and fourth quarters, at (-19%) and (-22%) respectively. An average of 99% of Guam's visitors come in by air. Cited as the primary reason for the drop in visitor arrivals was the ongoing Asian economic crisis. Overall, there was a significant decrease in arrivals of (-18%) as compared to 1997.

Total Japanese visitor arrivals dropped (-12%) in 1998, while Korean visitor arrivals dropped drastically by (-83%). The huge drop in Korean arrivals could additionally be explained by a reduction in airline seat capacity serving that market as well as other factors related to the Korean Air tragedy in 1997.

Figure T1
MONTHLY VISITOR ARRIVALS TO GUAM CY1997 AND CY1998

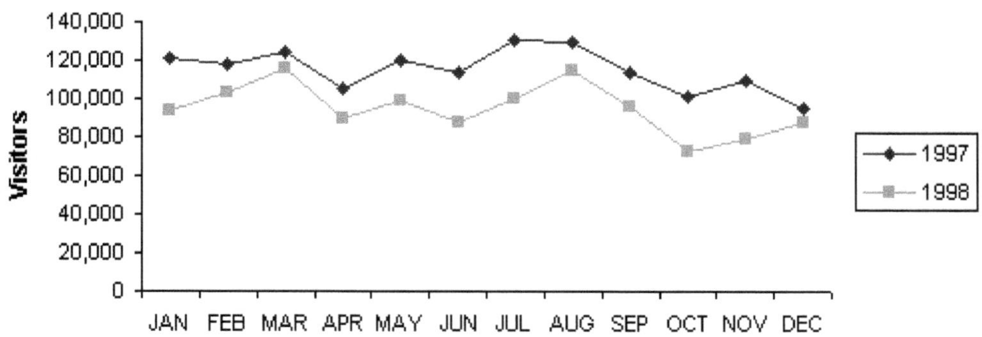

Source: Guam Visitors Bureau

Figure T2
ANNUAL VISITOR ARRIVALS TO GUAM 1978 - 1998

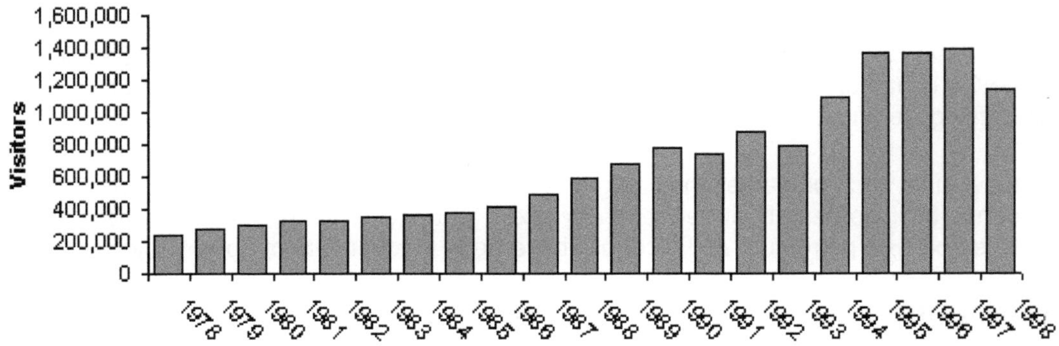

Source: Guam Visitors Bureau

VISITOR MARKETS

Figure T3 shows the percentage breakdown in Guam's major markets. Japan, Korea, Taiwan, the U.S. Mainland and Hawaii comprise Guam's primary markets in total visitor ***air arrivals.*** The major markets, Japan, Taiwan, the U.S. Mainland and Hawaii recorded decreases in visitor air arrivals for the year as compared to 1997. Another market, Thailand, produced the highest increase for 1998, although this was from a relatively small base number. Visitor arrivals from Korea and the CNMI also declined.

Figure T3
VISITOR AIR ARRIVALS TO GUAM BY PLACE OF RESIDENCE CY1997 AND CY1998

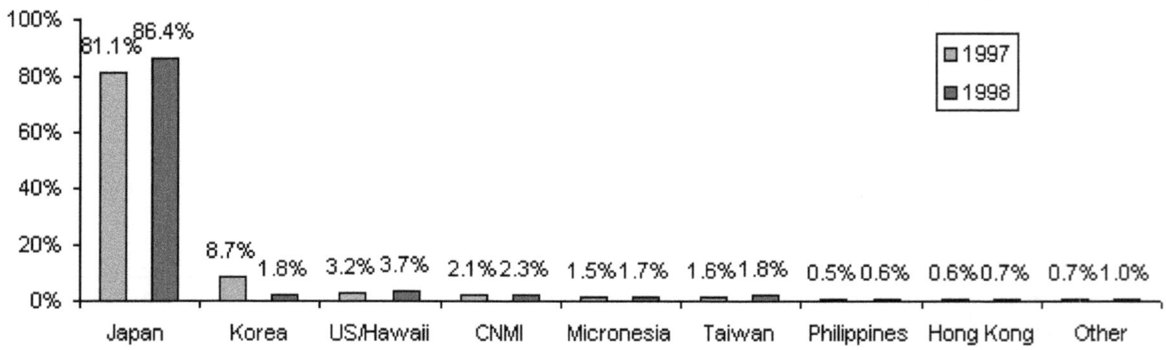

Note: Figures may not add exactly to 100 due to rounding

Source: Guam Visitors Bureau

JAPAN Japanese visitors continued to have the greatest impact on visitor arrivals as Guam's largest market, making up 86.4% of all visitor air arrivals, for a total of 975,402.

Figure T4 shows that Guam's share of the estimated 15.8 million outbound travelers from Japan was 6.2% for 1998. This is a decrease from the 1997 figure which was at 6.6%. According to the Japan National Tourist Organization, outbound travel decreased by approximately (-5.9%) in 1998.

Figure T4
GUAM'S SHARE OF JAPANESE INTERNATIONAL TRAVELERS 1988-1998

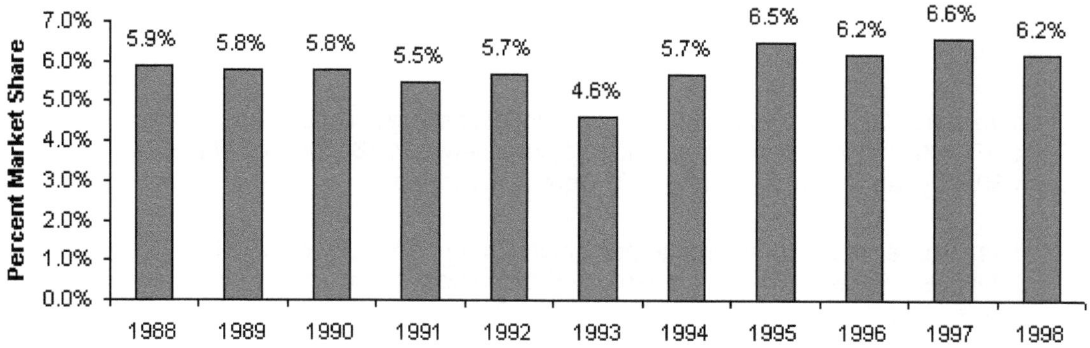

Source: Guam Visitors Bureau

BY REGION

For 1998, all regions except for Okinawa experienced declines. The highest single region percentage decline took place in Tohoku at (-23%), followed by Kyushu at (-20%) and Chubu (Nagoya) at (-19%). Arrivals from the highest percentage growth region, Okinawa, totaled 1,700 more visitors to Guam in 1998 (See Figure T5).

Figure T5
JAPANESE VISITOR ARRIVALS TO GUAM BY REGION 1997 AND 1998

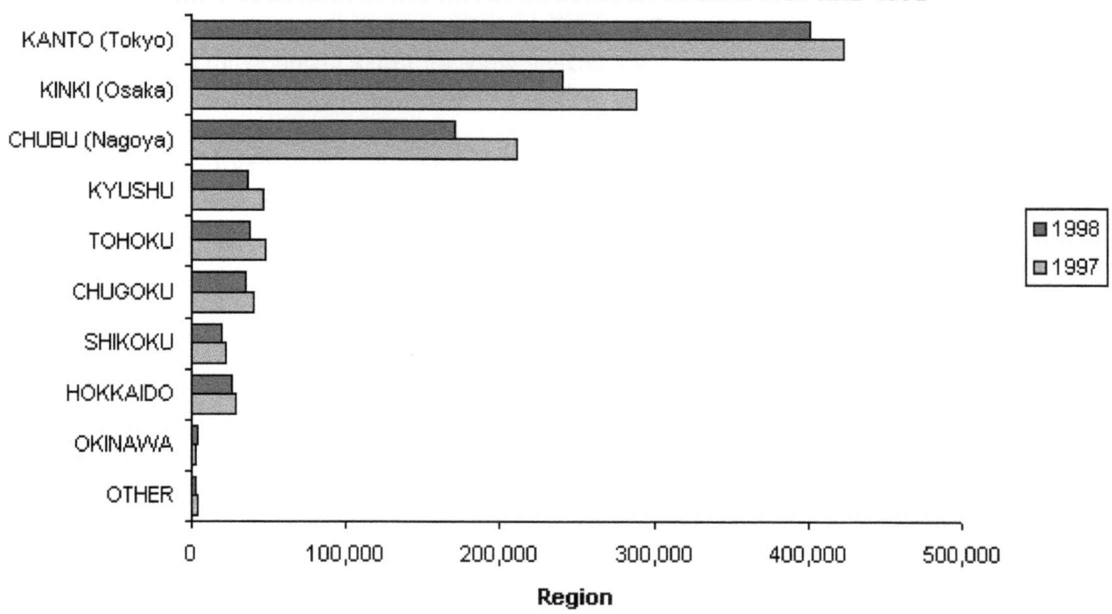

Source: Guam Visitors Bureau

DEMOGRAPHICS AND TRIP CHARACTERISTICS

Demographic characteristics of Japanese travelers to Guam based on the Guam Visitors Bureau quarterly exit surveys for FY1997 and FY1998 are shown in Table T1. Notable figures are presented below.

Gender - Males constituted 46% of the survey responses while females constituted 54%.

Age - There were notable changes in age breakdown of survey respondents as compared to 1997; For FY1998, 61% of survey respondents were between 18-29 years old, 33% were between 30-49 years old, and the other 6% were 50+ years old.

Occupation - There was a 7 percentage point increase in Office Ladies. Another notable increase was in Salarymen/women, which increased by 5 percentage points. The biggest decreases were in Housewives and Business Owners, which fell by 2 percentage points each. All the other categories recorded relatively slight changes.

Travel Purpose - There was a 1 percentage point increase in pleasure travelers. All other categories likewise recorded very slight changes.

Travel Arrangements - Exit survey questions for this category were revised by the Guam Visitors Bureau in FY98. Thus, responses are not necessarily comparable to those given in FY97. The highest recorded responses were Full Package Tour, at 57%, and Free Time Package Tour (airfare and hotel only), at 38%. However, a caveat to these figures is that to achieve economies of scale, unrelated individuals are often sold "packages" by tour operators. Thus, they appear to be on a "group tour", as would employees from the same company or students from the same school.

Repeaters - The percentage of repeat visitors decreased slightly to 28% of total survey respondents, as compared to 29% for FY1997.

Travel Companions - The most significant increase were for those visiting with Friends at 42% of survey respondents. All other categories recorded relatively slight changes.

Length of Stay - 11% of survey respondents stayed 1 to 2 nights, 61% stayed 3 nights and 28% stayed 4 or more nights.

Travel Motivation - Seas and Beaches and Proximity are the key motivators at 35% and 34% of respondents respectively. Relaxation and Tour Price were also strong factors at 29% and 25%.

Table T1 - JAPAN DEMOGRAPHICS AND TRIP CHARACTERISTICS (FY1998 - FY1997)

	FY1998	FY1997		FY1998	FY1997		FY1998	FY1997
GENDER			TRAVEL ARRANGEMENTS[1]			TRAVEL MOTIVATION		
Male	46%	47%	Full Package Tour	57%	N/A	Seas, Beaches	35%	42%
Female	54%	53%	Free Time Package Tour (airfare and hotel)	38%	N/A	Tour Price	25%	36%

			Individually Arranged Travel (FIT)	3%	N/A	Water Sports	11%	15%
AGE			Other	2%	N/A	Proximity	34%	45%
18-29	61%	51%				Relaxation	29%	17%
30-49	33%	42%	REPEATERS	28%	29%	Recommended by Family/Friends	8%	11%
50+	6%	8%				Golf	7%	7%
			TRAVEL COMPANIONS			Previous Trip	13%	6%
OCCUPATION			Office Mates	25%	24%	Business Trip	1%	16%
Salarypersons	31%	26%	Friends	42%	34%	Visit Friends/Relatives	2%	2%
Office Ladies	23%	16%	Spouse	18%	21%	Company Trip	21%	N/A
Executives	10%	11%	Family	20%	24%	SCUBA Diving	5%	N/A
Students	7%	6%	Children	N/A	19%	Other	21%	N/A
Business Owner	4%	6%	Alone	2%	N/A			
Professional	10%	9%	Other	2%	N/A			
Housewives	8%	10%						
Others	9%	16%	LENGTH OF STAY					
			1-2 Nights	11%	10%			
TRIP PURPOSE			3 Nights	61%	56%			
Pleasure	71%	70%	4 or more Nights	28%	34%			
Company Trip	18%	19%						
Honeymoon	6%	5%						
Business	1%	1%						
Visiting Friends and Relatives	1%	2%						
Other	3%	2%						

Notes: Some totals may not add to 100 due to rounding or multiple responses; in past surveys, Company and Business Trips as indicated under Travel Motivation were combined into one category.

N/A - Items not listed as possible responses in survey(s) due to revisions or other factors.

1/ No official fiscal year figures available; Travel Arrangement survey questions revised during FY98; data compiled from June 1998 and September 1998 Exit Survey Reports.

Source: Guam Visitors Bureau

KOREA Korean visitors totaled 20,268 in 1998, a drastic (-83%) decrease over 1997. Guam was still reeling from the Korean Air Flight 801 crash in August 1997, which led to subsequent cancellation of flights by the airline and cancellation of flights by other airlines serving the region. The ongoing Asian economic crisis was also another major factor cited for the decline. Korean visitors made up 1.8% of all visitor air arrivals to Guam in 1998.

Guam's market share for Korea likewise dipped tremendously, going from 2.6% in 1997 to 0.7% in 1998. However, there was also a significant decrease of about (-32.5%) for outbound Korean travelers in 1998. There is still room for growth in this market as recovery begins from both the Korean Air tragedy and the Asian economic crisis.

Demographics and Trip Characteristics

Demographic characteristics of Korean travelers to Guam based on the Guam Visitors Bureau quarterly exit surveys for FY1997 and FY1998 are shown in Table T2. Notable figures are presented below.

Gender - Guam attracted an equal number of men and women. The proportion of men declined considerably as compared to FY1997, where 54% of the respondents were men.

Age - 94% of Korean respondents were under 50 years of age, with 46% of the respondents between 18-29 years old and 48% between 30-49 years old. The largest increase was recorded in the 30-49 age group, which had increased by 4 percentage points as compared to FY1997.

Occupation - 36% of the survey respondents identified themselves as Salarymen/women while 16% identified themselves as Professionals. The most notable change was in Housewives, which increased to 12% in FY1998.

Travel Purpose - 47% of respondents listed Pleasure as their main purpose for traveling while Honeymoon came in second at 26%. The highest increase was recorded for those respondents Visiting Friends and Relatives, from 3% in FY1997 to 12% in FY1998.

Travel Arrangements - Exit Survey questions for this category were revised by the Guam Visitors Bureau for FY1998. Thus, responses recorded in FY1997 may not be directly comparable to those given under the new survey. The largest response recorded was for FIT's, at 47%.

Repeaters - 24% of Korean respondents were repeat travelers to Guam for FY1998, an increase of 10 percentage points over the previous year.

Travel Companions - Spouses were the most frequent travel companions for this market, being listed by 42% of the survey respondents. The second most cited travel companions were Friends, indicated by 20% of respondents.

Length of Stay - 64% of all respondents stayed 4 or more nights, while 28% stayed 3 nights.

Travel Motivation - Koreans indicated that Relaxation was the most important motivator for travel to Guam. Last year, Seas and Beaches was the most cited reason for visiting the island. Reasonable Tour Price appeared to be much less important to Korean survey respondents than it was for Japanese visitors.

Table T2 - KOREA DEMOGRAPHICS AND TRIP CHARACTERISTICS (FY1998 - FY1997)

	FY1998	FY1997		FY1998	FY1997		FY1998	FY1997
GENDER			TRAVEL ARRANGEMENTS[1]			TRAVEL MOTIVATION		
Male	50%	54%	FIT	47%	N/A	Seas, Beaches	17%	47%
Female	50%	46%	Group Package Tour	21%	N/A	Tour Price	7%	17%
			Group (Friends/Co-workers)	16%	N/A	Water Sports	8%	20%
AGE			Company Staff Tour	7%	N/A	Proximity	13%	23%
18-29	46%	50%	Company Paid	4%	N/A	Relaxation	32%	37%
30-49	48%	44%	Staff Incentive Tour	2%	N/A	Recommended by Family/Friends	12%	23%
50+	6%	5%	Client Incentive Tour	4%	N/A	Golf	2%	2%
						Previous Trip	3%	4%
OCCUPATION			REPEATERS	24%	14%	Business Trip	8%	7%
Salarypersons	36%	39%				Visit Friends/Relatives	15%	2%
Office Ladies	N/A	1%	TRAVEL COMPANIONS			Company Trip	10%	N/A
Students	8%	5%	Office Mates	11%	12%	SCUBA Diving	2%	N/A
Business Owners	4%	6%	Friends	20%	24%	Other	9%	N/A
Professional	16%	16%	Spouse	42%	48%			
Housewives	12%	6%	Family	18%	18%			

Others	22%	25%	Other	1%	1%			
			Children	N/A	12%			
TRIP PURPOSE			Alone	15%	5%			
Pleasure	47%	58%						
Company Trip	2%	4%	AVERAGE LENGTH OF STAY					
Honeymoon	26%	30%	1-2 Nights	8%	23%			
Business	8%	3%	3 Nights	28%	47%			
Visiting Friends and Relatives	12%	3%	4 or more Nights	64%	30%			
Other	5%	2%						
Notes: Some totals may not add to 100 due to rounding or multiple responses.								
N/A - Items not listed as possible responses in survey(s) due to revisions or other factors.								
1/ No official fiscal year figures available; travel arrangement breakdowns estimated from Guam Visitors Bureau Korean Exit Surveys for corresponding fiscal years.								
Source: Guam Visitors Bureau								

US MAINLAND/HAWAII The U.S. Mainland/Hawaii was the second largest market with 41,875 visitors. This market had experienced a slight decrease from 1997, when there were 43,316 visitors from the region.

DEMOGRAPHICS AND TRIP CHARACTERISTICS

Demographic characteristics of United States travelers to Guam based on the Guam Visitors Bureau Quarterly Exit Surveys for FY1997 and FY1998 are shown in Table T3. Notable figures are presented below.

Gender - Males constituted 83% of the survey respondents. This was a dramatic increase of 20 percentage points from FY1997.

Age - 56% of the survey respondents were between 30-49 years old, 29% were 50+ years of age and 14% fell into the 18-29 years age group. The lone increase was recorded in the 30-49 years age group.

Occupation - Most US/Hawaii visitors specifically identified themselves as Professionals at 21% of respondents; the next most cited occupations were Salarymen/women at 17% and Executives at 14%. However, 35% of the respondents either refused to disclose their occupation or identified themselves as "Other".

Travel Purpose - 52% of US/Hawaii travelers came to Guam for Business/Federal Assignments, while 15% came for Visiting Friends/Relatives. There was a notable decrease of 18 percentage points in Pleasure travelers to the island.

Travel Arrangements - No FY1998 figures were available for this category at time of publication; for FY1997, 94% of US/Hawaii travelers came in on Individual Tours, an increase of 11 percentage points over FY1996.

Repeaters - 60% of US/Hawaii visitors identified themselves as being repeat visitors. This is due in part to business travel and the purpose of visiting friends and relatives. Also, this market is the most mature and has had more time to travel.

Travel Companions - 58% of US/Hawaii visitors indicated they were traveling Alone, while 22% visited the island with Office Mates. The largest percentage point increase was also in Office Mates, increasing by 14 points.

Length of Stay - 83% of the respondents stayed 4 or more nights while 13% stayed 3 nights. The US/Hawaii sample had a significant number of short stay travelers but much longer average stays than the Asian markets.

Travel Motivation - 62% of the survey respondents indicated that they were on Guam for Business while 24% were here to Visit Friends/Relatives.

Table T3 - UNITED STATES DEMOGRAPHICS AND TRIP CHARACTERISTICS (FY1998 - FY1997)

	FY1998		FY1998		FY1998
GENDER		TRAVEL ARRANGEMENTS[1]		TRAVEL MOTIVATION	
Male	83%	Individual Tours	N/A	Seas, Beaches	9%
Female	17%	Group Package Tour	N/A	Tour Price	0%
				Water Sports	2%
AGE		REPEATERS	60%	Proximity	0%
18-29	14%			Relaxation	5%
30-49	56%	TRAVEL COMPANIONS		Recommended by Family/Friends	3%
50+	29%	Office Mates	22%	Golf	2%
		Friends	6%	Previous Trip	5%
OCCUPATION		Spouse	11%	Business Trip	62%
Salarypersons	17%	Family	4%	Visit Friends/Relatives	24%

Office Ladies	2%	Other	0%	Company Trip	7%
Executives	14%	Alone	58%	SCUBA Diving	5%
Students	1%			Other	17%
Business Owner	8%	AVERAGE LENGTH OF STAY			
Professional	21%	1-2 Nights	5%		
Housewives	1%	3 Nights	13%		
Others	35%	4 or more Nights	83%		
TRIP PURPOSE					
Pleasure	12%				
Company Trip	N/A				
Honeymoon	N/A				
Business/Federal Assignment	52%				
Visiting Friends and Relatives	15%				
Convention/Conference	1%				
Employment	7%				
Other	12%				

TAIWAN Taiwan represents 1.8% of total visitor air arrivals to Guam. There was a (-8.5%) decrease in visitor arrivals from the year before, totaling 20,545.

Guam's share of this market has not yet reached 1%. In 1998 there were over 5.9 million outbound travelers from Taiwan and Guam received only 0.4%, unchanged from the previous year. According to the Tourism Bureau Ministry of Transportation and Communications for the Republic of China, there was a 4.0% decrease in outbound travelers as compared to 1997.

DEMOGRAPHICS AND TRIP CHARACTERISTICS

Demographic characteristics of Taiwan travelers to Guam based on the Guam Visitors Bureau quarterly exit surveys for FY1997 and FY1998 are shown in Table T4. Notable figures are presented below.

Gender - Females constituted a majority of survey respondents at 54%.

Age - 54% of the survey respondents for this group fell into the 30 to 49 years age category while 40% were between 18 and 29 years old.

Occupation - 34% of the Taiwan visitors surveyed identified themselves as Salarymen/women; the next most cited response was Professional at 16%. The percentage of visitors identifying themselves as Salarymen/women increased by 7 points from FY1997.

Travel Purpose - 75% came to Guam for Pleasure, while 10% were here on Honeymoon. After recording the biggest drop in FY1997, those coming in on Company Trips experienced a 6 percentage point increase as compared to the year before.

Travel Arrangements - Exit Survey questions for this category were revised by the Guam Visitors Bureau for FY1998. Therefore, figures may not be directly comparable to the year before. 30% of respondents indicated they were FIT's, while 28% identified themselves as traveling in a Group (Friends/Co-workers).

Repeaters - 9% of the Taiwan survey respondents indicted that they were repeat travelers to Guam. This is a slight increase from the previous year.

Travel Companions - Most Taiwanese came to the island either with Friends, at 35% of survey respondents, or with their Family, at 33%. A significant 28% of Taiwan visitors arrived with their Spouse.

Length of Stay - 75% of all respondents stayed 3 nights, while 13% stayed 4 or more Nights.

Travel Motivation - Relaxation was a key motivator for Taiwanese visitors, indicated by 48% of respondents. Seas and Beaches came in second, being cited by 45% of Taiwanese visitors surveyed.

Table T4 - TAIWAN DEMOGRAPHICS AND TRIP CHARACTERISTICS (FY1998 - FY1997)

	FY1998	FY1997		FY1998	FY1997		FY1998
GENDER			TRAVEL ARRANGEMENTS[1]			TRAVEL MOTIVATION	
Male	46%	47%	Individual Tours	30%	N/A	Seas, Beaches	57%
Female	54%	53%	Group (Friends/Co-workers)	28%	N/A	Tour Price	18%
			Group Package Tour			Water Sports	28%
AGE			Staff Incentive Tour	4%	16%	Proximity	35%
18-29	40%	39%	Company Paid	27%	23%	Relaxation	46%
30-49	54%	53%	Company Staff	3%	6%	Recommended	

			Tour			by Family/Friends	
50+	6%	8%	Client Incentive Tour	3%	6%	Golf	23%
			REPEATERS	8%	8%	Previous Trip	4%
OCCUPATION						Business Trip	2%
Salarypersons	34%	27%	TRAVEL COMPANIONS			Visit Friends/Relatives	7%
Office Ladies	3%	4%				Company Trip	
Executives	13%	11%	TRAVEL COMPANIONS			SCUBA Diving	3%
Students	3%	4%	Office Mates	11%	36%	Other	3%
Business Owner	8%	8%	Friends	37%	29%		
Professional	16%	12%	Spouse	34%	35%		
Housewives	4%	6%	Family	24%	16%		
Others	21%	29%	Children	32%	23%		
			Other	2%	N/A		
TRIP PURPOSE			Alone	2%	8%		
Pleasure	75%	80%					
Company Trip	9%	3%	AVERAGE LENGTH OF STAY				
Honeymoon	10%	11%	1-2 Nights	18%	7%		
Business	5%	3%	3 Nights	36%	11%		
Visiting Friends and Relatives	2%	2%	4 or more Nights	46%	82%		
Other	0%	2%					

HONG KONG Hong Kong is starting to emerge as a new significant tourism market for Guam. Although other markets have larger numbers of visitor arrivals, the Guam Visitors Bureau had started to track Hong Kong tourists as this market cannot be ignored.

Hong Kong visitors accounted for 0.7% of total visitor air arrivals to Guam. In 1998, 7,906 arrivals were recorded from this area. This was a decrease of 5.0% from the previous year.

DEMOGRAPHICS AND TRIP CHARACTERISTICS

Exit surveys were conducted by the Guam Visitors Bureau for FY1998. The results are found in Table T5. Notable figures are presented below.

Gender - Males constituted a majority of survey respondents at 58%. This was an increase of 7 percentage points from the year before.

Age - 60% of the survey respondents for this group fell into the 30 to 49 years category while 34% were between 18 and 29 years old.

Occupation - 16% of the Hong Kong visitors surveyed identified themselves as Professionals; the next most cited response was Executives at 14%.

Travel Purpose - 82% came to Guam for Pleasure. The next most cited purpose was for Business, at 10%.

Travel Arrangements - Exit Survey questions for this category were revised by the Guam Visitors Bureau in FY1998. Therefore, results may not be directly comparable to the prior fiscal year. 48% of the survey respondents indicated that they had come in on a Packaged Tour, while 35% came in on a Partial Packaged Tour (hotel and airfare only).

Repeaters - 17% of the Hong Kong survey respondents indicated that they were repeat travelers to Guam.

Travel Companions - Most visitors from Hong Kong came to the island either with Family, at 30% of survey respondents or with their Friends, at 29%.

Length of Stay - 40% of all respondents stayed 1-2 nights, while 35% stayed 4 or more Nights.

Travel Motivation - Seas and Beaches was a key motivator for visitors from Hong Kong, indicated by 58% of respondents. Relaxation came in second, being cited by 47% of visitors surveyed.

Table T5 - HONG KONG DEMOGRAPHICS AND TRIP CHARACTERISTICS (FY1998 - FY1997)

	FY1998	FY1997		FY1998	FY1997		FY1998
GENDER			TRAVEL ARRANGEMENTS[1]			TRAVEL MOTIVATION	
Male	58%	51%	Packaged Tour	48%	N/A	Seas, Beaches	58%
Female	42%	49%	Partial Packaged Tour (hotel and airfare only)	35%	N/A	Tour Price	19%
			Non-Packaged Tour	15%	N/A	Water Sports	25%

AGE			Other	2%	N/A	Proximity	33%
18-29	34%	39%				Relaxation	47%
30-49	60%	57%	REPEATERS	17%	11%	Recommended by Family/Friends	14%
50+	7%	4%				Golf	3%
			TRAVEL COMPANIONS			Previous Trip	3%
OCCUPATION			Office Mates	5%	8%	Business Trip	11%
Salarypersons	12%	20%	Friends	29%	40%	Visit Friends/Relatives	7%
Office Ladies	13%	13%	Spouse	27%	37%	Company Trip	2%
Executives	14%	19%	Family	30%	17%	SCUBA Diving	8%
Students	6%	1%	Children	N/A	13%	Other	13%
Business Owner	7%	5%	Other	0%	15%		
Professional	16%	26%	Alone	15%	6%		
Housewives	2%	3%					
Others	31%	14%	AVERAGE LENGTH OF STAY				
			1-2 Nights	40%	45%		
TRIP PURPOSE			3 Nights	25%	31%		
Pleasure	82%	86%	4 or more Nights	35%	24%		
Company Trip	2%	3%					
Honeymoon	2%	3%					
Business	10%	5%					
Visiting Friends and Relatives	3%	2%					
Other	1%	1%					

ACCOMMODATIONS

In 1998, there were 8,667 hotel, motel and condo units available on a nightly basis, 428 more than tabulated the previous year. In terms of realistic capacity limits, this translates into approximately 3.10 million room nights available for use, with an allowance for 2% of rooms out of use for renovations, repairs or other reasons. If 80% of the units were occupied, Guam could accommodate approximately 1.65 million visitors, assuming an average of 2 persons per room and a 3 night average length of stay. Increasing the average occupancy level to 85%, Guam could accommodate 1.76 million visitors.

Additions and Deletions

Among the major changes to the accommodations inventory during 1998 included the following:

The opening of the Imperial Suites Hotel in Tumon, adding 142 rooms;
The opening of the Santa Fe Inn On The Bay in Tamuning, adding 112 rooms;
The opening of the Sherwood Resort Guam in Tumon, adding 332 rooms;
The closing of the Hotel Palmridge in Barrigada, deleting 66 rooms;
The demolition of a tower of the Guam Reef Hotel which suffered extensive typhoon damage in late 1997, deleting 158 rooms.

There were numerous other additions and deletions of hotel rooms which took place in 1998.

There are also other properties that have received approval from the Territorial Land Use Commission that appear definite but have not made formal announcements as to their opening date.

Under Construction/Renovation

Among the new units actively under construction or renovation at the end of 1998 included:

The Royal Orchid Guam in Tumon, with 200 proposed rooms;
The Outrigger Guam Resort in Tumon, with 600 rooms; facilities within the Outrigger complex include the Hard Rock Cafe;
The New Century Hotel in Tumon, with 100 proposed rooms;
The Hotel Accion in Yona, with 100 proposed rooms.

The completion of these projects will increase room capacity in Guam by a significant 12%.

There are also other properties that have received approval from the Territorial Land Use Commission that appear definite but have not made formal announcements as to their opening date.

HOTEL OCCUPANCY RATES

The Guam Hotel and Restaurant Association, which has 30 member hotels representing 96% of the total hotel/motel/condo units on Guam, reported a weighted average occupancy rate of 66% for 1998. This was a 13 percentage point decrease from 1997. However, because their membership includes both tourist and non-tourist hotels, the average occupancy rate for tourist hotels would be expected to be higher (See Figure T6).

Figure T6
GROSS WEIGHTED MONTHLY HOTEL OCCUPANCY RATES 1997 AND 1998

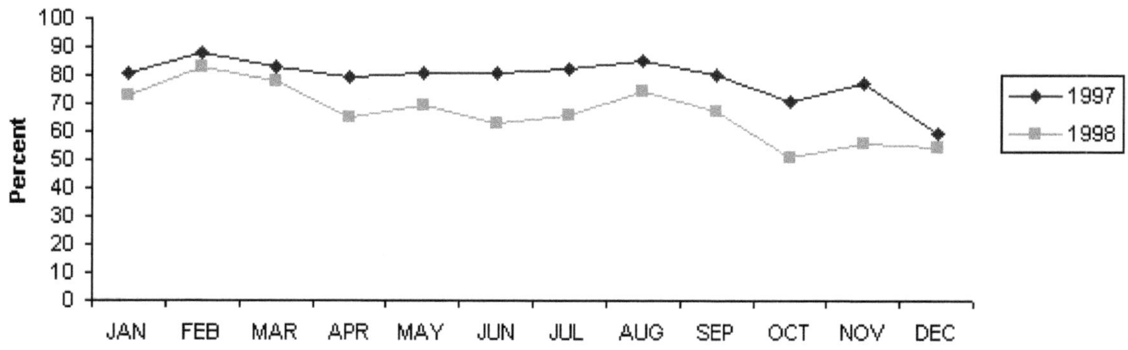

Source: Guam Hotel and Restaurant Association (GHRA)

GUAM AIRPORT PASSENGER MOVEMENTS

There was a 16.5% decrease in total passenger arrivals on flights to Guam, which in FY1998 numbered 1,374,927. The number of transiting passengers increased 14.9% to 336,049, while the number of departing passengers decreased 17.1% to 1,378,420.

In FY1997, total passenger arrivals to Guam numbered 1,646,126. The number of transiting passengers totaled 292,537 while the number of departing passengers totaled 1,646,126.

Figure T7
GUAM AIRPORT PAX MOVEMENTS FY1997 AND FY1998

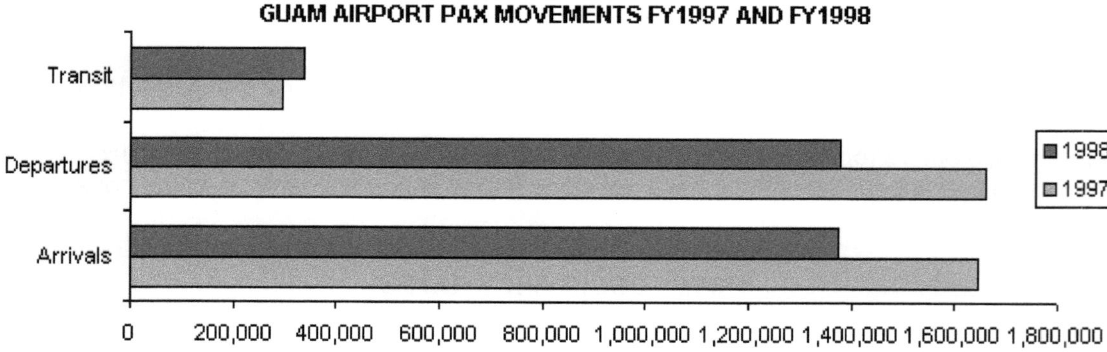

Source: Guam International Airport Authority

SCHEDULED AIR SEAT CAPACITY

Increases

The total number of average weekly seats originating from Japan decreased by 13.8% in 1998, from 36,178 to 31,172. Monthly, this would translate into approximately 124,689 seats. This total includes both direct and indirect flights from the country.

Decreases

In 1998, total scheduled seats per week from Taiwan declined by 2.5%, to 1,032 average seats. This figure includes both direct and indirect routes from the country. Total seats from Korea decreased dramatically by 75%, to 1,309 average seats per week.

Figure T8

1998 Average Number Of Airline Seats By Point of Origin

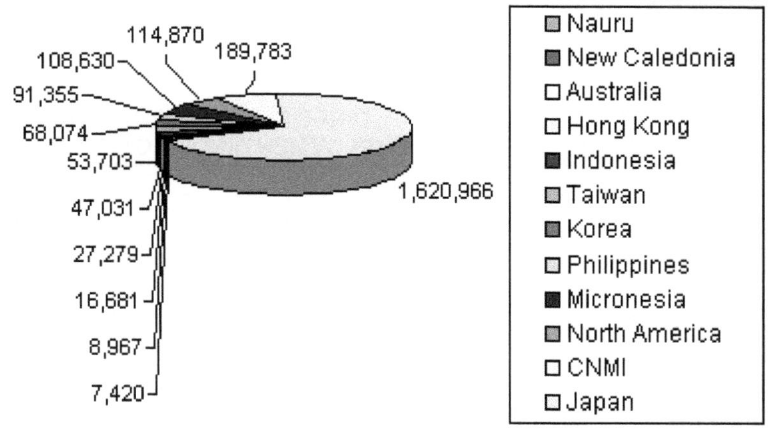

Source: Guam International Airport Authority

TOURISM RELATED EMPLOYMENT

Hotel Employment

The figure for employees on payroll for hotels in December 1998 was 5,730. This was a decrease of (-15.4%) from the December 1997 figure of 6,770. This represents the lowest amount of employees on hotel payrolls to date; the previous low was the December 1995 figure of 5,820 (See Figure T9).

Figure T9

HOTEL EMPLOYEES ON PAYROLL FOR DECEMBER 1988 - 1998

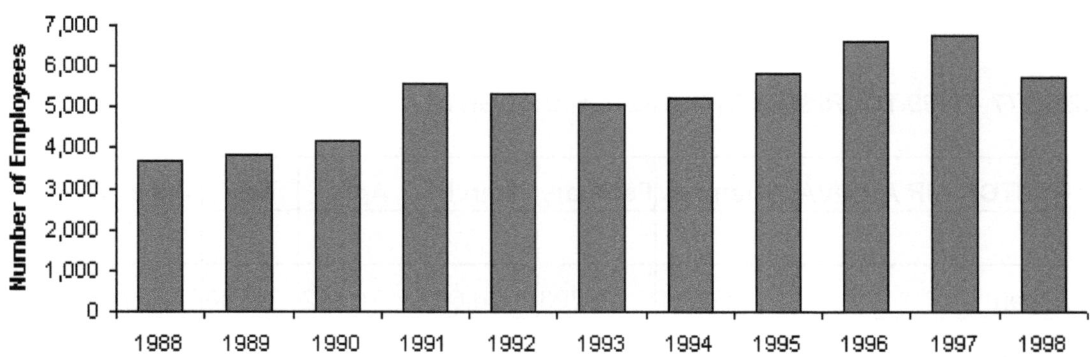

Source: Bureau of Labor Statistics, Department of Labor, Government of Guam

Indirect Employment

There were many jobs that were indirectly produced by tourism, and the Retail Trade sector had the highest number of indirect jobs at 3,717. Table T6, Estimated Direct and Indirect Tourism Related Private Sector Employment by Industry for September 1998, provides a more detailed breakdown of both direct and indirect employment generated by the visitor industry.

Table T6 - ESTIMATED DIRECT AND INDIRECT TOURISM RELATED PRIVATE SECTOR EMPLOYMENT BY INDUSTRY FOR SEPTEMBER 1998

INDUSTRY	TOTAL EMPLOYMENT	PERCENT DIRECT	DIRECT EMPLOYMENT	PERCENT INDIRECT	INDIRECT EMPLOYMENT	COMBINED	DIRECT & INDIRECT EMPLOYMENT
AGRICULTURE	300	0%	-	7%	21	7%	21
CONSTRUCTION	5,840	0%	-	11%	642	11%	642
MANUFACTURING	1,950	1%	20	24%	468	25%	488
TRANSPORTATION/ PUBLIC UTILITIES	5,570	43%	2,395	12%	668	55%	3,063
WHOLESALE TRADE	2,080	7%	146	26%	541	33%	687
RETAIL TRADE	12,390	24%	2,974	30%	3,717	54%	6,691
FINANCE, INSURANCE & REAL ESTATE	2,770	3%	83	11%	305	14%	388
SERVICES	14,440	38%	5,487	13%	1,877	51%	7,364
TOTAL	45,340	24%	11,105	18%	8,239	43%	19,344
Source: Bureau of Labor Statistics, Department of Labor, Government of Guam							

TOURISM STATISTICAL HIGHLIGHTS 1999

Table T7 provides a general highlight of tourism on Guam for the months of January to June 1999. Included in the table are visitor arrivals figures and brief demographics.

TABLE T7 - 1999 TOURISM STATISTICAL HIGHLIGHTS (JANUARY - JUNE)

VISITOR AIR ARRIVALS	January	February	March	April	May	June	TOTAL
Japan	72,611	70,296	86,607	70,422	73,748	74,117	447,801
Korea	2,210	2,116	1,977	2,475	4,225	2,943	15,946
Taiwan, R.O.C.	1,440	2,811	2,506	4,589	4,455	4,251	20,052
U.S. Mainland	2,726	2,622	3,590	2,587	3,101	2,875	17,501
Hawaii	775	589	1,031	678	845	866	4,784

CNMI	1,890	1,538	1,811	1,763	2,199	2,092	11,293
Palau	252	147	239	223	511	487	1,859
FSM	925	230	959	929	1,400	1,496	5,939
RMI	61	32	78	52	140	152	515
Philippines	525	579	829	552	580	449	3,514
Australia	164	134	139	133	213	187	970
Canada	70	34	60	51	34	45	294
Europe	125	164	185	141	133	114	862
Hong Kong	474	836	834	741	596	857	4,338
Nauru	38	11	23	15	184	74	345
Thailand	6	12	7	14	10	16	65
China, P.R.C.	23	118	28	92	55	94	410
Vietnam	1	6	3	2	6	0	18
Other/Unknown*	402	447	344	445	2,274	501	4,413
TOTAL AIR ARRIVALS	84,718	82,722	101,250	85,904	94,709	91,616	540,919
DEMOGRAPHICS**	GENDER		AGE				
Country of Origin	Male	Female	18-29 Yrs	30-49 Yrs	50+ Yrs		
Japan	46%	54%	56%	34%	10%		
Korea	53%	47%	47%	47%	6%		
Taiwan, R.O.C.	36%	64%	37%	60%	3%		
United States	N/A	N/A	N/A	N/A	N/A		
Hong Kong	56%	44%	40%	51%	8%		

HISTORICAL EVENTS

The following narrative provides a glimpse at key events that have shaped Guam's capacity to handle visitors. This includes primarily changes in accommodations, air transportation, entry requirements, attractions and activities.

GUAM TOURISM YEAR IN REVIEW

The Guam Visitors Bureau formulates a plan in early February to avert drops in tourism arrivals. The plan consisted of the following: Focus on Japan as a familiar market, maintain Guam's presence in South Korea - selling to niche markets including honeymooners, and increase arrivals from Taiwan.

In March, Far Eastern Air Transport Corporation announced that they were expected to commence direct flights from Taiwan to Guam.

On February 5, JetTour Corporation, a Tokyo based tour operator bringing in an average of tens of thousands of Japanese visitors monthly, filed for bankruptcy after it could not honor US$15.2 million in payments for airline tickets.

Seventy (70) tourist industry members met at the Hyatt Regency Guam to attend the "Tourism Industry Strategic Planning Summit". The event, sponsored by the Guam Visitors Bureau, was an industry-wide strategy session to come up with more precise ways to promote the island.

The Korean Association of Guam held an appreciation party on March 5 at the Pacific Star Hotel to thank the local community for its help after the Korean Air Flight 801 disaster.

DFS Guam lays off 45 employees, or about 3 percent of its work force, due to the effects of the Asian economic crisis.

Far Eastern Air Transport Corporation, based in Taiwan, inaugurated passenger service between Kaohsiung and Guam on April 24. The airline will serve Guam with twice weekly Boeing 757-200 planes capable of bringing in 207 passengers per flight.

Continental Micronesia Airlines inaugurated its first flight to Okinawa, Japan in April.

A February to March survey of 2,293 persons conducted by the Japan Travel Bureau revealed that 4.6 percent chose Guam and Saipan as the overseas destination where they planned to spend their honeymoon.

The $200 million Tinian Dynasty Hotel and Casino opened on April 25 after a construction period of almost two (2) years.

On April 30, Pacific Island Aviation started direct flights for Guam residents and tourists to Tinian.

For FY 1998, the Guam Visitors Bureau South Korea marketing Budget called for $1,038,025 with more than $800,000 earmarked for advertising and marketing.

On June 11, the U.S. dollar bought 141.76 Yen in Tokyo, an increase of 0.92 yen that had not been seen since June 1991.

On June 16, groundbreaking for a new building to house the "Crimes Against Tumon Tourists" program, a project by the Guam Police Department to actively deter crimes in Guam's main tourist areas, was held.

On July 2, Continental Air Micronesia added the Japanese cities of Okayama and Niigata to its list of destinations.

On August 15, Agana Bay Sunset Cruise, owned by Turtle Tours, began running its two hour dinner cruise in East Agana Bay. The boat, the "Hagan Tasi", was built in Arizona for Turtle Tours. It has a capacity of 150 people and can sail in 12 inches of water.

On September 4, Louis Vuitton, the parent company of DFS, announced an agreement for construction of a 50,000 square foot aquarium complex to be known as "Underwater World", to be located across Planet Hollywood.

In early September, hotel developers announced that construction was proceeding on the seven story Royal Riviera Hotel across the Pacific Islands Club. Opening was scheduled for April 1999.

Note: A more comprehensive review of historical events in Guam Tourism is available in the 1998-1999 Guam Annual Economic Review, a publication available from the Guam Department of Commerce.

ECONOMIC DEVELOPMENT CHALLENGES AND OPPORTUNITIES

An analysis of the environmental factors or conditions that are relevant to Guam's prospects for economic development is a good starting point for evaluating the challenges and opportunities that are available to Guam. In this regard, several descriptors have been identified to describe key characteristics of the Guam economy, with this paper focusing on the following six: (1) a small island economy that is relatively open that is (2) currently lacking economic diversification but (3) endowed with natural resources and a (4) multicultural society. It is (5) an unincorporated U.S. territory (6) located strategically in Asia-Pacific. Each descriptor presents Guam with challenges and at the same time opportunities. These descriptors and their implications for challenges and opportunities in economic development are discussed in the next section in turn.

SMALL DOMESTIC ECONOMY

Guam's smallness can be measured in several ways. First is in terms of its small population, which is estimated to be around 175,000 people and, consequently, a small labor force of around 74,950, of which 64,970 (86.7%) are employed and 9,970 (13.3%) are unemployed based on the latest unemployment report in March 2011 (Guam Bureau of Labor Statistics). During stronger economic periods when labor demand exceeds the available labor force, Guam has supplemented its local labor force with those from the U.S., neighboring islands that are freely associated with the U.S., and the use of foreign workers.

Guam is also small in terms of economic size. The latest estimate of its overall economy, its Gross Domestic Product, GDP (also referred to as Gross Island Product, GIP) is for the year 2009 and valued at $3.9 billion (U.S. Department of Commerce-Bureau of Economic Analysis, 2010). Per Capita Income for 2010 was $12,864, a decrease of $225 or 1.7% from calendar year 2008.

Guam's small population and relatively lower per capita income have prevented many businesses from achieving economies of scale and producing goods and services to local residents at lower prices. Not surprisingly, the cost of living on Guam is high but not different from other small island economies, including Hawaii. Guam's lack of economies of scale also presents challenges to autonomous government agencies that provide utilities and is also an obstacle from current efforts toward recycling, which have required recyclable materials to be gathered and then shipped off-island for recycling.

Guam's smallness also manifests itself in terms of its limited productive resources. The prospects of significant economic growth from the pending expansion of the U.S. military presence on the island have created expectations of shortage in available resources, including labor of different skills (including construction-related) as well as physical, social and institutional infrastructure. In addition, the limited productive resources available to Guam can be viewed as both cause and consequence for the island's lack of economic diversification.

OPEN ECONOMY

Like many small economies, Guam is a relatively open economy, especially in trade of goods and services. Guam imports around 36% of its GIP, showing a high dependence on imported supply but not quite common among small island economies in the Pacific. Guam's exports have primarily come from services to tourists, which account for 16.5% of its GIP (U.S. Department of Commerce-Bureau of Economic Analysis, 2010). The heavy reliance on tourism makes Guam vulnerable to external shocks that affect its main tourist markets, primarily Japan, including most recently the March 2011 earthquake and tsunami that devastated the northeastern part of Japan and led to a significant decline in tourist arrivals from Japan. These external shocks could also be positive for Guam such as the appreciation of the Japanese yen and Korean won against the U.S. dollar, which made tourism on Guam more affordable to Japanese and Korean visitors.

To some extent, Guam's openness applies to its labor market and migration, allowing from a free movement of labor among other island economies in Western Pacific which have free association with the U.S. (i.e. the Commonwealth of Northern Marianas, Federated States of Micronesia, Republic of the Marshall Islands and Palau) and the fifty states of the U.S. As already noted, this labor market arrangement has supplemented Guam's small labor force during times of high labor demand.

ISLAND ECONOMY

Guam is the largest island in the Micronesian region and is located in the Western Pacific region. Being an island is significant in that it implies some level of geographic isolation and distance from larger markets. It also suggests exposure to natural disasters such as typhoon, earthquakes and tsunamis.

Guam's smallness, openness and island-setting suggest benefits from attracting more resources, including foreign investments, which supplement its limited productive resources and also balance out the island's high imports. This descriptor of Guam, especially its implication for the lack of economies of scale, points to the absence of mass production of many products but suggests opportunities for niche markets and for small business participation. Although the government sector (a combination of U.S. Federal government agencies and local government agencies) continue to make up a significant share of the economy (48% of Gross Island Product in 2007, U.S. Department of Commerce-Bureau of Economic Analysis), the economy has made a notable shift toward a larger role of the private sector, including small businesses. Recent employment estimates show that 75% of jobs are provided by private businesses, 19% by the local government and 6% by the U.S. Federal government (Guam Bureau of Labor Statistics, December 2010). In terms of numbers, the private sector is comprised of 3,143 business establishments (U.S. Bureau of Census, 2007), with more than 90% of them classified as "small businesses" using the U.S. Small Business Administration definition.

LACK OF ECONOMIC DIVERSIFICATION

Guam's limited productive resources and lack of economies of scale prevent it from achieving the type of economic diversification that larger economies are able to enjoy. It would not be much of an over-simplification to view Guam's economy as a triad, comprised of three industries (tourism, military and local economy), or serving three groups of customers (tourists, military personnel and families, and local residents).

TOURISM

Tourism was very strong in 2010, with approximately 1.2 million tourists who visited Guam (Guam Visitors Bureau, December 2010). As already noted, tourism decreased this year, largely to the lower number of Japanese visitors. Prospects for tourism-related economic activities are not optimistic for the remainder of the year. It is unfortunate that Guam's comparative advantage as an island is so heavily dependent on tourism, which happens to be very unstable because it is hostage to factors outside of Guam's control and to external shocks. Tourism is an industry that is very sensitive to the income of the tourists' origin economy (one of the first activities to be cut out when times are tough) as well as health and safety threats (9-11, SARS, H1N1, etc.). It is in many economies, not only on Guam, a relatively low-paying, low-productivity service sector with little opportunity for innovation. It also puts Guam in direct competition with neighboring islands as well as Hawaii, although Guam's national tourism organization, the Guam Visitors Bureau, has not fallen short of exploring ways to further develop and diversify the tourism sector. While these efforts must be recognized and encouraged, other viable economic activities should be developed to provide the island with an alternative source of income, especially during times when the tourism sector is on a decline.

MILITARY

The military market is also significant in Guam. Expectedly, it claimed a larger share of the economy in the aftermath of World War II but has since decreased, although still notable. It usually reflects itself in construction and engineering services industries, although there are opportunities to get involved in military bases' maintenance and operation. The concern here is that decisions affecting the military presence on Guam are made externally, in this case, by the U.S. Federal Government, in consultation with foreign government(s). For instance, the U.S. and Japan entered an agreement in 2006 to realign U.S. military forces in Asia. Of particular interest to Guam is the proposal to relocate 8,000 military personnel and their families from Okinawa, Japan to Guam. Such military buildup on Guam was originally valued in excess of $10 billion (2.5 times the size of the current Guam economy) and was originally planned to take place over a short four-year period, after which the military-related construction boom would be expected to decline. More recently, there has been uncertainty regarding the terms, magnitude and timing of this military buildup, in part due to the recent natural disasters in Japan as well as to new developments in the U.S. Congress. Much depends on the fiscal health of both the U.S. Federal Government and the Government of Japan, which initially agreed to share the cost of the military buildup on a 40-60 basis (approximately). Any delay of the military buildup will likely increase earlier estimates of costs.

Local Economy

The instability of tourism, the unpredictability of the military buildup and the inability of Guam to significantly influence both economic sectors have made the third sector, which caters to the local residents, the more attractive sector. This sector provides strong support for retail trade and many different services including health, education, financial, legal, etc. This is also the most promising area for the strong majority of local businesses, which are small businesses.

All of the above brings to light the importance of self-reliance: the need to rely on the local economy, to develop it by identifying new industries, to enhance its purchasing power so that it will be the engine of growth that propels the entire economy into a sustainable and participatory development path that improves Guam residents' standard of living.

Opportunities for economic diversification would include those products that have potential to be exported but Guam's territorial status and the high transaction costs (including shipping) have presented challenges in this area. The more realistic option appears to be on the import side of trade where a search for ways to produce goods and services locally to reduce the current dependence on imported supply offers more promise. As discussions continue regarding the prospects of new industries on Guam, it would be helpful for these discussions to be guided by what emerged to be truly important to the island community

Increase in the standard of living and ability to provide materially for families
Smart management of the environment to ensure sustainability
Resurgence of pride in indigenous culture and resources

and pursue those new industries that are not economically viable but also encourage

High productivity and value-added, intensive use of human capital and technology
Use of "green" technology and practices, non-carbon printing and, if possible, carbon-reducing
Intensive use of indigenous resources including human talents and local materials.

Efforts to replace imports in a cost-effective manner will provide a boost to the local economy. Assuming a spending multiplier of 1.5, one is able to illustrate how significant the economic impact would be of shifting 10% of what is currently imported to a local source in terms of an increase in GIP by 25% (or $1 billion), an increase in the local government's revenue in terms of Gross Receipts Tax by 4% of $1 billion (or $40 million), and an increase in local jobs by 23% (or 14,000 jobs).

NATURAL RESOURCE ENDOWMENT

Guam's abundance in beaches, beautiful scenery, natural forests and marine life has made it an attractive site for tourism, military operations and for research and development. Opportunities exist in developing ecotourism that cater to all three segments of consumers, tourist, military and local residents. The availability of land, along with government incentives to use them productively, points to a continuous evaluation of prospects for expanding the agricultural sector. Of course, as natural resources are used to support economic activities, there is a need for effective management of natural resources in order to preserve their quality and sustain their usefulness. Guam has a long history of community activism to ensure that uses of natural resources are kept in check.

MULTICULTURAL SOCIETY

Guam's population is composed of 37% Chamorro (Guam's native culture), 27% Filipino, 7% other Pacific Islander, 6% non-Filipino Asians, 7% Caucasian, 2.2% all others (Guam Bureau of Statistics and Plans, 2010). One advantage of having a multicultural society is that the island becomes a melting pot of different ideas and talents. It also possesses richness in culture, which provides opportunities to incorporate "experience" in tourism, and a greater understanding and appreciation for diversity. All of these create flexibility and economic resilience. On the other hand, challenges arise as they are many differing opinions, perspectives and approaches, thus making reaching a consensus more difficult and time-consuming.

UNINCORPORATED U.S. TERRITORY

Guam's status as an unincorporated U.S. territory is both a blessing and a curse. On the positive side, it provides an attraction for both tourists and foreign investors, who benefit from having an English-speaking population, the presence of U.S. legal infrastructure, an economically free environment to do business, a democratic political structure and the presence of labor protection (e.g., minimum wage laws). As a territory, Guam receives funds from the U.S. Federal government that finances a significant portion of its physical infrastructure that are conducive for business. Guam also uses the U.S. tax system and is able to keep taxes collected from local residents as well as from U.S. military personnel who are stationed on Guam.

The downside of being a U.S. territory includes limits on the economic policy tools available to local policymakers and economic planners. As regards fiscal policy, Guam has its own elected legislatures that make budget decisions, with a lot of flexibility on spending decisions but have less flexibility on making revenue decisions because the primary source of revenue (income taxes) are set to follow the U.S. Federal system. Unlike politically-independent economies, Guam has no monetary policy to use to effectively manage the local economy and is subject to decisions made by the Washington, D.C.-based central bank, the Federal Reserve. This policy limitation extends to currency matters and exchange rate determination. In addition, being a U.S. territory has made Guam ineligible to access financial and technical assistance from international organizations, resources that other countries have used to support their economic development. For better or worse, Guam's minimum wage laws have priced it out of the of many labor-intensive industries in nearby Asian economies, effectively limiting the number of possible industries it could develop and, to some extent, forcing it to look at higher-paying industries that often require higher levels of human capital.

STRATEGIC LOCATION IN ASIA-PACIFIC

Guam's location in the Asia-Pacific region has been described to be strategic, thus making it an attractive site for military operations. In fact, the 2006 military forces agreement between the

U.S. and Japan is motivated largely by Guam's strategic location. This attractiveness to military operations brings with it both benefits and costs and hence requires a careful balance of these two effects. For example, the proposed military buildup on Guam has received numerous

scrutiny from those in favor of it as well as those opposed to it that achieving the balance has called for a need for strategically pacing the resulting economic development (e.g., adaptive program management) in order to match up the required resources (infrastructure, human capital) with their availability. Evaluating the benefits and costs of the military buildup (as well as other proposals for economic changes) have brought to light the need for current, reliable and relevant socio-economic data and models that can be used to accurately estimate the benefits and costs of military (as well as non-military) proposals/projects and to serve as evidence for effective policymaking.

Guam's location puts it in close proximity to the dynamic Asian markets, with several of them within a 3-5 hour direct flight distance. These point to opportunities to enhance travel infrastructure, for example, to explore additional air routes between Guam and important regional markets, thus having the effect of increasing competition among air carriers and potentially making travel more affordable to local residents as well as to tourists. On the other hand, proximity to Asia brings with to Guam the challenge of competing with other tourist destinations in Asia. It also causes a leakage from the local economy as local residents travel to the neighboring Asian destination to shop at much lower prices and enjoy a wider variety of goods and services.

Table 16 summarizes the challenges and opportunities associated with each characteristic/descriptor of Guam's economy.

Table 16: Summary of Challenges and Opportunities in Guam's Economic Development

CHARACTERISTICS/ DESCRIPTORS OF GUAM	CHALLENGES FACED BY GUAM	OPPORTUNITIES AVAILABLE TO GUAM
(1) Small, island, open economy	• Economic instability/vulnerability or exposure to external factors and external shocks • Small labor force and limited productive resources • Inability to engage in mass production has led to higher cost to operate business, provide utilities, recycle	• Increased outward orientation with regards to tourism, imported goods and services, foreign investment and military hosting • Opportunity for niche markets and greater small business participation
(2) Lack of economic diversification	• Heavy reliance on three sectors: tourism, military and local economy and increase exposure to shocks that negatively affect at least one sector	• Opportunity to explore new industries to supplement, complement and/or substitute existing industries • Opportunity to incorporate island community values to "designing" new industries
(3) Endowed with natural resources	• Need for effective management of natural resources	• Opportunity for more ecotourism • Opportunity to further develop the agricultural sector and other natural resources
(4) Multicultural society	• Many different opinions and difficulty to reach consensus	• Different ideas and talents, richness in culture, an understanding and appreciation of diversity, economic flexibility/resilience
(5) An unincorporated	• Limited economic policy	• Opportunity to strengthen

U.S. territory	tools • Ineligibility for international development assistance • Inability to compete directly with low-waged Asian countries in many labor-intensive industries	Guam's image as an attractive business/investment site and tourist destination
(6) Located strategically in Asia-Pacific	• Need for strategically pacing economic development • Need for current, reliable and relevant socio-economic data and models to accurately evaluate impacts of military and other economic changes • Direct competition with Asian markets	• Opportunity to benefit from hosting existing and increased military operations • Opportunity to access nearby Asian markets and to enhance travel infrastructure

ECONOMIC DEVELOPMENT GOALS AND OBJECTIVES

For years, strategies have been investigated to develop the economy, but Guam has yet to clearly define a strategy that it can be committed to, especially in light of having had a stagnant economy since 1996 and faced with the challenges and opportunities associated with the impending military buildup.

This is an opportune time to seriously evaluate what economic development strategies might work well on Guam in terms of economic growth that would be sustainable for a long period (beyond the military buildup) and where the benefits would be shared more broadly on Guam. What is the way forward for Guam?

In July 2009, a vision for Guam was proposed: Guam CAN be the first Pacific Tiger. To turn this vision into reality is a well-thought out economic development strategy, the Pacific Tiger strategy.[2]

The Pacific Tiger strategy is a plan to move the island's economy and society forward. Although it borrowed some elements from proven economic tigers in Europe (especially Ireland) and in Asia, it has been written specifically for Guam. Hirsch once said of Ireland, the Celtic Tiger... "Ireland didn't grow into the Celtic Tiger by growing bigger potatoes, or by implementing a better agricultural policy to keep more people at home on the farms. It went a totally different direction, getting into the globalization game and proving it could win."[3] A similar theme can be voiced for Guam... "Guam's becoming the Pacific Tiger will not happen on its own. It will require a well-thought out, broadly supported strategy toward a sustainable and participatory economic development as well as a long-term commitment by leaders and by all to see the strategy through its completion."

Because of the surprisingly striking similarities between Ireland and Guam and that, after careful scrutiny, it appears that the Celtic Tiger strategy represents nothing but "sensible policies" for enhancing economic growth. Guam can employ those elements of the Celtic Tiger strategy that worked, and modify those elements that did not. By doing so, Guam can transform itself into the Pacific Tiger. However, the road to becoming the Pacific Tiger would require strong leadership and political will toward deliberate policymaking and planning and making tough choices and the support and participation of the island community. Changes are always tough to make but are necessary. Timing is also very important since a delay in action is tantamount to a continuation of the current state, which deprives the community of the benefits of opportunities to improve Guam's livelihood and standard of living.

Why act now? First, Guam has momentum. The economy has been through a long period of stagnation since the 1990s, owing largely to BRAC in the early 1990s, the Asian crisis in the mid-1990s, and a number of natural disasters suffered in the 1990s and early 2000s. In addition, the impending military buildup has already provoked some serious dialogue and deep thinking by many in the community about the island's future socio-economic prospects.

Second, as the future continues to be discussed, a consensus has in fact been reached: that change is upon Guam – it is inevitable. In short, to resist change is already out of the question. It is no longer an option nor would it be a realistic response. However, discussion continues regarding the nature of the change that the island community would like to see happen on Guam and the choice on how best to respond to that change.

Third, although it would appear in discussions that Guamanians disagree a great deal, in the final analysis, Guamanians in fact all want the same thing: for the island economy to develop in a sustainable and participatory way. Sustainability would require a balanced approach toward the smart use of island resources (natural, human, fiscal), the continued regard for culture and tradition, and the pursuit of economic development over a long period of time, which would provide ample opportunities for a steady increase in quality of life. Participatory development suggests a process of decision-making and taking actions that involve the entire island community since Guamanians are all stakeholders of the island's future. It also calls upon all Guamanians for hard work and sacrifice, from which benefits come and can be shared.

GOALS AND OBJECTIVES

The 2011 Guam Comprehensive Economic Development Strategy is based on the concept of economic tigers in general and on Guam becoming the first Pacific Tiger in particular. The Pacific Tiger strategy is based on six overall economic goals that are designed to bring about a sustainable and participatory economic development process for Guam:

Openness of economy to global markets for goods and foreign investments
Investment in human capital
Availability of young, productive and creative labor force
Public sector reforms and fiscal discipline
Effective policymaking and social partnership
Hard work and sacrifice

It was first proposed in July 2009 and received favorable response from policymakers, local media, and the island community. The Pacific Tiger strategy found its strongest supporters in the current Calvo-Tenorio Administration whose economic platform "Blueprint 2020" provides details on how to begin the operations of the six Pacific Tiger goals into objectives in the following areas of concerns:

Trade in Goods & Services
Education
Training
Wages
Local Labor
Government Operations

Fiscal Management
Infrastructure
Veteran Affairs
Social Issues
Environment & Natural Resources
Military Buildup

The link between the Pacific Tiger goals and the Blueprint 2020 objectives is summarized in Figure 1. Examples of projects that support them are schematically presented in the Figure and are detailed in the Strategic Projects section of this report.

PRIVATE SECTOR AND COMMUNITY INVOLVEMENT

The Guam Economic Development Authority formed a strategy committee to assist with the development of the island's Comprehensive Economic Development Strategy. The selection team focused on bringing together a group of professional individuals from a variety of industries, Government of Guam, the federal government, military-related businesses, and the education community. This group was selected based on their professional credentials and years of experience in their industry or field and their reputation as industry, government, business and community leaders.

The selection team also considered the individuals' involvement in the Guam community and professional organizations and their history of serving on a variety of boards and in professional and civic organizations, including but not limited to:

Professional Organizations Guam Chamber of Commerce Guam Contractors Association Guam Hotel and Restaurant Association American Marketing Association (Guam Chapter) Society for Human Resource Management (Guam Chapter)

Civic Organizations Rotary Clubs of Guam Lions Club International Red Cross Make a Wish Foundation

Below is the list of members, their place of employment, and the industry or institutions which they represent:

Robert "Bob" Barber, Jr., University of Guam Manuel Duenas, Guam Fishermen's Cooperative Association Anthony Godwin, Guam Association of Realtors Dan Moffat, GTA TeleGuam Joaquin Cook, Bank of Guam Tom Maxedon, Marianas Cable Vision Dana Gutierrez, Mair, Spade & Thompson Jessica Leon Guerrero, Cassidy's Insurance Andrew Mariano, A&E Engineering Beatrice "Tricee" Limtiaco, Guam Cornerstone Sammy Sotelo, Atkins Kroll Noel Enriquez, AECOM Len Isotoff, Matson Navigation Lourdes Sanchez, Continental Airlines David Leddy, Guam Chamber of Commerce James Martinez, Guam Contractors Association Herbert Johnston, Guam Trades Academy Kenneth Lujan, Guam Small Business Administration Casey Jeszenka, Guam Small Business Development Council Ramona L.E. Jones, Jones & Guerrero Joseph Diego, USDA Anthony Barcinas, USDA

STRATEGIC PROJECTS

The Comprehensive Economic Development Strategy will be realized through the implementation of a series of specific projects. These projects are intended to address the core development objectives of the Six Point Action Plan and to meet both near and longer term objectives for Guam's economy. Each project was evaluated against EDA's Investment Policy Guidelines and against Guam's needs.

EDA POLICY INVESTMENT GUIDELINES

The following are EDA's Policy Investment Guidelines criteria:

The proposed investments are market-based. The investment should capitalize on the community's unique regional assets and strengths to build comparative advantages for future business investment.

The proposed investments are proactive in nature and scope. The investment should support and advance innovation and increased productivity. It should enhance a community's success in achieving a high and rising standard of living.

The proposed investments look beyond the immediate economic horizon, anticipate economic changes, and diversify the local and regional economy. The investment should be part of an overarching, long term regional strategy that includes expanding existing industry clusters and developing emerging, new clusters. Investments should create the conditions for sustained productivity.

The proposed investments maximize the attraction of private sector investment and would not otherwise come to fruition absent EDA's investment. EDA should serve as a unique public sector source of "venture capital" to assist distressed communities that otherwise would be at a distinct competitive disadvantage in attracting the higher levels of private capital investment in facilities and equipment that drives the creation of higher skilled, higher wage jobs.

The proposed investments have a high probability of success. The investment should have high level of local matching funds; should have high degree of local political capital (support); should have significant commitment of human resources talent to ensure achievement; and should have strong local leadership.

The proposed investments result in an environment where higher skill, higher wage jobs are created. The jobs created or retained should have a higher than average wage and skill level than that of the community.

The proposed investments maximize Return on Taxpayer Investment. Investments should generate a return for the taxpayer by attracting private capital investment and high wage jobs that promote regional prosperity through consumer demand they create. Successful economic development investments promote economic self-sufficiency; provide the resources for building safe, healthy, and attractive communities; and minimize poverty.

The projects are presented below in order of priority based upon an evaluation that was conducted of each project against EDA's Investment Policy Guidelines and against Guam's needs.

	CEDS PROJECT	EDA Policy Investment Guidelines Criteria							Total	Priority
		1	2	3	4	5	6	7		

	Infrastructural Development -PREREQUISITES TO ALL PROJECTS LISTED BELOW									
	Maritime Development	X	X	X	X	X	X	X	7	H
	Hågatña Revitalization	X	X	X	X	X	X	X	7	H
HIGH	Education Tourism	X	X	X	X	X	X	X	7	H
	Agriculture	X	X	X	X	X		X	6	H
	Information Technology	X	X	X	X		X	X	6	H
	Green Technology	X	X	X	X		X	X	6	H
	Business Hub									
	Industrial Park	X	X	X	X	X			5	M
MEDIUM	Conference Center	X	X	X	X	X			5	M
	Cottage Industries	X	X	X	X	X			5	M
	Ecotourism	X	X	X		X			4	M
	Sports Tourism	X		X	X	X			4	M
	Manufacturing & Exporting	X	X	X					3	L
LOW	Financial & Legal Services	X					X	X	3	L
	Medical Tourism	X					X		2	L
	Film Industry			X					1	L

INDUSTRIES AND DETAILS OF PROJECTS

High Priority

Maritime Development

The purpose of the Guam Fishermen's Cooperative Association's master plan is to establish goals by which the local fishing capacity could be enhanced. Guam imports on average, over $30 million of marine-harvested food products a year. Nearly 75% of the imports are processed fish species available in the waters surrounding Guam.

Project Name: Construction of New Wharf and Land Reclamation

Situation Statement: The Base Realignment and Closure (BRAC) decision of '95 resulted in the closure of the former Naval Ship Repair Facility which was to have been transferred to the

Government of Guam, thereby increasing wharf space by 3,251 linear feet. Navy has since decided to retain the lands, wharves and buildings associated with this facility due to the strategic value of Guam. In addition, the Navy has decided to dredge the inner Apra Harbor to accommodate additional vessels in 2006. This proposal is intended to create new wharf space at the Port Authority of Guam to replace those wharves that will not be returned under the Base Realignment and Closure (BRAC). The additional wharf space will be available for Navy use.

Objectives: Construction of new wharfage totaling 2,900 lineal feet and 3,000 lineal feet of reclaimed land at the Commercial Port of Guam under the auspices of the Port Authority of Guam.

Description: The Port Authority of Guam is developing architectural and engineering plans under a grant from the Economic Development Administration, for the construction of new wharfage totaling 2,900 lineal feet of sheet piles with tie-rods anchored to sheet pile dead-men, and 3,000 lineal feet of reclaimed land at the Commercial Port of Guam. Funding is needed for wharf construction and purchase and installation of cranes at the new wharf.

Anticipated Impacts and Benefits: Upon completion of the project, congestion at the Port would be alleviated, room for additional economic activity would be created, thereby generating additional jobs. New wharf construction, especially in the proposed area which is characterized by deep water draft will also provide the U.S. Navy with the opportunity to utilize wharf facilities that can accommodate larger military vessels, such as aircraft carriers that cannot enter the inner harbor even after Navy's dredging project is completed.

Deliverable: 2,900 lineal feet of new wharf space; new cranes for cargo off-loading; and reclamation of 3,000 lineal feet of land for industrial development.

Timing and Responsibilities: Construction of the new wharf and installation of cranes will be completed within 36 months of receiving funding.

Budget: The project is estimated to cost $35,000,000.

PROJECT NAME: GUAM FISHERMEN'S COOPERATIVE ASSOCIATION MARINA AUTHORITY

Description: To revitalize the Agat Marina and expand the Greg D. Perez Marina in Hågatña under a public-private partnership. Each marina will have a council (community-based oversight) to manage the marinas along with the GFCA Board of Directors.

Current Conditions: Both the Agat Marina and the Hågatña Marina have suffered numerous typhoons and years of neglect. The conditions are hazardous and the main concern is that the next major typhoon will not only destroy the docks but a large majority of the vessels as well.

Estimated Cost: $7,500,000

Funding Source: GEDA Fishery Development Program/Department of Agriculture Sportfish Restoration Funds

Revenue Forecast: $500,000 annually; user fees

Revenue Potential: $15,000,000 for tourism and domestic activities annually

PROJECT NAME: MARINA DEVELOPMENT

Situation Statement: With Guam's current economic difficulties, there is a need to enhance economic opportunities within its fisheries industry through the expansion of marina facilities. The current facility is inadequate and is unable to withstand typhoon conditions. The construction of typhoon-proof docks and additional boat slips and services will enable Guam's marine tourism activities and its local boating and fishing industry to expand, flourish and prosper.

Objective: To design and construct a 150-boat-slip marina and shore-line facility to promote marine industry, stimulate job growth through the revitalization of Guam's capital city of Hågatña, and to promote long-term economic benefits that will advance Guam's efforts to diversify its economy and stimulate growth.

Description: The project has two phases. Phase I: The Hågatña Revitalization Authority, in conjunction with the Guam Fishermen's Cooperative Association, would issue a Request for Proposals to contract the services of an architectural and engineering (A/E) firm to prepare the design for the marina and facility, prepare the Environmental Impact Statement (EIS), secure all federal and local permits, and serve as contract/construction manager during the construction phase of the project. Phase II: Construction of the 150-boat-slip marina and shore-line facility.

Anticipated Impacts and Benefits: The project will create additional jobs. In addition, the economy will realize $25 million in annual revenue from tourism activities within the marina, alleviate over-crowding and provide for an opportunity for larger scale domestic commercial fishery, not to mention, global exposure as a marine activity destination.

Deliverable: The completion of an EIS and A/E design for the complex, the securing of all federal and local permits, and the construction of the facility.

Timing and Responsibilities: The Hågatña Revitalization Authority, in conjunction with the Guam Fishermen's Cooperative Association, will oversee the contracts for the Environmental Impact Statement (EIS), the A/E design, and the construction of the facility. The total project is anticipated to take 36 months to complete the A/E design and EIS, secure permits, and complete construction.

Budget: The project is estimated to cost $4,500,000.

PROJECT NAME: GUAM FISHERMEN'S COOPERATIVE ASSOCIATION BUILDING COMPLEX

Description: 20,000 sq. ft., 2-story building. GFCA headquarters, fish market, marina offices, multipurpose room, restaurant, snack bar, dive and tackle shop, and gift shop.

Current Conditions: The GFCA is operating out of a 1,200 sq. ft., 30-year-old rusted structure. The refrigeration and freezing systems are in need of upgrading. The processing room as well as the retail space are no longer adequate to accommodate the growth in membership and consumer base.

Estimated Cost: $3,500,000

Funding Source: U.S. Housing and Urban Development (HUD) Section 108/GEDA Fishery Development Program

Revenue Forecast: $10,000,000 annually

PROJECT NAME: GUAM'S LIMITED ENTRY LONGLINE FLEET (5 LONGLINE ICE VESSELS)

Description: To establish a longline fleet to operate in Guam's waters. These vessels shall be limited to ice for on-board handling and storage of harvested fish. This project shall assist in capacity building of the domestic fishery and provide the community with fresh, locally harvested fish.

Current Conditions: There are no vessels operating out of Guam. The foreign vessels curently fish in outside areas. Estimated Cost: $1,750,000 Funding Source: GEDA Fishery Development Fund Revenue Forecast: $2,000,000 annually Growth Potential: 5 vessels by year 2015

Project Name: Marine Small Loan Revolving Fund

Description: Establish a revolving low-interest loan fund to assist small-boat fishermen with making necessary repairs to their vessels or purchasing needed equipment.

Current Conditions: No such program exists, resulting in fishermen obtaining loans from institutions other than recognized banks. Often the interest rates are cost-prohibitive that fishermen either lose their vessels or quit fishing altogether.

Estimated Cost: $500,000

Funding Source: GEDA Development Program

Revenue Forecast: Fishing ability $5,000 to $50,000 based on reduced down fishing time. 100 x $5,000 = $500,000

PROJECT NAME: MULTIPURPOSE VESSEL DEVELOPMENT

Description: To establish a vessel that is able to perform multiple missions. To establish a baseline survey of Guam's off-shore seamounts and other research programs. This vessel could augment the rescue operations of the Guam Fire Department while fostering support and development of the community-based fishery.

Current Conditions: The Guam Fire Rescue and the Guam Police Harbor Unit both have multiple missions and often responding to none life or death requests may conflict with a more serious request. The services also are limited in range which also limit the fishing areas. The community lacks the ability to further explore or address the scientific concerns.

Estimated Cost: $500,000

Funding Source: GEDA Fishery Development Fund

Revenue Forecast: $200,00 annually

Growth Potential: 2 vessels by year 2015

PROJECT NAME: GUAM DOMESTIC FISHERIES (INCLUSIVE OF AQUACULTURE AND DOMESTIC OCEAN FISHERIES)

Situation Statement: Guam's domestic ocean fisheries consist of a few hundred small-scale fishermen operating personal trolling and bottom fishing boats. The Guam Fishermen's Cooperative Association coordinated the maiden efforts of this industry and grosses approximately $1.5 million annually. A key issue for Guam fisheries identified by the Western Pacific Regional Fisheries Management Council is that there are no domestic purse seine operators. Guam's aquaculture fisheries operate mostly on a small-scale basis and consist of roughly 100 farmers, with less than 25 farmers comprising the most of the $300,000 to $750,000 in gross annual sales. The main species farmed are tilapia, freshwater shrimp, catfish and milkfish. Information is difficult to obtain due to the seemingly uncoordinated efforts of the farmers and lack of technical business expertise.

Objective: Diversify the Guam economy and create jobs uncorrelated with tourism and military spending.

Description: Identify assistance needs of the industry; facilitate needed financing of projects; coordinate outreach to remote farmers and fishermen; assist in compliance with federal environmental regulations.

Anticipated Impacts and Benefits: There is capacity for increase of Guam's ocean fisheries. The opportunity for the development of a Guam longline fleet, the further development and increased capacity of the Guam Fishermen's Cooperative Association are a few possibilities. This industry is underutilized and Guam relies heavily on imported seafood. There is also much room for development in Guam's aquaculture industry. Farmers can take advantage of technical advice and business expertise provided by the development of this facet. The low cost of entry into this industry makes this a viable opportunity.

Deliverable: Develop and implement a fisheries feasibility study.

Timing and Responsibility: 24 months by GEDA, the Guam Fishermen's Cooperative Association, and Guam Aquaculture Growers Association.

Budget: The project is estimated to cost $200,000.

Hågatña Revitalization

Discussion: The city of Hagåtña has served as downtown, a central location for the Chamorros the indigenous people of Guam -dating as far back as the sixteenth century before Spanish settlers arrived on Guam. As its capital, Hagåtña serves an important role as the center of government. In 1668, Padre San Vitores, a Spanish missionary, was instrumental in establishing the first Spanish (Catholic) church in Hagåtña, forcing most of the indigenous population of Guam to relocate to the city.

Hagåtña has been the capital of Guam since the Spanish-American War of 1898 when the United States captured Hagåtña from the Spanish. The result of World War II, from the Japanese occupation of Guam to its recapture by the U.S. military, left many of Hagåtña's historical sites and the city itself damaged. However, there are still a number of historical monuments and remains that can be viewed, including sections of buildings left over from the time of Spanish rule, such as the Plaza de Espana near the cathedral of the Archdiocese of Agana, and Latte Park, where visitors can see pre-Spanish stone pillars referred to as Latte Stones. The devastation of the city, however, forced the once most populated village prior to World War II, to the least populated area that serves primarily as a center for government and business.

In the past decade, many loosely related efforts have been made towards the redevelopment of the once vibrant capital. A serious commitment towards the need to restore and redevelop Guam's capital was first codified in Guam Public Law 24-110, known as the Hagåtña Restoration and Redevelopment Act ("the Act"). The Act created an autonomous agency, the Hagåtña Restoration and Redevelopment Authority ("HRRA"), to carry out the purposes of the legislation. Other government agencies have also addressed redevelopment efforts for Hagåtña. The Guam Economic Development Authority, charged with economic development initiatives for Guam, has directed redevelopment efforts toward Hagåtña, via Kottura. The Guam Visitors Bureau, responsible for developing Guam's visitor industry, has also addressed the development potential of downtown Hagåtña. Additionally, market forces evidenced through private organizations such as the Guam Chamber of Commerce, have made it a priority in recent years to redevelop the flailing downtown as a counterpoint to the tourist attraction of Tumon.

The Hagåtña Restoration and Redevelopment Act, Title 21 Guam Code Annotated Chapter 79, was enacted with the dual intent to protect and promote restoration and development of Hagåtña. The overarching concerns for protection of downtown were to remedy the injurious conditions of homeless in the area and the poor subdivision and zoning layouts of the village that had led to serious deterioration and disuses. The intent to redevelop Hagåtña was simply stated so that it would be better put to public use and purpose. Projects included towards these purposes include the alteration, improvement, modernization, reconstruction, rehabilitation, or any combination of these, of existing structures in Hagåtña. It also calls for the provision for open-space types of use, such as streets and other public grounds and space around buildings, and public or private buildings, structures and improvements, and improvements of public and private recreation areas and other public grounds. Also included is the re-planning or redesign or original development of areas in Hagåtña as to which either of the following conditions exist: (1) The areas are stagnant or improperly utilized because of defective or inadequate street layout, faulty lot layout in relation to size, shape, or accessibility, or usefulness, or for other causes; and (2) The areas require re-planning and land assembly for reclamation or redevelopment in the interest of the general welfare because of widely scattered ownership, tax delinquency, or other reasons.

Within the same act, it cites that the Guam Legislature deems a fundamental purpose of redevelopment is to expand the supply of low-and moderate-income housing, to expand employment opportunities for the jobless, underemployed, and low-income persons, and to provide an environment for the social, economic, and psychological growth and well-being of all citizens.

The Hagåtña Restoration & Redevelopment Authority, a public corporation and autonomous instrumentality of the Government of Guam, was established to carry out and perform the purposes and provisions of Chapter 79, except the power to levy and collect taxes or special assessments. It is charged to develop a Plan to carry out the purposes of Chapter 79, to include the planning, preparation, development, construction, acquisition, lease disposition, reconstruction, improvement, alteration, extension, repair, maintenance and operation of the Hagåtña Restoration and Redevelopment Project; shall include the terms and conditions for the reuse of the properties; shall include standard of eligibility for ownership or occupancy of housing, dwellings and facilities; shall include installation, construction or reconstruction of streets, utilities, parks, playgrounds and other public improvements. In developing the Plan, according to public law, the Authority is authorized to conduct surveys, appraisals, surroundings, test borings or any other technical investigations.

A draft Hagåtña Land Use Plan 2006 served as an important part of the broader planning process in the Hagåtña Restoration and Redevelopment Authority's (HRRA) Hagåtña Master Plan effort. The Land Use section of the plan focuses on the arrangement and types of land use types, their impact upon the environment, and relation to community development. This is opportune, in light of the potential to expand Guam's tourism base by capitalizing on the Hagåtña attraction as a historic center of religion, government and cultural heritage. Many existing land uses in Hagåtña, however, do not comply with Guam's Zoning Law.

Another serious effort towards the restoration or revitalization of Guam's capital is through a proposal developed by the Guam Economic Development Authority, entitled *Kottura: Cultural Destination Development.* This document has a threefold focus which addresses economic development, cultural preservation, and artistic accessibility. It is intended to convert Guam's downtown area to a cultural destination for residents, visitors, and tourists. It is designed to integrate economic zoning in its layout, which will then provide incentives to entice businesses to locate or relocate to Hagåtña.

Another strategic view of Downtown Hagåtña's restoration is captured in the Guam Visitors Bureau's Five Year Strategic Plan (2007). It cites the need to execute the Hagåtña Master Restoration Plan. According to this document, Hagåtña, the seat of government for over 400 years during the Spanish, U.S., and eventually Guam's elected government administration has deep rooted historical and cultural significance. The document implies that the city of Hagåtña should be developed not only as good counter-balance to Tumon's attractiveness but also, more importantly, for the people of Guam to regard their capital city as one of the most beautiful capitals in the world. Further, it proposed a partial list of the many significant landmarks and visitor attractions to be highlighted in Hagåtña.

Create another village attraction to complement Tumon
Focus on historical significance of Guam's capital city
Home of colonial Spanish government
Cultural and social center of pre-war Guam
Governor's Office, Legislature, Supreme Court
U.S. District Court, U.S. Post Office, and other Federal offices
Government House overlooking Hagåtña skyline
Houses most of Government of Guam offices
Site of the Catholic Archdiocese of Agana
Site of Dulce Nombre de Cathedral-Basilica Catholic church
Establish a historic walking tour of Hagåtña with interpretive signage
Has many historic preservation sites
Future home of Guam National museum
Historic sites, parks, cemeteries, and monuments
Y Seng Song Chamorro and Wednesday night market
Hosts many shopping and dining establishments.

A recent initiative to restore Downtown Hagåtña is to capitalize on its unique package of historical sites. The launch of the Hagåtña Heritage Walking Trail, which comprises 17 historical sites, in March 2010 is hoped to transform what one person coined a "ghost town" to a bustling center. One way of restoring the capital city of Hagåtña is by bringing back government agencies downtown. The 2.5 mile Hagåtña Heritage Walking Trail is anticipated to provide economic stimulus through increased local government revenue, through tourists who spend an extra half day to experience the walk. This will be a result of increased hotel and tax revenues.

There are many attributable factors for the stalling of revitalization efforts. The anticipated military buildup on Guam has surfaced is the highest priority with the local government, given the need to prepare the island's infrastructure for a 40 percent population growth and resulting social-cultural, economic, and environmental impacts to the civilian community. However, it is these very same factors that necessitate more immediate action for implementation. One of the problems may have been that there was a lack of direction in which way to move. Government intervention, by its very nature, is not market driven. It seeks to drive the market. However, it is still necessary to know what the demand is in order to meet the supply. Therefore, a study gathering informational/generational/xxx factors was necessary to provide the impetus for revitalization.

EDUCATION TOURISM

Discussion: Education tourism is a fairly new phenomenon as a revenue option, but it is beginning to gain a great deal of universal popularity. It is the concept in which students travel to other academic institutions to study abroad. It is similar to student exchange programs yet much more expansive since it encapsulates bringing revenue to the economy as a whole rather than just to the sponsoring institution. Education tourism has grown into an industry that is highly marketed and sold as an overall attractive package promising education, culture, travel, and recreation. Travelers spend money for leisure activities, food and beverage, housing, and shopping.

Currently, tourism in general is a market that earns billions of dollars per month. According to the Department of Commerce, International Trade Association (2011), 55 million people traveled to the United States and spent over $11.4 billion in the month of November 2010 alone. The top five places in which visitors are coming from, listed in order of precedence, are People's Republic of China (excluding Hong Kong), South Korea, Brazil, Australia, and Argentina. In an analysis report that compares monthly and year-to-date figures of current to previous year, there is consistent percentage growth in travelers to the U.S. as well as visitor spending. These figures are reflective of registered, non-resident, countries with double-digit increases to the U.S. as compared to the previous year. Clearly, there is an evident market and demand for this industry with tons of potential for growth and development. Additionally, there are opportunities for specialized or niche tourism markets such as education tourism.

Economists and analysts have forecasted very positive growth statistics for inbound travel to the

U.S. It is anticipated that the U.S. will return to positive growth mode in 2010 and continue to increase six to nine percent throughout 2015. This rebound will definitely offset the five percent decline in 2009, which marked the first decline since 2003. The forecast for 2010 through 2015 predicts that international travel will attract 83 million visitors, which would be a 51% increase from 2009-2015. Increases are expected to come from China (40%), Brazil (35%), Korea (35%), Hong Kong (27%), New Zealand (24%), and Australia (19%). These trends were prepared by the staff of the Department of Commerce, Office of Travel and Tourism, using economic, demographic, social factors, historical visitation trends, input from overseas staff, and other numerous and varied sources. Visitor spending is not forecasted but typically moves in the same relative direction as changes in visitor arrivals.

Just as tourism is increasing and forecasted to continually increase in the U.S., the same can be expected for Guam. In fact, it is plausible to speculate that this increase will be phenomenal for Guam since it is a highly desired location for experiences in tropical weather, ethnic heritage, local foods, and customs. It is less populated than the more common destinations such as Hawaii and we have the privilege to offer pristine beaches as well as a warm, unique, culture. According to the Guam Tourism Economic Impact report, a summary of the key findings state that the total spending in 2005 was $1.15 billion in revenues. There are further details of this figure as it is analyzed by direct, indirect, and induced spending as well as expenditure categories of transportation, lodging, food and beverage, shopping, and entertainment. Specifically and more pertinent to this research, a total of $26.8 million was spent in education and health services. This figure certainly provides support that there is a noteworthy economic impact and value-added service we can further develop for Guam. Moreover, according to the recent Calvo-Tenorio Blueprint 2020, there is notable interest from leaders to capitalize on this potential market for Guam. Calvo-Tenorio's (2010) plans state the following:

Education Tourism: We must work with the University of Guam and explore the potential of partnering with Asia to market educational exchange programs. We must also explore the potential of establishing Guam as a destination for learning English as a second language (ESL) for Asian markets.

AGRICULTURE

Objective: To further develop Guam's agriculture industry through organization and expansion of current resources and the introduction of new technology.

Discussion: Guam has traditionally been an agricultural society. Ironically, Guam now imports a majority of its agricultural products. There are still a good number of farmers on island and there has also been a movement and renewed interest in aquaculture and mariculture. P.L. 30-228 provides an authorization for bond funding, "for the design and construction of a Guam Farmers Cooperative Association facility and the relocation of the Dededo Flea Market."

Strengths:

Large domestic market for farm-raised products

Farming and exporting are favorable for Guam as it is a domestic U.S. port

Farming experience with vegetable and fruit crops

Existing facilities, such as the University of Guam's Hatchery at Fadian Point and other farms around Guam

Guam is duty-free (import and export)

Tax incentives are available

Tropical climate is conducive to farming

Weaknesses:

Funding

Centralized distribution

Limited technical expertise

Limited government support Draft as of 8/3/11 77

Limited acreage/resources

Opportunities:

Increased demand due to population increase and transportation costs

New farming technologies (e.g. hydroponics)

Growth opportunities include domestic market, hotel and restaurant network, and export (American markets)

Threats:

Regulatory concerns

Collaboration of all parties involved

Inclement weather

Increased competition from established markets and nearby upstarts

Sustained funding

Recommendation: Continue the development of agricultural cooperatives to their fullest potential by providing funding and support. Promote expansion into new fields and technology in agriculture, with the cooperation of the UOG College of Agriculture and the Department of Agriculture.

Information Technology

PROJECT NAME: TELECOM INDUSTRY TRAINING PROGRAM

Situation Statement: To insure Guamanians benefit from the development of the telecom industry as expected as a result of other proposed telecom projects, a training center would be established jointly at the University of Guam and the Guam Community College to accommodate the various levels of skills necessary to fulfill the needs of the IT and telecom industries that will surely develop in the immediate future.

Objectives: Obtain a funding source to conduct a program development study that would identify the program training needs in the telecom industry and prescribe a step-by-step program to accommodate those needs, utilizing the training environment and facilities currently available at the local college institutions mentioned above.

Description: Issue a request for proposal (RFP) to obtain the services of a consultant to develop the program development study. Assess the University of Guam and Guam Community College's contribution to providing technical assistance in this type of industry, conducting applied research, and disseminating program results.

Anticipated Impacts and Benefits: Project would create 50 -100 certified technicians.

Deliverable: Program Development Study for the proposed Telecom Industry Training Program.

Timing and Responsibilities: The selected consultant would be required to complete the project 78 within six (6) months from time of grant approval.

Budget: The project is estimated to cost $205,000.

PROJECT NAME: REGIONAL SOFTWARE SUPPORT CENTER

Situation Statement: Interest has been raised by several U.S.-based software companies interested in exploring the possibility of using Guam as a hub for their software support and marketing activities. These companies have existing clients in Asia and would like to use Guam as a software support center for these clients. Guam needs to assess the potential for this type of activity.

Objective: To assess the potential for this type of activity and to evaluate the benefits and costs for the development of such an industry.

Description: Feasibility study and cost-benefits analysis for the development of Guam as a center for software support for U.S.-based software companies doing business in Asia.

Anticipated Impacts and Benefits: Creation of jobs in the field of information technology.

Deliverable: A report analyzing the feasibility of such an endeavor, inclusive of costs and benefits.

Timing and Responsibilities: As interest has been expressed, Guam needs to complete this study in 6 months.

Budget: The project is estimated to cost $150,000.

GREEN TECHNOLOGY RESEARCH, DEVELOPMENT AND MANUFACTURING

Objective: To market Guam as a destination for the research, development and manufacturing of green technologies.

Discussion: The need to reduce the usage of energy, water and waste has prompted the need to look into green technology. Projects that involve ocean thermal energy conversion, solar power, and the use of environmentally responsible building materials help reduce energy usage and the depletion of Guam's limited natural resources. Promoting the research, development and manufacturing of green technology on island would not only reduce consumer costs for energy, but may provide regional exporting opportunities for Guam.

Strengths:

Promotion of economic development activities in the research, development and manufacturing of green technology

Guam's proximity to the Northern Mariana Islands, Federated States of Micronesia, and Asia should exporting become feasible

Lack of professional personnel on island to fill the manufacturing and research positions

Prevailing wage requirements versus other regional and Pacific Basin wage scales

Cost of transporting and maintaining specialized machinery

Opportunities:

The lack of competition increases success of venture

The need to retrofit homes and offices with energy efficient materials

Creation of jobs

GEDA Qualifying Certificate available for manufacturing

Threats:

Sourcing of similar products abroad at lower prices may undercut the market for locally produced goods

Weaknesses:

Recommendations: GEDA and the Guam Energy Office should work collaboratively and attend international trade expos focusing on renewable energy or green technology, and market Guam as a destination for the research, development and manufacturing of green technologies in the Asia-Pacific region.

Medium Priority

Business Hub

PROJECT NAME: INDUSTRIAL PARK

Discussion: 12 GCA Section 50103(h) provides that the Guam Economic Development Authority (GEDA) is authorized to obtain land owned by the Government of Guam as required to carry out its purposes and objectives, under such terms and tenures as the Legislature through appropriate legislation may prescribe.

Since the 1970s, GEDA has managed three industrial parks, the E.T. Calvo Memorial Park, the Harmon Industrial Park and the Cabras Industrial Park, and then in the late 1990s, the Guam Shipyard. Annually, on average, the leases on these properties have generated about 740 jobs, $21.7 million in gross payroll, over $55.7 million in gross sales and $2 million in Gross Receipts Tax. Leveraging GEDA's Industrial Park Program in 2006, GEDA's Real Property Division engaged in a management Memorandum of Understanding (MOU) with the Guam Ancestral Lands Commission (GALC) to lease and manage 135 acres of Spanish Crown properties. As a result of this management agreement, for the period October 2007 to February 2011, GEDA leased 49 acres and collected $768,882 in ground lease and participation rents of which $656,719 was remitted to GALC, while the balance was retained by GEDA as provided for in the MOU. Remaining properties will be leased as the market improves. GEDA is currently looking into similar management agreements with other GovGuam agencies with land inventory that could generate lease revenues at fair market value rates.

Some of the services provided by GEDA's Real Property Division include:

Management of leases and licenses

Evaluation of real property opportunities Draft as of 8/3/11 80

Advertising availability of properties for commercial leases and licenses

Evaluation and negotiation of lease agreements

PROJECT NAME: CONFERENCE CENTER

Discussion: With the construction of a small conference facility that can accommodate 1,500 to 2,500 conference attendees, Guam has the ability to compete and market the island to companies and organizations throughout the Pacific Asia region. This offers job opportunities in destination marketing as well as conference planning and event coordination.

PROJECT NAME: COTTAGE INDUSTRIES

Consolidation of miscellaneous business opportunities that may not have an impact on the island but have the potential to create business niches and small business opportunities.

ECOTOURISM

Discussion: Ecotourism is a growing segment of the global tourism industry that is making significant positive contributions to the environmental, social, cultural and economic well-being of destinations and local communities around the world. It offers long-term solutions by helping protect natural and cultural heritage. It appeals to travelers of all ages who are interested in social, economic and environmental sustainability. These travelers seek authentic local experiences and opportunities to give back to the communities they visit.

During a PATA Micronesia chapter quarterly membership meeting, Duncan Morris, CNN vice president of research, presented some significant highlights of a 2006 CNN Guam Tourism Survey. Most respondents (50% or higher) were aware of Guam's beautiful beaches and scenery, and agree that it is a desirable destination for diving. However, most did not know that Guam is eco-friendly, good for hiking, rich in culture/heritage, and has good food. Sustaining or growing Guam's market share will be difficult in the future as other competing destinations increase in number and marketing sophistication. The proliferation of many beach and cultural destination resorts in the Asia-Pacific region pose a challenge to Guam. To meet the challenge of existing and emerging destination competitors, Guam must deliver a brand promise supported by destination improvements.

Tumon is the center of leisure activity on the island. It is internationally recognized for the white sandy beach and blue waters of Tumon Bay, and the variety and quality of activities and attractions available to visitors. For instance, the Guam Zoological, Botanical and Marine Garden (better known as Cushing Zoo) is located in the heart of Tumon, surrounded by a high-rise hotel on one side and a high-rise condominium unit on the other. Despite the difficulties of its location, Cushing Zoo owners have worked hard to maintain the tranquil setting. A large variety of Guam's indigenous species of plants and animals can be found here, including some marine life. Gun Beach lies north of Tumon Bay. Although less developed than Tumon Bay, it is a good getaway for those who do not mind less traveled spots. Fai Fai (part of Gun Beach) is a private eco-cultural retreat that features a beautiful sandy beach, a reef worth snorkeling, and coconut trees for shade. For an even more isolated beach experience, low tide allows for a trek around the rocks at the north end of Gun Beach.

In addition, Gun Beach will now be the home of Lina'La, a new cultural and eco-adventure park. Mark Baldyga, owner and founder of Tumon's SandCastle entertainment complex, wants to bring a unique tourist attraction that showcases Guam's culture. "This is a living, interactive, highly immersive, very exciting Chamorro cultural center," Baldyga said. The highlight of the project will be the "living village" that will resemble an ancient, pre-contact village. The park will also include a history and nature eco-walk along an outdoor trail, building that will feature artifacts and a theater, exhibits of animals native to Guam, Chamorro cultural demonstration area, and proa canoe rides. Furthermore, the cultural park will include a beach bar, volleyball court, and zip line from the top of a hillside behind the cultural park for thrill seekers. The extensive archaeological work on the project has contributed to a two-year time frame for the project. According to Baldyga, the clientele for the beach bar will mostly be local, while the demographic for the cultural village and eco-park will be off-islanders and tourists.

Visitors may opt for eco-cultural attractions located in the northern and southern area of Guam as well. Ritidian Point lies on the northernmost tip of Guam and is the sight of the Guam National Wildlife Refuge, which is dedicated to the conservation of Guam's indigenous animals and plant life. This 772-acre refuge consists of 371 acres of native limestone forest, home to the endangered Mariana fruit bat, and 401 acres of marine habitat for the endangered hawksbill and green sea turtles. Visitors can arrange a guided tour of the limestone forest and caves where ancient Chamorros once lived and decorated cave walls with petroglyphs (cave drawings). Ritidian Point is also open to the public for fishing, picnicking, swimming, and snorkeling.

The Guam Historical Village at Gef Pa'go Park in Inarajan is known for its buildings made solely of natural materials. Bamboo and other woods serve as pillars of many shelters, each topped by a traditional thatched palm roof. Visitors can learn about Guam's history and culture through exhibits, dances, and demonstrations. For instance, demonstrations reveal how natives use coconut for something more than just food. Talofofo Falls Park is another favorite day-long excursion for the entire family. Ugum River waters cascade into a deep pool framed by steep bluffs and level rock ledges. There is a cable car to transport visitors while enjoying stunning views of the landscape. In addition, there is a museum, wild pigs and geese, children's rides, and a replica of Sergeant Shoichi Yokoi's cave. A leisure boat ride through Talofofo River can expose visitors to more of the island's beauty. Family and friends can explore the jungle and creatures that use it as their natural habitat. The Jungle River Boat Cruise will take visitors to the ruins of an ancient Chamorro village, and they will be able to enjoy demonstrations of traditional craft making.

Guam has an array of accommodations including luxury hotels and resorts that have the latest in amenities, including boutiques, restaurants, swimming pools and water parks. Hilton, Westin, Hyatt Regency, Outrigger, Nikko, Marriott, Pacific Islands Club, and other international and regional hotel chains have beach front properties on the island. Visitors can also stay at the Guam Garden Villa, Guam's only licensed bed and breakfast establishment located in Ordot. It is a unique form of travel accommodation because it provides guests with an opportunity to meet people from Guam who are happy to share their home and knowledge of the island. Guests have free access to living and dining areas, patios, and garden grounds where there are exotic fruit trees, such as mango, banana, jackfruit, sour sap, breadfruit and coconut. Although Guam currently offers a number of eco-cultural attractions, it lacks unique travel accommodations like the Guam Garden Villa B&B Homestay where guests are fully immersed in the cultural and environmental life of Guam. As ecotourism continues to establish itself in the global economy, the demand for environmentally sound lodging facilities like ecolodges is at an all time high. Ecolodges enable the visitor to interact with the natural and cultural surroundings of Guam.

Sports Tourism

Objective: Develop Guam as a destination for sports tourism

Discussion: Guam's temperate climate encourages major sports teams throughout Asia to visit for spring training exercises, as well as an opportunity for the enjoyment of outdoor sports on a year-round basis by locals and visitors alike. In an effort to promote such activities, the University of Guam (UOG), in cooperation with the University of Guam Endowment Foundation (UOGEF) have embarked upon the development of an outdoor multipurpose sports complex. The UOG physical master plan calls for a UOG Sports Complex to meet the physical education, athletic and sports needs of the UOG student population, general public and international athletes. The site for this development is a parcel directly adjacent to the UOG Fieldhouse. Outdoor sports, such as football, soccer, rugby, track, tennis, baseball, softball, volleyball and basketball are envisioned to be accommodated at the UOG Sports Complex. The direct adjacency of the existing UOG Fieldhouse and its amenities, such as locker rooms, weight and aerobic rooms, meeting rooms and a 4,000-seat Fieldhouse complement and enhance the viability of this project.

Strengths:

Guam's temperate climate, adjacency of the proposed Sports Complex to the existing Fieldhouse, passage of P.L. 27-130 that provides seed funding via the issuance of $1 million in tax credits should be sufficient for the A&E design and construction of the first phase of the project.

Existing recognition of Guam as a venue for training and the hosting of sporting events from major sports teams throughout Asia.

Recent construction of the outdoor sporting facilities at Okkodo High School (NCS road in Dededo), with brand new lights surrounding the baseball, softball, football, soccer and track field.

Weaknesses:

Inability to maintain sports venues, such as Southern High School's Olympic swimming pool.

Inability to consistently maintain the sports fields on island, such as the Eagles field in Mangilao.

Opportunities:

Sports tourism is a growing segment of the entire travel market and is in support of Guam's efforts to enhance the island as a vacation destination and promote local sports enthusiasm.

P.L. 30-228 supports funding for improvements to the Hågatña Pool and Tennis Court, and the Community Sports Recreational Improvement Fund for the construction and/or renovation of sports and community recreational facilities.

Draft as of 8/3/11 83

Guam Visitors Bureau funding in the form of approved grants that support sports tourism.

Construction of a new JFK High School campus in Upper Tumon will also include a new outdoor sporting facility surrounded by lights and a seating section.

Threats:

Possible competition with existing destination resorts, such as Leo Palace, and the development of similar projects that could erode the potential for securing full use and the maximizing of revenues derived from the use of the UOG Sports Complex.

Current Status: The UOG Outdoor Sports Complex tax credit rules and regulations have been approved by the Governor, and is now undergoing Legislative review in accordance with the Administrative Adjudication Law.

Low Priority

MEDICAL TOURISM

Objective: To further develop and expand medical initiatives for Guam, including increased education, services and capacities, and the utilization of the visitor industry to attract new and innovative medical technologies and services.

Discussion: The medical industry has been identified as having exceptional potential for Guam, as it will provide continued diversification of the economy, increased stability for our environment and improve the quality of life. Guam's civilian population has grown steadily over the years and is expected to surpass 180,000 by the end of the decade. Population in the secondary market (Saipan, Palau and the Federated States of Micronesia) is estimated to be around 196,000. The growth in the island's population and visitor industry indicates a need to develop and expand Guam's healthcare services, facilities and education. In addition, current medical insurance statistics indicate that approximately 35% of medical cases leave off-island for in-patient services (surgeries or procedures not available on island). For out-patient services (includes annual physical examination, secondary medical opinion, etc.), approximately 20% travel off-island. Guam's medical community is also currently experiencing a shortage of physicians in the field of family medicine. In addition to the shortage, the average age of these physicians is 55+ years. The additional resident doctors would create a larger resource for this discipline on island. There are still other critical physician shortage areas within the community that need to be filled, such as orthopedics, neuro-surgery, cardiac surgery and urology. The University of Guam (UOG) and the Guam Community College (GCC) are the only primary educational institutions in this region that provide training and support for healthcare professionals. GEDA has also met with representatives of James Cook University (JCU) in Cairns, Australia who are interested in setting up a student exchange program where Guam interns could be sent to JCU to participate in its medical programs.

Strengths:

Community of doctors (family practitioners) is adequate to support academic initiatives

Available working facilities (Guam Memorial Hospital, Skilled Nursing, Public Health)

Institutional resources (UOG, GCC, Guam Medical Society)

Attractive location to Asia Draft as of 8/3/11 84

Weaknesses:

No existing professional programs locally

Limited resources

Venture has no feasibility study or business plan to support claims

Capital-intensive industry

Opportunities:

Guam residents will further benefit from the development of the healthcare industry due to the following advantages:

o Easier and increased access to quality, specialized healthcare services

o Reduction in expenses associated with going off-island for medical diagnosis and treatment

o Availability of a larger pool of physicians with the most current medical knowledge

o Increased exposure to large healthcare corporations and industry professionals

o Adequate healthcare is a requirement for sustainable economic growth; healthier workers result in reduced absences and higher production levels

o Guam's close proximity and low cost fares to major Asian markets, combined with U.S. standards, could influence increased medical business activity

Attract a pool of physicians (private and military) that might opt to remain on or return to Guam

Supportive component for Guam Memorial Hospital and Public Health

Will provide alternative careers and employment opportunities, and promote the creation of an educated, qualified workforce

Creation of new business/clinics

Importation of new technology

Threats:

Lack of financing interest or grants for such funding

Tendency of local government to interfere and over-regulate

Depressed economy

Guam Memorial Hospital Authority issues

Recommendation: By further developing Guam's healthcare industry, the local population would then receive enhanced and expanded medical services usually sought off-island. Additionally, these added services will also act as an enticement for investors and visitors as they look to Guam as a Pacific Rim destination. It would also add a new dimension to the visitor industry other than strictly leisure. In order to expedite the educational component of this initiative, GEDA along with UOG and GCC, should aggressively pursue the offer by James Cook University to set up a student exchange program.

MANUFACTURING AND EXPORTING

Objective: Identify potential areas of high-tech, light manufacturing applicable to Guam's unique environment in an effort to further diversify Guam's economy.

Discussion: While Guam faces stiff competition within the Pacific Basin in accessing affordable labor and materials necessary to establish and maintain profitable production and manufacturing facilities, niche areas do exist that allow for the local production of goods needed in the construction industry whose cost is comparable or below prices for the same items sourced abroad. A good example of successful light manufacturing is the current production of typhoon shutters, locally produced doors and windows, and the recent investment in a steel rebar forming company. Another venture is the production of steel framing for use in the installation of drywall for construction and renovation projects.

Strengths:

Proven ability to find areas of profitable manufacturing/production

Ability to leverage the influx of labor associated with the military buildup

Geographic proximity to the Northern Mariana Islands, Federated States of Micronesia, and Asian nations should export become feasible

Weaknesses:

Lack of trained labor force

Prevailing wage requirements versus other regional and Pacific Basin wage scales

Cost of land and transport of specialized machinery

Opportunities:

Lack of competition adds to increased success of venture

Military buildup will assist in initial success of such ventures given the tremendous amount of work necessary to accommodate the Marine relocation from Okinawa

GEDA Qualifying Certificate available for manufacturing

Threats:

Similar products could be sourced abroad and undercut market for locally produced goods

Timeframe for committing to projects, as further delay could result in the inability to sell locally manufactured products for use in the military buildup

Recommendation: Suggest that GEDA work with the Chamber of Commerce and other private sector partners and participate in international trade expositions, in an effort to identify viable manufacturing opportunities. GEDA will continue to promote the Qualifying Certificate program as a means to incentivize entrepreneurs in pursuing local manufacturing ventures.

Financial & Legal Services

Discussion: Guam provides the economic cluster of American stability and soil. The biggest components of that are the military buildup/construction, American dollars (banking and financial services), and American legal infrastructure (alternative dispute resolution and court services). Together, these components meet the common cluster development objectives creating an internationally attractive destination for Asian countries that would like to utilize American economic and legal infrastructure. Meanwhile, federal resources for the military buildup will be maximized as a result of Guam's proximity to Asia.

Film Industry

Objective: To create the first Guam Film Commission that will become the lead entity in the development and organization of Guam's film industry, overseeing all film, video and photographic projects and activities on Guam.

Discussion: U.S. and international film markets are always looking for new locations to film motion pictures, TV shows or commercials, and production events. Additionally, in light of global security issues, production companies are also looking for scenic locations that are safe for visiting talent and crews and that feature supporting service infrastructure and business-friendly environments. Directors, specifically, are looking for locations that allow for shooting a variety of scenes in one location. Guam was the location for the 1970's feature film "Noon Sunday," and has since been a common filming location for Japanese and Korean television and production companies. Guam's domestic infrastructure has also grown to support a more sophisticated local market and the growth of the niche foreign production market. Identified target markets include the U.S., Japan, Hong Kong, Korea, India and the Philippines. In 2004, Guam hosted the filming of "Max Havoc: Curse of the Dragon" which featured David Carradine and Carmen Electra. Guam has received inquiries from large Hollywood production companies and the Philippines about filming in Guam, how to contact the Guam Film Commission, and how to purchase a "Guam Film Guide" (a resource guide for local production infrastructure).

Strengths:

Guam is a virtually new filming location

Guam is a safe destination protected by U.S. laws

Guam has talent, technology and facilities to support activities

Guam has experienced professionals that can contribute to this industry

Guam has the support of private and corporate sponsors

Weaknesses:

Currently no commission and regulatory body

No "Film Guide"

No film school or professional technical school

Limited equipment (rental houses, lighting rigs, trailers, etc.)

Limited support facilities (sound stage, film processing, editing, etc.)

Opportunities:

Guam can become a centralized hub for stateside productions and Micronesian area productions

Guam offers a mix of tropical, urban, domestic and Asian nuances for a multitude of filming options to include:

o Tropical rainforest

o Urban city setting

o Resort and beach

o Underwater

o Military

Guam can develop more professional service infrastructure (technical sectors, equipment, talent and labor hiring, catering, logistical support, and others that lead to job creation)

Growth in foreign (Asian) film market

More global recognition of Guam through visual and artistic promotion

New revenue center for the island (film guide sales, fees and indirect tax collection)

Threats:

Commitment of local professionals

Regulatory concerns

Inclement weather

Increased competition from established markets and nearby upstarts

Recommendation: Create a Guam Film Office, under the Government of Guam or GEDA, as the one-stop central coordinator for film and photographic use of government-administered parks, beaches, roads, and facilities. The office will work closely with local government agencies to assist filmmakers with acquiring the necessary permits and resources to shoot on Guam. The creation of a Guam Film Office website that can inform interested parties of the opportunities and incentives available on Guam is recommended. This website will serve as the main marketing center for interested investors; it will feature pictures of locations, incentives and tax credits, permit requirements, information about Guam, contact information, and other necessary resources.

STRATEGIC INFORMATION

GUAM POWER AUTHORITY (1 of 2) Generation Capital Improvement Projects for New Bonds FY 2011 -FY 2014 (x $1,000)

Item	Capital Improvement Project Name	FY11	FY12	FY13	FY14	Project Total
1	Cabras 3&4 Facility Improvements -New Storage Building, HVAC Replacement, Plant Security System	460		550		1,010
2	Provide Fire Protection for Transformers and Fire Detection System for Boiler Burner Area - Cabras 1&2	650				650
3	Cabras 1&2 Facility Improvements -New Plant Maintenance Shop, Plant Paging System, A/C for Office and Lab, New Chemical Storage Facility	838	200			1,038
4	Replace Existing Yard Fire Hydrant System - Cabras 1&2	420				420
5	Install Generator On-Line Monitoring System for Unit 1&2 and Provide Electrical Testing and Measuring Equipment	165		63		228
6	Fire Alarm / Suppression System Upgrade Phase 2 -Cabras 3&4	640	160			800
7	Waste Oil Facility Improvements -Cabras 1&2	150				150
8	Cabras #2 Reheater Tubes Replacement	1,113				1,113
9	Replace Cabras Unit #1 Feedwater Heater #2 and Unit #2 FWH #4	1,090				1,090
10	Replace Cabras Unit #2 Hydrogen and CO2 piping	75				75

11	Replace Cabras Unit #1 Instrument Air Compressor 1B & Cabras Unit #2 Service Air Compressor	85	180			265
12	Cabras Unit #2 Heater Drain Pump & Motor Replacement	240				240
13	Replace one (1) Boiler feed Pump Motor for Cabras Unit #1	275				275
14	Replace Battery Bank "A", "B" & "C" -Cabras 3&4	50		100		150
15	Governor Control System Replacement - Cabras 3&4	600				600

GUAM POWER AUTHORITY (2 of 2) Generation Capital Improvement Projects for New Bonds FY 2011 -FY 2014 (x $1,000)

Item	Capital Improvement Project Name	FY11	FY12	FY13	FY14	Project Total
16	Homogenizer Replacement -Cabras 3&4	500				500
17	Sea Water Travelling Screen A,B, C Replacement -Cabras 3&4	400	800			1,200
18	CEMS Replacement -Cabras 3&4		150			150
19	New Hydraulic Press for Waste Oil Recovery - Cabras 3&4		50			50
20	Lube Oil Storage and Maintenance Facility for WSD					0
21	Replace One (1) Forced Draft Fan Motor for Cabras Unit #1		275			275
22	Design and Construct Chemical Storage Facility for Cabras Unit #1&2		250			250
23	Generator Protection Relay Panel Replacement -Cabras 3&4		250			250
24	Distributed Control System(DCS) Replacement - Cabras 3&4		1,200			1,200
25	Turbochargers Replacement -Cabras 3&4		1,400			1,400
26	Air Cooler 2 sets Replacement (Phase 1) - Cabras 3&4		250			250
27	Replace Service Water Cooler for Cabras Unit #1			500		500
28	Replace Unit #1 Auxiliary Transformer -Cabras 1&2			500		500
29	Exhaust Gas Silencer Replacement -Cabras 3&4			150		150
30	Fuel Oil Purifier Feed Pumps Replacement - Cabras 3&4			150		150
31	Installation of Vent Fan for Turbochargers - Cabras 3&4			300		300

32	Debris Filter Replacement -Cabras 3&4			250		250
33	Cabras #3 Bearing Temperature Monitoring System			380		380

Guam Waterworks Authority Capital Improvement Projects (1 of 3)
PW 05-01 Ground Water Disinfection
PW 05-02 Water Reservoir Condition Assessment
PW 05-03 Santa Rita Springs Booster Pump Rehabilitation, Phase II
PW 05-04 Ugum Water Treatment Plant Refurbishment
PW 05-05 "A" Series Well Transmission Line
PW 05-06 Water Booster Pump Station
PW 05-07 Meter Replacement Program
PW 05-08 Barrigada Tank Repair/Replacement
PW 05-09 Leak Detection / Line Replacement
PW 05-10 Potable Water System Planning
PW 09-01 Ugum Water Treatment Plant Intake Modifications
PW 09-02 Water Wells
PW 09-03 Water Distribution System Pipe Replacement
PW 09-04 Pressure Zone Realignment/Development 2005
PW 09-05 Northern System Water Distribution System 2005 Improvements
PW 09-06 Central Water Distribution System 2005 Improvements
PW 09-07 Southern Water Distribution System 2005 Improvements
PW 09-08 Mechanical/Electrical Equipment Replacement
PW 09-09 Water Reservoir Internal/External Corrosion Asmt
PW 09-10 Water Reservoir Internal/External Corrosion Rehabilitation
PW 09-11 Water System Reservoirs 2005 Improvements
PW 11-01 Distribution System Upgrades
PW 11-02 Ugum Water Treatment Plant Reservoir Replacement
WW 05-01 Old Agat Wastewater Collection (I/I reduction)
WW 05-02 Collection Line Upgrade/ Collection System Upgrades

Guam Waterworks Authority Capital Improvement Projects (2 of 3)
WW 05-03 NDWTP Diffuser Installation
WW 05-04 Wastewater System Planning
WW 05-05 Wastewater Vehicles
WW 05-06 Wastewater Pump Station Upgrades
WW 05-07 NDWWTP -Chlorine Tanks
WW 05-08 Umatac-Merizo STP Improvements
WW 09-02 Moratorium

WW 09-03 Old Agat Collection Continuation (III)
WW 09-05 Agat Manhole Rehabilitation
WW 09-06 Wastewater Collection System Replacement/Rehabilitation
WW 09-07 Tumon Bay Sewer Upgrades
WW 09-08 Facilities Plan/Design for Baza Gardens STP Replacement
WW 09-09 Facilities Plan/Design for the N. District STP Bio-solid
WW 09-10 Facilities Plan/Design for Agat-Santa Rita STP Replacement
WW 09-11 WWTP Priority 1 Upgrade
WW 11-01 Priority 1 Sewer Upgrades – Agat District
WW 11-02 Priority 1 Sewer Upgrades – Baza Garden District
WW 11-03 Baza Gardens STP Replacement
WW 11-04 Facilities Plan/Design for the Umatac-Merizo STP Improvements
WW 11-05 Facilities Plan for Hågatña STP Improvements & Effluent WWPS
WW 11-06 Hågatña STP Improvements and Effluent WWPS
WW 11-07 Northern District STP Expansion – Biosolids Electrical
MC 05-01 Laboratory Modernization
EE 05-01 Well Electrical Protection
EE 05-02 SCADA Pilot Project
EE 09-01 Wastewater Pumping Station Electrical Upgrade

Guam Waterworks Authority Capital Improvement Projects (3 of 3)

EE 09-02 Electrical Upgrade -Water Wells
EE 09-03 Electrical Upgrade -Water Booster Pump Stations
EE 09-04 Electrical Upgrade -Water Booster Pump Stations
EE 09-05 Electrical Upgrade -Other Water Booster Pump Stations
EE 09-06 SCADA Improvements – Phase 1
EE 09-07 SCADA Improvements – Phase 2
EE 09-08 SCADA Improvements – Phase 3
EE 09-09 SCADA Improvements – Phase 4
DOD FUNDED PROJECTS
WW 05-02 Collection Line Upgrade/ Collection System Upgrades
WW 05-03 NDWTP Diffuser Installation
WW 05-06 Wastewater Pump Station Upgrades
WW 09-01 LS Priority 1 Upgrades
WW 09-02 Moratorium
WW 09-04 Manhole Frame Seal Repair
WW 09-06 Wastewater Collection System Replacement/Rehabilitation
WW 09-09 Facilities Plan/Design for the N. District STP Bio-solids
WW 11-05 Facilities Plan for Hågatña STP Improvements & Effluent WWPS
WW 11-06 Hågatña STP Improvements and Effluent WWPS
WW 11-07 Northern District STP Expansion – Biosolids Electrical

Draft as of 8/3/11 103

Department of Public Works Capital Improvement Projects (1 of 2)

Construction of Emergency Shelter/Tanks @ Astumbo Elementary School
Construction of Emergency Shelter/Tanks @ Wettengel Elementary School
Construction of Emergency Shelter/Tanks @ Maria Ulloa Ellementary School
Construction of Emergency Shelter/Tanks @ George Washington High School
Construction of Emergency Shelter/Tanks @ MU Lujan Elementary School
Construction of Emergency Shelter/Tanks @ Carbullido Elementary School
Construction of Emergency Shelter/Tanks @ Talofofo Elementary School
Construction of Emergency Shelter/Tanks @ Inarajan Elementary School
Construction of Emergency Shelter/Tanks @ Harry S. Truman Elem. School
Construction of Emergency Shelter/Tanks @ Merizo Elementary School
Construction of Emergency Shelter/Tanks @ FQ Sanchez Elementary School
Construction of Emergency Shelter/Tanks @ Machananao Elementary School
Construction of Emergency Shelter/Tanks @ J.M. Guerrero Elementary School
Construction of Emergency Shelter/Tanks @ UPI Elem. Sch.
Construction of Emergency Shelter/Tanks @ Chalan Pago Ordot Elem. School
Construction of Emergency Shelter/Tanks @ F.B. Leon Guerrero Middle School
Construction of Department of Parks & Recreation/ Historic Preservation Guam Sports Complex Baseball Park (Design-Build)
Renovation and Miscellaneous Repair at DPHSS (Design-Build)
Typhoon Shutters @ GUAM DOE HMPG-GU-DR-1446, PW # 12 for M.U. Lujan
Construction of Guam Heritage Walking Trail
Emergency repairs at various facilities of GUAM DOE, Maria Ulloa Elementary school
Emergency repairs at various facilities of GUAM DOE, Finegayan Elementary school Boys and Girls Bathroom
Emergency repairs at various facilities of GUAM DOE, Finegayan Elementary School Perimeter Fence

Department of Public Works Capital Improvement Projects (2 of 2)

Emergency repair at various facilities of GUAM DOE, JM Guerrero Elementary School
Emergency repair of various facilities at GUAM DOE, Simon Sanchez High School (Roof Repair)
Construction of New Nursery at Dept. of Agriculture (Design-Building)
Construction and Restoration of Masso River Reservoir, Piti, Guam
Santos Memorial Park Improvements
As-Atdas Apartment Complex-Renovation of Bldg A
Renovation of Guma As-Atdas Apartment Complex Bldg 5, A & B, Yigo
Guam Heritage Walking Trails
Procure/Construct Generator Room and Generator at Dept. of Agriculture (Design-Building)

Construct Guam Sports Complex Baseball Park (Design-Building)
Construction of New Fisheries Office Building @ Department of Agriculture
New Chain Link Fence at Masso River Reservoir
Repair of Merizo Pier and Merizo Boat Ramp
Renovation and Upgrading of Building "E" @ the Dept. of Youth Affairs (Design-Building)
F.B. Leon Guerrero Middle School Roofing (Under Contractor's warranty)
Agat Marina Public Boat Ramp
Building Renovation of WIC Facilities (Electrical), Tiyan
Building Renovation of WIC Facilities , Tiyan
Building Renovation of WIC Facilities (Electrical), Santa Rita
Construction of New John F. Kennedy High School Finance, Demolition, Design, Build, Maintain & Leaseback (FDDBML)
Construction of Guam Forensic Science Laboratory in GCC Campus, Mangilao
King Fisheries Holding Enclosures, DOAG,
Upgrade and Installation of Electronic Locking System @ the Dept. of Correction Facilities (Design-Building)
Retrofitting Public Buildings
LED Streetlights in Marine Drive

Guam International Airport Authority Capital Improvement Projects

Extend Runway 6L/24R
Rehabilitate Runway 6L/24R
Install Instrument Landing System Runway 6L
Noise mitigation for residence
Improve Airport Utility Infrastructure (Sewer and storm water design only)
Collect airport data for the Airports Geographic information system (AGIS)
Install Instrument Landing System Runway 6L Phase II
Conduct Environmental Assessment for Sewer and Storm drainage

Port Authority of Guam Capital Improvement Projects

Port Modernization -Acquisition of Two (2) New Container Cranes
Port Modernization -Operating Systems for Terminal ad Gate/OCR Canopy Portals
Port Modernization: Container Yard and Existing Reefer Upgrade
Port Modernization -Building Renovation & Construction
Port Modernization -Wharf Rehabilitation and Dredging for F4, F5 & F6

Guam Memorial Hospital Authority Capital Improvement Projects

Chiller Replacement

Fire Sprinkler System Upgrade
Infusion Pump Replacement Project
3rd and 4th floor A-wing wall hardening
A/E design services to replace electrical power distribution system
Portable X-Ray Machines
Procure & Install (by Owner) Touchless Faucets and Water Closets
Replace Laboratory Information System (LIS)
Replace Ultrasonic Cleaning System
Replace Patient Room Doors
Vertical Transportation Elevator Modernization Project
ER & CCU/ICU Expansion/Upgrade Project
Replace Main Electrical Distribution System & one (1) 1.6 Megawatts Generator Set

Medical Equipment and Furnishings for the ED and CCU/ICU Expansion
Medical Equipment for the various inpatient and outpatient Nursing Units
The 1st & 2nd Floors HVAC Upgrade (A/E & Construction)
Removal and replacement of built up roofing system 3rd & 4th floors
Replace the Hospital and SNU Nurse Call / Code 72 / Intercom Systems
Replace the SNU Chiller System
Replace the SNU Fire Alarm System
Office and interior furnishings for general care areas
Replacement of various air handling units throughout facility
Upgrade typhoon shutters from panel type to roll up SNU
Replacement of roof coating system SNU
Replacement of hot water system SNU
Replacement of water softener system SNU
Replacement of dishwasher system SNU

One Guam Report of Capital Improvement Projects (1 of 2)

Tier	Department	Prioritization of Government of Guam Projects
1 FY 2012 2014	DPW	School Bus Fleet & Maintenance Facility
	DMHSA	Mental Health & Substance Abuse Facility
	DPHSS	CDC Lab & Medical Healthcare Campus Master Plan
	GCA	Cultural Repository
2 FY 2013 to 2015	OOG	Program Management Office
	GWA	Sixteen (16) New Production Water Wells
	PAG	Port Modernization -Acquisition of Two (2) New Container Cranes
	GC&QA	Biosecurity Enforcement Needs
	GEPA	Military Buildup Related Resource Needs
	DPW	Highway Maintenance & Construction Enhancements
	BSP	Capacity Assistance for Project Review & Monitoring

PAG	Port Modernization -Operating Systems for Terminal ad Gate/OCR Canopy Portals
PAG	Port Modernization: Container Yard and Existing Reefer Upgrade
PAG	Port Modernization -Building Renovation & Construction
PAG	Port Modernization -Wharf Rehabilitation and Dredging for F4, F5 & F6
GEDA	Polaris Point Infrastructure Improvements
DPW	Information Technology Systems Infrastructure Enhancements/Upgrade
DPW	Fleet Management and Inventory System
DPW	Warehouse Inventory & Fixed Asset System
DRT	Department and Revenue Tax Building (New)
GPD	GPD Headquarters
GMHA	Guam Memorial Expansion
DPHSS	DPHSS Facility & Central Health Clinic
DOL	Labor Resource Needs

One Guam Report of Capital Improvement Projects (2 of 2)

Tier	Department	Prioritization of Government of Guam Projects
	GPD	Crime Laboratory Expansion
	GPD	Vehicle Fleet Augmentation
	GFD	New Fire Stations & Equipment for Military Growth Areas
	GIAA	Passenger Concourse Construction -Gates 1, 2 & 3
	GFD	Fire Apparatus-Ambulance Fleet Upgrade
	UoG	School of Engineering Annex Expansion
	DOE	Construct Four (4) Schools
	GIAA	Outbound Baggage System Improvements
	GPD	Central Precinct Facility (Relocation/New)
3 FY 2014 to 2016	DPR	Expansion of Historic Preservation Office
	GPD	Yigo Precinct Command Facility (New)
	DYA	Construction/Expansion of Youth Correctional Facilities -NEW
	GPD	Marine Enforcement Facility -Boat House
	DPW	New School Buses
	DPHSS	Improvements for the Office of Vital Statistics
	GIAA	Integrated Cargo Aprons
	GIAA	North & South Ramp Pipeline and Hydrant System
	DOC	Adult Correctional Facility Phase One
	SCOG	Hagatna Judicial Center
4 FY 2015 to 2016	UOG	Triton Engagement Center
	GIAA	Military Specifications Runway Retrofit
	DPR	Construct Olympic Pool Facility
	DPR	Paseo Stadium Upgrade/Renovation
	DPR	Guerrero Field Upgrade/Renovation
	DPR	Dededo Sports Complex Upgrade/Renovation

DPR	Hagatna Pool Upgrade/Renovation
DPR	Tennis Centers Upgrade/Renovation
DPR	Inarajan Pool Upgrage/Renovation
DPR	Support Equipment Acquisition
DPR	Construct/Expand Warehouse

GUAM TAX REGULATIONS: BASIC INFORMATION

GENERAL INFORMATION

The U.S. Congress created the Territorial Government of Guam as a separate taxing jurisdiction by enactment of the Organic Act of Guam in 1950. Section 31 of the Act provides that the income tax laws in force in the United States shall be the income tax laws of Guam, substituting Guam for the United States where necessary and omitting any inapplicable or incompatible provisions. The U.S. Internal Revenue Code with such changes constitutes the Guam Territorial Income Tax Law.

There is the usual range of other types of local taxes, such as, liquor, tobacco, gasoline, real property, gross receipts, use, admissions, amusement, recreational facilities, and hotel occupancy. However, there is only one taxing authority in the Territory, the Government of Guam. There are no separate municipal, county, school district or improvement district taxes. Other than admissions, use, and hotel occupancy taxes, there is no general sales tax imposed directly on the consumer.

Foreign Sales Corporation (FSCs) which are licensed to do business on Guam may qualify for certain exemptions or rebates of income, real property, gross receipts and use taxes. Information concerning this can be obtained from the Director of Revenue and Taxation.

Personal and Corporate Income Tax

1. Bona fide residents of Guam are subject to special U.S. tax rules. In general, all individuals with income from Guam will file only one return—either to Guam or the United States.

   If you are a bona fide resident of Guam during the entire tax year, file your return with Guam. This applies to all bona fide residents who are citizens, resident aliens, or nonresident aliens of the United States.

   For more information, see Publication 570, *Tax Guide for Individuals with Income from U.S. Possessions*, or Publication 54, *Tax Guide for U.S. Citizens and Resident Aliens Abroad.*

2. Guam corporations are subject to income tax on their income from all sources. Other corporations doing business on Guam incur income tax liabilities to Guam on all Guam source income. Corporations not engaged in business on Guam are liable to a 30% tax on certain types of income from Guam sources. The tax rates for corporations doing business on Guam can be found in Section 11 of the Guam Territorial Income Tax Law.
3. Filing dates of Income Tax Returns are as follows:

   a. Individual income tax returns for the calendar year are due on or before April 15 of the following year. Individuals reporting on a fiscal year basis must file their returns on the 15th day of the fourth month following the close of the fiscal year. When the due date for doing any act for tax purposes -- filing a return, paying taxes, etc. -- falls on a Saturday, Sunday, or legal holiday, you may do that act on the next business day.

   b. Corporations are required to file an income tax return for the calendar year on or before March 15 of the following year. Corporations on a fiscal year basis must file income tax return on the 15th day of the third month following the close of the fiscal year.

Guam has its own tax system based on the same tax laws and tax rates that apply in the United States.

Requests for advice about Guam residency and tax matters should be addressed to:

Department of Revenue and Taxation
Government of Guam
P.O. Box 23607
GMF, GU 96921
Telephone: (671) 472-7471
Fax: (671) 472-2643

If you are a U.S. citizen with income from sources in Guam and the United States, you must file your income tax return as explained below with either Guam or the United States, but not both. You are not liable for any income tax to the jurisdiction with which you do not have to file.

If you are a resident of Guam on the last day of your tax year, you should file your return with the:

Department of Revenue and Taxation
Government of Guam
P.O. Box 23607
GMF, GU 96921

Include income from worldwide sources on the Guam return. Include any balance of tax due with your tax return.

If you are a resident of the United States on the last day of your tax year, you should file your return with the:

Internal Revenue Service
Philadelphia, PA
19255-0215

Include income from worldwide sources on the U.S. return. Include any balance of tax due with your tax return.

If you are neither a resident of Guam nor a resident of the United States at the end of your tax year, you should file with Guam if you are a citizen of Guam but not otherwise a citizen of the United States (born or naturalized in Guam). If you are a U.S. citizen or resident but not otherwise a citizen or resident of Guam, you should file with the United States.

U.S. MILITARY EMPLOYEES

If you are a member of the U.S. Armed Forces stationed on Guam, you are not considered a resident of Guam and you must file your return with the United States. However, if you are a member of the military and a citizen of Guam, or if you are a civilian employee of the military, you are subject to the same rules described in the previous paragraphs.

INCOME TAX WITHHELD

Take into account tax withheld by both jurisdictions in determining if there is tax due or an overpayment.

INFORMATION RETURN

If your adjusted gross income from all sources is at least $50,000, your gross income consists of at least $5,000 from sources in Guam, and you file a U.S. income tax return, attach Form 5074 , Allocation of Individual Income Tax to Guam or the Commonwealth of the Northern Mariana Islands (CNMI) to Form 1040.

JOINT RETURN

If you file a joint return, you should file it (and pay the tax) with the jurisdiction where the spouse who has the greater adjusted gross income would have to file (if you were filing separately). If the spouse with the greater adjusted gross income is a resident of Guam at the end of the tax year, file the joint return with Guam. If the spouse with the greater adjusted gross income is a resident of the United States at the end of the tax year, file the joint return with the United States. For this purpose, income is determined without regard to community property laws.

Note

Guam and the United States have entered into an implementing agreement. The effective date of the agreement, however, has been indefinitely postponed. When the agreement goes into effect, the following rules may apply.

Guam may enact its own laws for taxing residents of Guam as well as for taxing income sourced in Guam (or income effectively connected with a trade or business in Guam) and paid to a nonresident.

Individuals who are bona fide residents of Guam and have income sourced outside Guam, the CNMI, or American Samoa may have to file a U.S. tax return.

Individuals who are bona fide residents of Guam and have income sourced in any of the three possessions may be able to treat that income as exempt from U.S. income tax under the possession exclusion rules.

DOUBLE TAXATION

A mutual agreement procedure exists to settle cases of double taxation between the United States and Guam. See Double Taxation under Filing U.S. Tax Returns, earlier.

The Department of Revenue and Taxation, Government of Guam, is the primary agency for all taxation related matters in Guam. For such information, please contact them at the following:

Department of Revenue and Taxation
Government of Guam
P.O. Box 23607
GMF, BARRIGADA, GUAM 96921 U.S.A.

Tel: 1 (671) 475-1817 Fax: 1 (671) 472-2643 The U.S. Congress created the Territorial Government of Guam as a separate taxing jurisdiction by enactment of the Organic Act of Guam in 1950.

Section 31 of the Act provides that the income tax laws in force in the United States shall be the income tax laws of Guam, substituting Guam for the United States where necessary and omitting any inapplicable or incompatible provisions. The U.S. Internal Revenue Code with such changes constitutes the Guam Territorial Income Tax Law.

There is the usual range of other types of local taxes, such as, liquor, tobacco, gasoline, real property, gross receipts, use, admissions, amusement, recreational facilities, and hotel occupancy. However, there is only one taxing authority in the Territory, the Government of Guam. There are no separate municipal, county, school district or improvement district taxes. Other than admissions, use, and hotel occupancy taxes, there is no general sales tax imposed directly on the consumer.

FOREIGN SALES CORPORATIONS

Foreign Sales Corporation (FSCs) which are licensed to do business on Guam may qualify for certain exemptions or rebates of income, real property, gross receipts and use taxes. Information concerning this can be obtained from the Director of Revenue and Taxation.

PERSONAL AND CORPORATE INCOME TAX

Individuals who are citizens or residents of Guam are required to report their income from all sources when computing their Guam taxes. Their income taxes must be paid into the Treasury of Guam. Non-residents except those who acquired their U.S. citizenship through the Organic Act, or through naturalization proceedings in the District Court of Guam, incur income tax liability to Guam only on income derived from Guam sources. Self-employed individuals who are covered by the Federal Old Age Insurance and Schedule C of individual income tax return Form 1040.

A U.S. citizen who is a resident of Guam at the last day of the taxable year (usually December 31) will be required to file an individual income tax return in Guam reporting his or her worldwide income. In such case the U.S. Internal Revenue Code provides that no return need be filed with the U.S. Internal Revenue Service.

Guam individual tax rates are the same as those in the U.S. Internal Revenue Code and can be found in Section 1 of the Guam Territorial Income Tax Law. Guam corporations are subject to income tax on their income from all sources. Other corporations doing business on Guam incur income tax liabilities to Guam on all Guam source income. Corporations not engaged in business on Guam are liable to a 30% tax on certain types of income from Guam sources. The tax rates for corporations doing business on Guam can be found in Section 11 of the Guam Territorial Income Tax Law.

FILING DATES OF INCOME TAX RETURNS

Individual Income Tax Returns: Individual income tax returns for the calendar year are due on or before April 15 of the following year. Individuals reporting on a fiscal year basis must file their returns on the 15th day of the fourth month following the close of the fiscal year. When the due date for doing any act for tax purposes -- filing a return, paying taxes, etc. -- falls on a Saturday, Sunday, or legal holiday, you may do that act on the next business day.

Corporations: Corporations are required to file an income tax return for the calendar year on or before March 15 of the following year. Corporations on a fiscal year basis must file income tax return on the 15th day of the third month following the close of the fiscal year.

TAXES AND TAX RATES APPLICABLE IN GUAM INCOME WITHHOLDING TAX

Less than $500 at end of quarter: If at the end of the quarter your total undeposited taxes for the quarter are less than $500, you do not have to deposit the taxes. You may pay the taxes with Form W-1 or you may deposit them by the end of the next month.

$500 or more but less than $3,000 at end of any month: If at the end of any month your total undeposited taxes are $500 or more but less than $3,000, deposit the taxes within fifteen (15) days after the end of the month.

If your taxes are less than $500, carry them over to the next month. (This deposit requirement does not apply if you made a deposit for an eighth-monthly period during the month under the $3,000 rule).

$3,000 or more at end of the eighth-monthly period: If at the end of any eighth-monthly period your total undeposited taxes are $3,000 or more, deposit the taxes within three (3) banking days after the end of the eighth-monthly period.

Eighth-monthly periods end on the 3rd, 7th, 11th, 15th, 19th, 22nd, 25th and last day of each month. (Do not count as banking days legal holidays observed by authorized financial institutions, Saturdays and Sundays).

Gross Receipts Tax: All individuals and entities doing business or performing services on Guam are subject to a four percent (4%) gross receipts tax. This tax is levied on the gross receipts from business or professional services on Guam.

The tax is to be reported and paid no later than the 20th day of the month following the month in which the gross receipts were received or accrued, depending upon the accounting method elected by the taxpayer.

The first $1,200 of rental income in a year is exempted.

Banks and lending institutions are taxed on annual net income. Reports for banks and lending institutions are due on the 90th day following the taxpayer's tax year.

Use Tax: All personal property imported into Guam for use or consumption by the person importing it is subject to four percent (4%) tax on the landed cost. Property imported for resale is not subject to this tax.

The tax does not apply to property having had a substantial use by the person bringing it into Guam before importation, or to machinery and other moved when the contract or other work is completed.

No tax is imposed when the total value of all property imported by any one person in any one calendar month is $100 or less.

Purchase of personal property on Guam for use or consumption from a person not liable for Gross Receipts Tax is also subject to the four percent (4%) use tax. The $100 exemption also applies to such purchases.

Real Property Tax: A real property tax is levied upon land at a fixed rate of one-half percent (1/2%) of the assessed value, which is thirty-five percent (35%) of the appraised value, or an "economic rate" of 0.175%; the tax on improvements is a fixed rate of one percent (1%) of the assessed value which is thirty-five percent (35%) of the appraised value or an "economic rate" of 0.35%.

(1) Properties which are used exclusively for educational; religious or eleemosynary purposes are exempt from Real Property Taxes.

(2) A home owner, provided he is occupying the home, may apply for a home exemption up to $15,000 of the appraised value.

OTHER TAXES AND RATES

Alcoholic Beverage Taxes :$10.00 per wine gallon of distilled beverages; $2.75 per wine gallon for vinous beverages; $0.04 per each twelve (12) fluid oz. malted fermented beverages.

Tobacco Tax: $0.35 for each 100 cigarettes; 40% of landed cost of cigars; $0.35 per pound all others.

Liquid Fuel Tax: This tax is levied on the distributor of liquid fuel. Diesel Fuel -- $0.10 per gallon; all other liquid fuel -- $0.11 per gallon.

Consumers using liquid fuel for marine or aviation purposes may obtain a tax drawback of $0.02 per gallon.

Consumers using liquid fuel for non-highway agricultural purposes may obtain a tax drawback of $0.04 per gallon.

Users of diesel fuel for marine or aviation purposes may obtain a tax drawback of $0.01 per gallon.

Users of diesel fuel for non-highway agricultural purposes may obtain a tax drawback of $0.02 per gallon.

Admission Tax : $0.01 for each $0.10 admission in excess of $0.25. This tax applies only to spectacle amusement, such as, movies, boxing and similar events.

Amusement Taxes: $100.00 single coin pinball machine and juke box; $250.00 multiple coin pinball machine; $100.00 plus $15.00 for extra coin slots for coin activated music producing machines; $50.00 kiddie rides; $350.00 poker machines, video horse or greyhound racing machines; $100.00 all others.

Recreational Facilities Tax: $10.00 for each bowling alley $100.00 for each nine holes of golf course or fraction thereof and driving range on miniature golf course. $5.00 for each pool or billiard table $100.00 for each skating rink, dance hall, or shooting gallery.

Hotel Occupancy: 10% of rental price charged each transient occupant.

Vehicle Transfer Tax: 2% of market value. Tax occurs upon transfer of vehicle. Not applicable upon transfer of title directly from a licensed dealer.

DEPARTMENT OF REVENUE AND TAXATION'S SERVICES

I. LICENSES AND REGISTRATION

A. Business Licenses (Title XVII, Government Code of Guam)

1. To obtain a business license, a business license application form must be completed in full (name of individual or corporation, address, SSN or EIN, telephone number, description of activity, etc.). The application then must be routed through the various government agencies for clearance by either the applicant or the License and Registration Branch. The license will be issued after all clearances are completed. Applicable fees are made payable to the Treasurer of Guam.
2. There is no citizenship requirement for the application of a business license.
3. Annual fees for business licenses are as follows:

4.	Banking	$ 500.00
5.	Small Lending Institution	250.00
6.	Wholesale	100.00
7.	Retail	40.00
8.	Hand Manufacture	5.00
9.	Machine Manufacture	40.00
10.	Service	25.00
11.	Coin-operated Machines	5.00
12.	Service Rental (One family residential unit) .	5.00
13.	Home Industry	25.00
14.	Large Foreign Sales Corporation (FSC)	1,000.00
15.	Small Foreign Sales Corporation (FSC)	400.00
16.	Temporary - one-fourth of license fee	
17.	of type of license desired.	

License fees are prorated and one-fourth of the annual fee is charged for each quarter or portion of a quarter remaining in the fiscal year from date of issuance. All business licenses expire on June 30 of each year. A penalty of $1.00 per day is assessed after June 30 for failure by an ongoing business to renew its license.

18. Individuals or firms engaged in certain professions must obtain a permit in lieu of a business license. These include architects, engineers, surveyors, and contractors. This permit can be obtained from the Department of Public Works.
19. All corporations and partnerships must be registered on Guam with the Licenses and Registration Branch prior to being issued a business license. See I(c) below for requirements for corporations.

B. Alcoholic Beverage Control Licenses (Title XXVI, Government Code of Guam)

1. Individuals applying for an Alcoholic Beverage Control license must have resided on Guam for at least one year at the time of application. If the applicant is a partnership, then each partner must satisfy the same requirement. If the applicant is a corporation, the majority of the members of the Board of Directors must meet this requirement.
2. General On-Sale and General Off-Sale licenses are issued on a municipality basis. One of each license per one thousand persons or fraction thereof is issued. However, a

special provisions of the law allows application for a license if the establishment is a hotel with at least twenty(20) rooms or if it is a public restaurant where the investment in the building is not less than $50,000.

3. The fees for various classes and kinds of Alcoholic Beverage Control licenses are as follows:
4.
5. Class 1 Manufacturer's License $100/year
6. Class 2 Agent's License $250/year
7. Class 3 Wholesale Dealer's License $500/year
8. Class 4 Retail Dealer's On-Sale License:
9. Beer $150/year
10. Wine $150/year
11. General $500/year
12. Class 5 Retail Dealer's Off-Sale License:
13. Beer . . . . $ 50/year
14. General $400/year
15. Class 6 Special Alcoholic License . . . . $ 25/year
16. Class 7 Temporary Beer License . . . . $ 10/day
17. Class 8 Public Warehouseman's License . . . . . $ 25/year
18. Class 9 Club License $250/year
19. Class 10 Temporary General License . . . . $ 10/day
20. Zoning Requirements. Applicant must comply with Health and Safety Laws. Inquiries regarding health, safety and zoning laws should be made at the Departments of Public Health and Social Services, Public Safety, and Land Management, respectively.
21. The Alcoholic Beverage Control Administrator is responsible for the enforcement of the Alcoholic Beverage Control Laws.
22. The Alcoholic Beverage Control Board meets regularly each month to consider applications and reports of violation of the ABC laws and regulations.

C. Corporations (Title I, Civil Code of Guam)

1. Prior to conducting business on Guam, a corporation must be registered with the License and Registration Branch.
2. Domestic Corporations:

a. Corporations may be formed by voluntary association of three or more persons as prescribed by law and for any lawful purpose.
b. The Articles of Incorporation shall be filed in the License and Registration Branch, duly executed and acknowledged before any person authorized to administer oaths.
c. The Articles of Incorporation shall state:
(1) The name of the corporation.
(2) The purpose for which it is formed.
(3) The place and where the principal office of the corporation is to be established or located, which place must be on Guam and must be an address where service of process or other legal documents can be served.
(4) The term for which it is to exist, not exceeding 50 years, except as otherwise provided.
(5) The names and residences of the incorporators.
(6) Unless otherwise provided, the number of its directors, which shall be not less than three (3) nor more than seven (7), and the names and residences of the persons who are appointed to act as such until the first annual meeting of the shareholders or until the election and qualification of their successors as provided by the bylaws: Provided, however, that at any time during the existence of the corporation the number of directors

may be increased to any number not exceeding fifteen (15) or diminished to any number not less than three (3) in the case of a non-stock corporation by the formal assent of a majority of the members at a regular or special meeting of the membership, and in the case of a stock corporation the number of directors may be increased to any number not exceeding eleven (11) or diminished to any number not less than three (3) by the formal assent of the stockholders of the corporation at a regular or special meeting of stockholders representing or holding a majority of the stock; and provided, further, that a certificate setting out such increase or diminution in the numbers of directors of any corporation shall be duly signed and sworn to by the president, managing agent, secretary or clerk, or treasurer of such corporation and forthwith filed in the Department of Revenue and Taxation.
(7) If it be a stock corporation, the amount of its capital stock in United States currency, and the number of shares into which it is divided.
(8) If it be a stock corporation, the amount of capital, stock actually subscribed, the names and residences of the persons subscribing, the amount subscribed by each, and the sum paid by each on his subscription.
(9) Before filing, a fee of fifty dollars ($50.00) shall be collected for such filing.
(10) Each person named in the articles as a director must sign the Articles of Incorporation.
(11) The treasurer must execute a sworn statement to the effect that at least 20 per centum of the total capital stock has been subscribed and at least 25 per centum of that subscribed has been paid in for the benefit of and to the credit of the corporation.
(12) Bylaws must be filed withing one (1) month after the filing of the Articles of Incorporation. The fee is ten dollars ($10.00).

3. Foreign Corporations: Foreign corporations are permitted to register in Guam provided they meet the following requirements:

a. Specifically, the managing agent of the foreign corporation is required to file a statement verified under oath setting forth, the following information:
(1) The name of the corporation.
(2) The purpose for which it was organized.
(3) The location of its principal or home office.
(4) The capital stock of the corporation and the amount thereof actually subscribed and paid into the Treasury on the (Day) (Month) (Year)
(5) The net assets of the corporation over and above all debts, liabilities, obligations and claims outstanding against it on the (Day) (Month) (Year)
(6) The name of the resident agent authorized by the corporation to accept summons and process in all legal proceedings against the corporation and of all notices affecting the corporation.
b. The notarized statement must be accompanied by:
(1) A certified copy of the Articles of Incorporation.
(2) Certificate under notarial seal that the corporation has been established pursuant to the laws of the place where incorporated. In the case of an alien corporation, certificates must be issued by a United States Consul. (A currently dated certificate of good standing issued by the governmental department having jurisdiction over corporations in the state or country of incorporation may be accepted in satisfaction of this requirement.)
(3) Designation by the corporation of a resident agent to accept service of summons and process in all legal proceedings against the corporation and notices affecting the corporation, and an acceptance of such appointment by the resident agent.
(4) Certified check or money order payable to the Treasurer of Guam in the amount of $105. (Fees for the issuance of the Certificate of Registration - $5.00 and Foreign Corporation license - $100.00)

(5) A balance sheet detailing the assets and liabilities of the corporation as of the last accounting period.

Upon satisfaction of the above requirements, the foreign corporation shall be properly registered upon direction by the Governor of Guam.

4. Misleading Name & Title

No corporation shall be registered which set forth a name that is likely to mislead the public or which is the same as or resembles so closely as to deceive:

(1) The name of a domestic corporation; or
(2) The name of a foreign corporation which is authorized to transact business in Guam.
(3) The use by a corporation of a name in violation of this Section may be enjoined, notwithstanding the filing of its articles of incorporation by the Director of Revenue and Taxation.
(4) The Director of Revenue and Taxation shall not file articles of incorporation setting forth a name in which the words "trust" or "trustee" appear, unless upon a certificate of approval by the Governor of Guam.

5. 5. Miscellaneous:

(1) Every domestic corporation must within one month after filing the Articles of Incorporation, file its Bylaws.
(2) Every director in a domestic corporation must own in his own right at least one share of the capital stock of the stock corporation of which he is director. (This requirement does not apply to Foreign Sales Corporations (FSCs)).
(3) The secretary or treasurer of a domestic corporation must be a resident of Guam.

II. TAX STRUCTURE OF GUAM

The U.S. Congress created the Territorial Government of Guam as a separate taxing jurisdiction by enactment of the Organic Act of Guam in 1950. Section 31 of the Act provides that the income tax laws in force in the United States shall be the income tax laws of Guam, substituting Guam for the United States where necessary and omitting any inapplicable or incompatible provisions. The U.S. Internal Revenue Code with such changes constitutes the Guam Territorial Income Tax Law.

There is the usual range of other types of local taxes, such as, liquor, tobacco, gasoline, real property, gross receipts, use, admissions, amusement, recreational facilities, and hotel occupancy. However, there is only one taxing authority in the Territory, the Government of Guam. There are no separate municipal, county, school district or improvement district taxes. Other than admissions, use, and hotel occupancy taxes, there is no general sales tax imposed directly on the consumer.
Foreign Sales Corporation (FSCs) which are licensed to do business on Guam may qualify for certain exemptions or rebates of income, real property, gross receipts and use taxes. Information concerning this can be obtained from the Director of Revenue and Taxation.

A. Personal and Corporate Income Tax

1. Individuals who are citizens or residents of Guam are required to report their income from all sources when computing their Guam taxes. Their income taxes must be paid into the Treasury of Guam. Non-residents except those who acquired their U.S. citizenship

through the Organic Act, or through naturalization proceedings in the District Court of Guam, incur income tax liability to Guam only on income derived from Guam sources. Self-employed individuals who are covered by the Federal Old Age Insurance and Schedule C of individual income tax return Form 1040.

A U.S. citizen who is a resident of Guam at the last day of the taxable year (usually December 31) will be required to file an individual income tax return in Guam reporting his or her worldwide income. In such case the U.S. Internal Revenue Code provides that no return need be filed with the U.S. Internal Revenue Service.

Guam individual tax rates are the same as those in the U.S. Internal Revenue Code and can be found in Section 1 of the Guam Territorial Income Tax Law.

2. Guam corporations are subject to income tax on their income from all sources. Other corporations doing business on Guam incur income tax

   liabilities to Guam on all Guam source income. Corporations not engaged in business on Guam are liable to a 30% tax on certain types of income from Guam sources. The tax rates for corporations doing business on Guam can be found in Section 11 of the Guam Territorial Income Tax Law.

3. Filing dates of Income Tax Returns are as follows:

   a. Individual income tax returns for the calendar year are due on or before April 15 of the following year. Individuals reporting on a fiscal year basis must file their returns on the 15th day of the fourth month following the close of the fiscal year. When the due date for doing any act for tax purposes -- filing a return, paying taxes, etc. -- falls on a Saturday, Sunday, or legal holiday, you may do that act on the next business day.
   b. Corporations are required to file an income tax return for the calendar year on or before March 15 of the following year. Corporations on a fiscal year basis must file income tax return on the 15th day of the third month following the close of the fiscal year.

4. Taxes and Tax Rates Applicable in Guam Income Withholding Tax

   a. Employers who have employment taxes of less than $500 in a calendar quarter are not required to make deposits.
   b. Less than $500 at end of quarter. If at the end of the quarter your total undeposited taxes for the quarter are less than $500, you do not have to deposit the taxes. You may pay the taxes with Form W-1 or you may deposit them by the end of the next month.
   c. $500 or more but less than $3,000 at end of any month. If at the end of any month your total undeposited taxes are $500 or more but less than $3,000, deposit the taxes within fifteen (15) days after the end of the month. If your taxes are less than $500, carry them over to the next month. (This deposit requirement does not apply if you made a deposit for an eighth-monthly period during the month under the $3,000 rule.)
   d. $3,000 or more at end of the eighth-monthly period. If at the end of any eighth-monthly period your total undeposited taxes are $3,000 or more, deposit the taxes within three (3) banking days after the end of the eighth-monthly period. Eighth-monthly periods end on the 3rd, 7th, 11th, 15th, 19th, 22nd, 25th and last day of each month. (Do not count as banking days legal holidays observed by authorized financial institutions, Saturdays and Sundays.)
   e. Gross Receipts Tax. All individuals and entities doing business or performing services on Guam are subject to a four percent (4%) gross receipts tax. This tax is levied on the

gross receipts from business or professional services on Guam. The tax is to be reported and paid no later than the 20th day of the month following the month in which the gross receipts were received or accrued, depending upon the accounting method elected by the taxpayer. The first $1,200 of rental income in a year is exempted. Banks and lending institutions are taxed on annual net income. Reports for banks and lending institutions are due on the 90th day following the taxpayer's tax year.

f. Use Tax. All personal property imported into Guam for use or consumption by the person importing it is subject to four percent (4%) tax on the landed cost. Property imported for resale is not subject to this tax. The tax does not apply to property having had a substantial use by the person bringing it into Guam before importation, or to machinery and other moved when the contract or other work is completed. No tax is imposed when the total value of all property imported by any one person in any one calendar month is $100 or less. Purchase of personal property on Guam for use or consumption from a person not liable for Gross Receipts Tax is also subject to the four percent (4%) use tax. The $100 exemption also applies to such purchases.

g. Real Property Tax. A real property tax is levied upon land at a fixed rate of one-half percent (1/2%) of the assessed value, which is thirty-five percent (35%) of the appraised value, or an "economic rate" of .175%; the tax on improvements is a fixed rate of one percent (1%) of the assessed value which is thirty-five percent (35%) of the appraised value or an "economic rate" of .35%.

(1) Properties which are used exclusively for educational; religious or eleemosynary purposes are exempt from Real Property Taxes.

(2) A home owner, provided he is occupying the home, may apply for a home exemption up to $15,000 of the appraised value.

h. Other taxes and rates are as follows:

(1) Alcoholic Beverage Taxes

$10.00 per wine gallon of distilled beverages $2.75 per wine gallon for vinous beverages $.04 per each twelve (12) fluid oz. malted fermented beverages

(2) Tobacco Tax $.35 for each 100 cigarettes 40% of landed cost of cigars $.35 per pound all others

(3) Liquid Fuel Tax

This tax is levied on the distributor of liquid fuel.

Diesel Fuel -- $0.10 per gallon. All other liquid fuel -- $0.11 per gallon.

Consumers using liquid fuel for marine or aviation purposes may obtain a tax drawback of $0.02 per gallon.

Consumers using liquid fuel for non-highway agricultural purposes may obtain a tax drawback of $0.04 per gallon.

Users of diesel fuel for marine or aviation purposes may obtain a tax drawback of $0.01 per gallon.

Users of diesel fuel for non-highway agricultural purposes may obtain a tax drawback of $0.02 per gallon.

(4) Admission Tax

$0.01 for each $0.10 admission in excess of $0..25. This tax applies only to spectacle amusement, such as, movies, boxing and similar events.

(5) Amusement Taxes

$100.00 single coin pinball machine and juke box $250.00 multiple coin pinball machine $100.00 plus $15.00 for extra coin slots for coin activated music producing machines $50.00 kiddie rides $350.00 poker machines, video horse or grey- hound racing machines $100.00 all others

(6) Recreational Facilities Tax

$10.00 for each bowling alley $100.00 for each nine holes of golf course or fraction thereof and driving range on miniature golf course. $5.00 for each pool or billiard table $100.00 for each skating rink, dance hall, or shooting gallery.

(7) Hotel Occupancy

10% of rental price charged each transient occupant
(8) Vehicle Transfer Tax
2% of market value. Tax occurs upon transfer of vehicle. Not applicable upon transfer of title directly from a licensed dealer.

III. INSURANCE, SECURITIES & BANKING

A. Insurance
An insurance company which has complied with the Civil Code of Guam by registering, if a foreign corporation; by filing its Articles of Incorporation, if a domestic corporation, must apply to the Insurance Commissioner for licensing under Title XXXIX of the Government Code.

1. Foreign Insurance Companies

   An Insurance Company incorporated in any state of the United States or any territory of the United States shall file with the Commissioner the following additional information:

(a) Application for Certificate of Authority (Form 1-1)
(b) Agreement and Power of Attorney (Form 1-2)
(c) File a copy of its latest Annual Statement in the form prescribed by the National Association of Insurance Commissioners.
(d) File Insurance Company's Bond (Form 1-3) or in Lieu of the bond, deposit with the Commissioner acceptable, unencumbered securities or other unencumbered assets of value of Fifty Thousand Dollars ($50,000.00) (Form 1-4).
(e) File appointment of General Agent; Authority to Appoint Sub-Agents and Solicitors; Authority to Accept Service of Legal Process; Authority to Countersign policies of insurance (Form 1-5).
(f) File General Agent's or Sub-Agent's applicaiton (Form 1-10).
(g) Copy of latest examination report conducted by the NAIC certified by the Commissioner of the Domestic State.
(h) Check in the amount of $75.00 payable to Treasurer of Guam.
(i) File all insurance policies and rate manuals for coverages to be written. Guam Insurance Law requires approval of all insurance policies and rates.
(j) The company must, in writing, agree that the company will actively engage in business here on Guam and that all income earned from Guam shall be subject to the Corporate Income Tax Law.

2. Alien Insurance Companies

   In addition to all requirement provided for foreign companies, alien companies are required to make additional deposits of securities with the Commissioner of a class or classes authorized for investment of the assets of domestic insurers in an amount equal to the minimum amount of paid-in capital required of domestic insurers. Securities will be valued at the current market value.

3. Insurance Agent, Sub-Agents and Solicitors-Adjusters applicants applying for the first time for a license shall either pass an examination or show evidence that he is presently licensed by another state or territory. The fee for this license is $10.00 per year.
4. All insurance licenses are issued to expire on July 1 every year.
5. Other fees.

(a) Renewal of Certificate of Authority $37.50
(b) Filing of any certificate, statement paper or exhibit $10.00
(c) Filing of new application after refusal to issue original certificate $75.00.
(d) Filing of applicaiton for issuance of Certificate after revocation or expiration $250.00.
(e) Filing of application for withdrawal $10.00
(f) Furnishing copies of papers filed per page $.50.
(g) Certifying copies of papers filed per document $2.00. The fees are not refundable under any circumstances.
B. Securities.

1. Registration of Securities

   Unless specifically exempt all securites be sold on Guam must be registered. The Law provides for three methods of registration:

   1. By Notification
   2. By Coordination
   3. By Qualification.

   Copies of the Law will be available for interested parties.

2. Registration of Broker-Dealer, Agent or Investment Advisor

   Sale of most securities would require licensing by NASD and the Territory of Guam. Guam acts as proctors for NASD examinations. Evidence of NASD licensing is required for Guam license. Those wishing to sell Guam securities will be required to take the Government of Guam Securities Examination. The fee for Broker-Dealer and Investment Advisor License is $25.00 per year. Agent License is $10.00 per year. A bond in the amount of $10,000.00 may be required for Broker-Dealer depending on the paid-in capital of the corporation.

C. Banking
Parties interested in establishing a local bank or a branch operation of United States Banks should write to the Banking Commissioner, Department of Revenue and Taxation.
D. Consumer Credit Code (Title XIV, Government Code of Guam)
Guam presently has a Consumer Credit Code which regulates all lending operations. Since it is a very comprehensive law, interested parties should contact the Director of Revenue and Taxation for information.

REAL PROPERTY TAXES

Hafa Adai!
Each year, Guam propery owners make an investment in their island when they pay their property taxes. Every dollar is returned in the form of vital services such as education for our children, fire and police protection, street maintenance and repairs, refuse collection and other public services. These services are financed especially by real property tax revenues.
PROPERTY TAX AUTHORITY
The Real Property Tax Division of the Department of Revenue and Taxation administers and enforces the Real Property Tax Laws as mandated by Section 19300, Title XX, Chapter IV of the Government Code of Guam. This pamphlet has been prepared in an effort to familiarize you with Real Property Taxes.
PROPERTY VALUATION

The value on your property provides the single most imporant element in computing your tax assessment. Generally, value is reflected at the most current appraisal or full cash value. Full cash value, or the price most people would pay for your property, is the standard used to measure equity in property assessments. Your tax assessments are computed only to the extent of the first theirty-five percent (35%) of the full cash value (appraisal). Thus, if land or building appraisal of property were $100,000, then the taxable value for computing taxes would be $35,000. (100,000 x .35) Authority: Section 19301(f), P.L. 6-95. The Mass Appraisal Method of valuation is primarily used at developing appraisal/full cash value for your property. As recently as September 1987, a mass reappraisal of our taxable properties was completed to update our valuations. Zoning changes, changes in property use, improvements and additions, destruction and/or demolition will definitely affect values and tax assessments. Because the department accounts for over 50,000 parcels of land and structures, a personal inspection of your property is normally undertaken only at the time construction is completed. Property owners are encouraged to visit the Real Property Tax Division located at the Former El Gecko Building at Tiyan to inform Division personnel of any changes or transactions. Property records will be updated accordingly and this would ensure correct and timely billing statements. Recorded Deeds or Maps, Occupancy Permits for buildings and Certificates of Title are generally the required documentation needed for the updating of property records.

HOMEOWNERS EXEMPTIONS

If you own and occupy your property as your principal residence, you may be eligible for a $52.50 credit against your tax assessment. For example, if your residence is valued at the following:

	BUILDING	LAND
APPRAISAL VALUE	$75,000.00	$25,000.00
ASSESSMENT RATIO	X .35	X .35
ASSESSED VALUE	$26,250.00	$ 8,750.00
TAX RATE	X .01	X .005
TAXES LAND/BUILDING	$ 262.50	$ 43.75

TAX ASSESSMENT..........................$306.25
HOMEOWNER EXEMPTION....................(52.50)
ADJUSTED TAX ASSESSMENT................$253.75

You must file an Application for Homeowners Exemption on or before March 15. Once filed and approved, no additional action is required until the status or use of the property as your principal residence changes. Failure longer qualify for the Homeowners Exemption will result in a fine. (Section 19330.8).

For more information on other tax exemptions and tax credits please contact the Real Property Tax Division.

ASSESSED VALUE AND TAX RATES

The laws of Guam specify that assessed values shall be thirty-five percent (35%) of the property's appraised value. A property valued at $100,000 would therefore have an assessed value of $35,000. (Section 19301(f)) By law, tax rates have been established at one percent (.01) for buildings and one half of one percent (.005) for land. (P.L. 12-52, 123) Thus, continuing with the example above, the assessed values and taxes would be as follows:

	APPRAISED VALUE	35% ASSESSED VALUE	RATE		TAX TAXES
LAND	$ 25,000	$ 8,750	X	.005	$ 43.75
BUILDING	75,000	26,250	X	. 01	262.50
TOTAL	$100,000		$35,000		$306.25

TAX ROLL, STATEMENTS AND APPEALS

Annually, on or before September 1st of each year, the Real Property Tax Division makes available a TAX ROLL LISTING identifying all taxable properties by lot number, owners of record and assessed values. We encourage all property owners to review their tax assessments, values, lot description and name(s) so as to be aware of their tax responsibilities and inform this office of any discrepancies that require correction. The Tax Roll is also made available to each village Mayor for their respective municipalities in an effort to facilitate public inspection of the Roll. If you feel an error was made in the assessment, the description of your property, please contact the Real Property Division so that we may make corrections where needed. Should you want to appeal the assessment of your property, an appeals process is made available to all taxpayers. The appeals are heard by a five-member Board of Equalization composed of property owners such as yourself. Taxpayers are asked to state their case while the Department also explains how the tax assessments was determined. The Division would be happy to explain the appeals process and procedure for you should you need more information. Please remember the tax assessment appeals can only be made between September 15 and October 15 prior to the issuance of your tax bill.

IMPORTANT DATES TO REMEMBER

SEPT 1	Publication of the Annual Real Property Tax Assessment Roll
OCT 15	Deadline for filing Appeal Application
OCT 30	Certification of the Real Property Tax Assessment Roll
DEC 15	Payment due date for 1st Installment
FEB 20	Delinquency date for 1st Installment, and Payment due date for second Installment
MAR 15	Deadline for filing Home Exemption Application
APR 1	Publication of the 90-Day Delinquency Notice and of the Termination of the Right of Redemption
APR 20	Delinquency date for 2nd Installment
JUN 8	Publication of Delinquency list of taxes still not paid after April 20
JUL 6	Property becomes Tax Sold to the Government if taxes are still unpaid
MARCH *	Tax Assessments become a lien on the property as of noon the first Monday in March

Your property's legal description is very important. Property owners should know the municipality and Lot Number when inquiring about their taxes. Real Property is indexed according to legal lot number which is needed for its identification. All matters concerning your property should be addressed in reference to your lot number.

EXAMPLES:

Municipality	Lot ID#
Dededo	#5118-3-NEW-1
Sinajana	TRACT #232,BLK 3, LOT 4
Agana(Urban)	BLOCK 1, LOT 4

For additional information please visit us at:

Department of Revenue and Taxation

Real Property Tax Division
(Former El Gecko Building)
Tiyan, Guam 96913
Tel: (671)475-1890/1891/1752/1765
Fax: (671)472-2643

GUAM TAX INCENTIVES

The Government of Guam, through the Guam Economic Development Authority, is authorized by law to allow tax rebates to qualified investors. Qualifying Certificates for tax incentives are granted on the basis of investment commitment as well as the potential for creating new employment and expanding the base of the island's industry. These incentives are aimed primarily at manufacturers,insurance companies, commercial fishing companies, corporate headquarters, specialized medical facilities, high technology, agricultural and tourism development firms.

Qualified firms may be granted up to 100% income tax rebates for a maximum of 20 years; up to 100% abatement on real property tax for a maximum of 10 years; up to 75% rebate on corporate dividend tax for a maximum of 5 years; and abatement on gross receipts tax on petroleum and alcoholic beverages made in Guam for a maximum of 10 years.

Public Laws 23-135 and 24-266 allow developers of qualified hotels and tourist facilities to provide funds needed to "jump start" the construction of affordable housing on Guam, in exchange for enlarged tax benefits.

These two laws also provide a two-year period (extendible for another two years at the discretion of the GEDA Board) whereby eligible developers of hotels and tourist facilities may apply for these benefits under GEDA's Qualifying Certificate program. These expanded benefits include:

- Exemption of Gross Receipts Taxes for suppliers of building materials & supplies, contractors for labor/supervision furnished for a qualified project.
- Exemption of Use Tax by the owner of the hotel/tourist facilities
- Rebate of Rental Income, up to 50% for the first 5 years and up to 25% for the next 5 years, to the lessor of land, buildings, machinery/equipment to QC holder for hotel/tourist facilities.
- Rebate of Capital Gains, up to 50%, to the seller of land and other real property to hotel/tourist facility of affordable housing developer.

Other tax incentives qualified firms may take advantage of are:

- Firms licensed to do business on Guam pay a territorial income tax based on a tax code that mirrors the U.S. Internal Revenue Service Code; however, they do not pay federal income taxes;
- Tax aspects of off-shore lending, whereby interest earned by a bank through the operation of an off-shore lending facility in Guam is not treated as a Guam source income for tax purposes.

TAX STRUCTURE

GENERAL

U.S. citizens file only one tax return to that jurisdiction (Guam or U.S.) in which they reside on the last day of the tax year. Pursuant to Section 32 of the Organic Act, Guam uses the income tax laws enforced in the United States. Income taxes applicable in Guam are determined by applying the U.S. tax law (Internal Revenue Code) and substituting the word "Guam" for the words "United States." The Department of Revenue and Taxation through its Taxpayer Assistance and Processing Branch issues official pamphlets with detailed income tax information and provides assistance to taxpayers.

PERSONAL INCOME TAX

U.S. citizens residing in Guam on the last day of the year, unless exempt, are required to file a tax return (Guam Form 1040) with the Government of Guam reporting all world-wide income. Their personal income taxes must be paid into the Treasury of Guam.

CORPORATE INCOME TAX

Guam corporations unless exempt, are subject to income tax on their income from all sources. Other corporations doing business in Guam incur income tax liabilities to Guam for all Guam source income. Most Guam sourced income of alien corporations are subject to tax at the same rates as for U.S. corporations if "effectively connected" with the conduct of a Guam trade or business.

LOCAL TAX

Guam has the usual range of local taxes found in the U.S. states, such as gasoline, real property, gross receipts, admissions, hotel, occupancy, etc. However, there is only one legal taxing authority. There are no separate municipal, county or district taxes. Other than admissions, use and hotel occupancy taxes, there is no general sales tax imposed directly on the consumer.

GROSS RECEIPTS TAX

Unless exempt by law, all persons (individual, professions, partnerships, corporations, etc.) doing business or performing services in Guam are subject to a 4% monthly privilege tax on their gross receipts or gross income. Banks and other lending institutions report their income on an annual basis and are taxed at the rate of 4% on their net income. In general, retailers must report quarterly and pay the tax required on the gross proceeds of sales on a monthly basis. Wholesale sales, although generally exempt from Gross Receipts Tax, need to be reported quarterly. Petroleum and alcoholic beverages manufactured on Guam are exempt.

USE TAX

All personal property imported into Guam for use or consumption by the person importing it is subject to a 4% tax on the landed cost, payable upon importation. The tax does not apply to property having previous substantial use by the person bringing it into Guam or to certain other property specifically exempt. No tax is imposed when the total value of all property imported by any one person in any one calendar month is $1,000 or less, not to exceed $5,000 in any calendar year. Purchase of personal property in Guam from a person not liable for the gross receipts tax is also subject to the 4% use tax. A Use Tax return is due quarterly.

REAL PROPERTY TAX

A real property tax is levied upon land and/or improvements and is significantly lower than similar taxes encountered in the United States. The rates are: one percent of the assessed value of the land and one-half of one percent of the assessed value of the improvements on the land. The assessed value is 35% of the appraised value. Typically a tax of $600 in California would be equivalent to a tax of $90 in Guam.

OTHER TAXES

Guam has an Alcoholic Beverage Tax, Tobacco Tax, Liquid Fuel Tax, Admission Tax, Amusement Tax, Recreation Tax, Facilities Tax, Hotel Occupancy Tax and Vehicle Transfer Tax.

GUAM: A TAX HAVEN[1]

Pacific Islands Tax Haven is not a new term to many island residents. However a Relative Guam Tax Haven has its own significance. The Relative Guam Tax Haven concept is introduced here with a 12% flat tax structure (10% after five (5) years). When this tax structure is aided by the best judicial protection of the United States, Guam could eventually become a world class U.S. tax haven. Guam's unique location and political relationship with the United States should allow this tax haven to happen. Flat tax would attract more businesses to establish their operations and more quality individuals to claim Guam residency. Flat Tax is a step further in Guam's quest for hosting off-shore banking facilities. Flat Tax will not endanger the existing tax collection so there is no immediate drawback to the existing Government of Guam operations. Implementing the Flat Tax structure, as presented in this paper, would greatly improve Guam's economic conditions by stimulating the influx of well-to-do residents therefore causing the increase in business and population, thus tax revenues. With a better tax structure, improved business and living climate, Guam should be able to survive and compete in this integrated and interdependent world market and eventually become an important international and financial center within the Asia-Pacific Region, or call it a U.S. version of Hong Kong. The author does realize the difficulties in implementing this idea, however, Guam scholars and politicians should initiate further studies.

INTRODUCTION AND AN INTERNATIONAL SETTING

1. A WORLD CLASS U.S. TAX HAVEN

The Island of Guam is faced with one tough road ahead. The Asia Crisis has finally hit us and we are feeling the pain now. Nothing seems to be able to save anybody anything. The market is winding down so quickly that all of us are worried. We are waiting for other nation's mercy (maybe Japan). Where is the Federal Government, we need you. This is indeed an economic survival cross road.

The small Catholic society has been frequently presented with one serious challenge – whether to legalize gambling so the island can generate more revenues. But so far the society has resisted. Nevertheless we have got to do something. We have to break this so called "status quo" and think of ways to improve our existing economic condition as well as create a road map for our future, fast.

[1] By Mark Zhao, Vice President Bank of Hawaii(Excerpts)

Guam's economic activities are dominated by two factors: tourism and military. Is there a third factor? Some experts say that if Guam ever reaches the level of 2 million tourist count, everybody should have a piece of cake with comfort. The same experts say that if Guam's population ever reaches 230,000, we should arrive at the same conclusion. Well, we have been trying to increase the tourist count and look what happened (though we shall continue to try to bring in more). Maybe it is time to think about the third factor: increase our population. But how ?

One of the ways this U.S. Territory after all could do to increase population and related businesses is to adopt a world class relative tax haven under the best known and the most reliable judicial protection of the United States. Is it possible? Yes, it is.

2. A LOW FLAT TAX RATE SYSTEM

Tax haven is not a new term in international economics or in the international business community. There are many existing tax havens around the world, even right here in the Pacific Region. We know that the Republic of Palau is a tax-free nation, Saipan offers a 75% tax rebate (not long ago it was 95%), Cook Island and Vanuatu all have laws exempting taxes for offshore banking facilities. It may be very difficult for the United States to have a pure tax haven (Congress would not easily approve that). During the past several years, the Guam Legislature along with GEDA enacted laws creating tax concessions for the insurance industry and investment trusts. In the early 1980s, when Congress approved the Foreign Sales Corporation (FSC) for the nation's exporters, it barred any state from taxing these entities until 1987. The Guam Legislature in 1984 enacted laws to make permanent tax exemptions for FSCs. Suddenly Guam became a well-known place. Island politicians obviously realized the need to offer tax incentives to bring in more businesses, investors and wealthy individuals.

However here we are talking about a relative tax haven or a less taxed environment. It would attract more businesses and quality residents and it could make a significant difference in our island's future. A low flat tax system. If implemented, this tax system should be simple, fair, pro-growth and obviously affordable to island residents and new businesses, investors and wealthy individuals.

3. THE U.S. VERSION OF HONG KONG

Hong Kong for so long has had a flat tax structure (but was never a tax haven). This simple and one-of-a-kind tax structure has made Hong Kong what it is today (obviously among other elements). Hong Kong was able to afford this because of the boom in society as a whole brought property values up thus higher property taxes are possible. Businesses and individuals in Hong Kong are used to not paying significant income taxes.

However, Hong Kong is changing. Due to its revert back to the People's Republic of China (PRC) in 1997, it now has to deal with a new tax relationship with PRC and it has to amend many tax treaties with various countries. Hong Kong's tax structure has changed and will continue to change unfavorably. The most significant change, however, is the Sino-U.S. trade relationship and even the political standings. The recent bombing of the Chinese Embassy in Belgrade, Yugoslavia by U.S. led NATO and the Chinese Nuclear Espionage case have both very seriously altered many conventional thinking in both countries and policies toward each other. As a result, many U.S. and western nation corporations may have to rethink their trade strategies toward China. They may also face retaliations from China in every possible way, certainly including business activities. So there may be some "moving" initiatives again.

Well, Guam is not a bad place for a retreat. We are an English speaking environment. We have up-to-date communications systems. We have a great airport and a well-connected transportation network. Most importantly, we have a stable government and the U.S. judicial system to ensure the smooth operations of all lines of businesses. If we offer a competitive low flat tax rate along with other incentive measures and a well-designed business climate, we may be one step further in our direction to increase our chance of becoming the U.S. version of Hong Kong.

4. COMPETITIVENESS

Why a flat rate? Because it is simple, fair, pro-growth and it causes fewer headaches. This is a big competitive factor. When it is simple, it saves a lot of compliance costs. When it is fair, there is no need to hire more accountants and lawyers. After all, when all the dollars are saved, they get right back into investments therefore stimulating more growth and more profits. This is definitely what businesses and investors are looking for. As we mentioned earlier. Hong Kong has been a free trade region that offers flat tax rates. Hong Kong's corporate tax rate is 16%, and the individual tax rate is 15%. Guam's tax rate, if changed to a flat tax rate, should be lower than Hong Kong's rate. This would only be fair. Why should someone seek a place to do the same business if he would have to pay higher taxes? Our flat tax rate should weigh the similarities and differentials among our neighboring islands, Asian countries and other tax havens in the world.

On the U.S. continent, as the Republicans are eager to regain power in the political stage, there is a loud voice in Capitol Hill calling for tax reforms. As a matter of fact, both the Republicans and the Democrats are feeling the pressure from the American people who want to have a simplified and fair tax system. The flat tax has been mentioned more than ever now, both in the Senate and in Congress. In 1995, a bill called "The Freedom and Fairness Restoration Act" was proposed by Rep. Dick Armey and Sen. Richard Shelby promoting a 17% flat tax on all income. In more recent discussions, this rate has been lowered to 15%. Although there is a reasonable level of difficulty in getting this huge task in a relatively short period of time and there are different interest groups still fighting for this bill, there are already insurmountable Americans supporting it. If the U.S. adopts the flat tax rate on income, then Guam would immediately lose all significance. Therefore, we need to be competitive. Put in a simple term, Guam as a relative tax haven has to have a flat tax rate of lower than 15%, if not significantly lower.

A LOW FLAT TAX PROPOSAL

5. THE DEFINITION OF FLAT RATE TAX

By definition, the flat tax is referred to a tax structure that collects a flat tax on all income earned both for taxable individuals and businesses. To be more specific, the individuals will be taxed a flat rate on their total income less a specified sum of exemption, and the businesses on their total revenues less certain allowable deductions. This U.S. version of the flat tax concept was originally conceived by Stanford economist Robert Hall and political scientist Alvin Rabushka in the early 1980s. This Hall-Rabushka model has been used by many including U.S. Rep. Richard Armey and Sen. Richard Shelby in introducing a legislative bill in Congress to promote flat tax as a way to reform the U.S. tax structure.

There are still many details that need to be worked out about this flat tax structure. For the purpose of this article, we now assume that all of these have been worked out. And for Guam's situation, we will start our discussion from the individual's taxable income and business's net profit before income taxes therefore ignoring the arguments in what should be included in expense deductions and what compensations should be granted for losing certain deductions (as they are being argued upon in Capitol Hill).

6. SOME DISCUSSION ABOUT THE POLITICAL POSSIBILITIES

Guam has a history of fighting for political independence. Within this difficult task, a "for Guam only" tax code was also mentioned. Local politicians want to de-link the Guam tax code from the federal code. Well, this was successfully done. Just a couple of years ago, Congress approved the "de-link" with conditions. Since Guam has no state tax, would the "de-link" actually create a "Guam State" tax code? Obviously that's not what Guam wants. Well then, which American is not paying federal tax? If the people of Guam are U.S. citizens, they have to pay federal income taxes. The most we can ask for or change to is not to pay less than what we are paying now. So what is the significance in de-linking? We have yet to see any development on this issue between Guam and Federal politicians. However, one thing is sure, we are not going to pay more than what we are paying. Within the existing tax code, we can design our tax code to make tax paying more simple and cost saving, and at the same time attract more new businesses and investors.

A flat tax structure is one alternative to this Guam tax code. While it is too complicated for Congress to adopt the flat tax because too many issues and too many interest groups' would have to be taken care of, Guam is a relatively simple society. Guam has only the rich and the poor. A lower flat tax would tend to satisfy both. After all, the rich may not pay more taxes anyway so they should be glad to pay the low flat tax. For the poor, their tax rate is always low after tax credits and government assistance. For the few middle class people, they may be looking for an easy time in filing their tax returns anyway. (So long as no one is paying more than what he or she is paying right now).

7. SOME RELATED DISCUSSIONS

The fact that Guam has more low income wage earners than middle income wage earners suggests that most people here are paying the minimum 15% tax rate. Let's assume that the rich find ways also to pay the minimum rate. so if the flat tax is set at 15%, we are not going to see any significant changes in the total amount of taxes paid. In the calculations shown later, indeed Guam residents are paying less than 15% tax on the average because of various exemptions, deductions and tax credits. The range would seem to be between 12% to 15%.

On the business side, few companies are paying the majority corporate taxes. If a business makes money, it may pay a minimum of 15%. However, to what level of certainty does the government have on the true picture of a business' operations if at the end the books would not show any profits to minimize taxes? At a lower flat tax rate, some of the concerns may be gone so as the costs associated with them. The business may report true operation results. Tax revenues may actually increase.

The relationship between the flat tax and the increase of new businesses and quality residents is a big variation. Some say that there is no direct link between the two. This is basically to say that lower flat tax is not enough or is not the reason why businesses flow in. This paper tends to disagree with this view. All countries around Guam have higher taxes so there are obvious advantages in coming to Guam.

However, we also have to note that the business climate and the true desire of the local politicians are very important in determining the relation between flat tax and influx of dollars. We have to clearly see the new trend and the interdependence in today's world market. We have to take the stand that we want to change for the better. We have to not worry about the population increase. We have to continue to modernize and beautify our island. We have to improve on our schools and hospitals. We have to negotiate our ticket prices with the airlines to make travel in and out of our island affordable. We have to work out ways to bring the U.S. Immigration on our side when dealing with visas. These non-tax issues are also important in attracting businesses and quality residents. Flat tax is an important vehicle in accomplishing this huge task.

8. THE ASSUMPTIONS

For the discussion of the flat tax proposal, we have to make certain assumptions and limitations. The issues discussed in the last section are also the pre-requisites to our flat tax proposal.

We are to examine the changes that the flat tax brings on total tax revenues both from increase in business and quality residents;
That the current tax collection is equivalent to or less than 15%;
Guam is going to impose a new flat tax rate of **12% (10% after five years);**
With the lower flat tax rate, Guam is going to receive more new businesses and quality residents. The first year is 200 new businesses and 1,000 new quality residents. Second year the numbers increase to 400 and 2,000. By the fifth year, Guam should have 1,000 new businesses and 5,000 new quality residents;
Each new business has an average net income of $0.5 million per year and each quality resident has a taxable income of $40,000;
Government and Legislature are pro-growth;
No other major changes occurred during the five-year period.

9. THE EXPLANATIONS

With the assumptions made above, now we can derive the changes that would occur to the total income tax collections. At a flat rate of 12%, there will be more businesses established here on Guam. As they report their net income to be $0.5 million, each will have to pay a flat tax of $0.06 million for a total of $12 million. These same 200 companies would have paid $16 million if they filed their tax forms in Hong Kong. Since they saved $4 million in total, they are satisfied. Within five years, the total new businesses in Guam would reach 1,000, and Guam would generate $60 million more tax revenues than what we have collected before we start the low flat tax program. Likewise, each new quality resident would have to pay $4,800 annually on his or her $40,000 taxable income for a total of $4.8 million. Within the five year period, when total new quality residents reach 5,000, Guam would be able to collect $24 million in total individual taxes. If we combine the two figures, Guam is going to have an increased tax revenue sum between $16.8 million and $84 million for the five year period after the flat tax structure is implemented. This explanation can be presented in the following graph.

If indeed tax revenues are increasing as the graph shows, further cuts in the flat tax rate is warranted. At the flat rate of 10%, Guam shall become more attractive to more businesses and individuals. At that time, quality of life should be lifted even more and infrastructure and other living accommodations should be improved even further.

10. ECONOMIC IMPACT OF THE FLAT TAX PROPOSAL

At the extra $16.8 million increase per year of its tax revenue, the Government of Guam is going to reap much economic benefits. Looking at a slightly longer period (5 years), Guam is going to more than double its income tax revenues. *But how about the extra money that those 1,000 companies and 5,000 quality residents spend on the island*? How about the extra office spaces and residential units that they are going to occupy? How about the employment opportunities that those companies provide? Most importantly, what would the $84 million mean to our economy when we calculate the impact multiplier?

As indicated by the Guam Department of Commerce, the savings rate on Guam is 10 percent. In other words, Guam residents would spend 90 cents of every dollar in income. This further shows that for every extra dollar brought into the economy, the frequency of multiple use of that dollar is very high. If we apply equations in our economics theory, the impact can be shown as follows:

K = 1/MPS = 1/1-MPC

Since Marginal Propensity to Save (MPS) is said to be 10 percent, then the Marginal Propensity to Consumption (MPC) must be 90 percent.

Therefore, the multiplier (k) is:

K = 1/1-0.9=1/0.1=10

So within a five year period, there would be a positive economic impact from the flat tax of between $168 million to $840 million.

The greater the total amount of tax collected from new business and quality residents (or the greater the influx of fresh money), the greater is the total economic impact of the flat tax on Guam.

Guam's major tax revenues are from business privilege taxes and individual income taxes. There are 17,650 businesses out there but the corporate tax collected is only one fourth of the individual income taxes. Flat tax is going to make more businesses honest and generate more taxes from them. On the individual income tax side, the average percentage of tax paid against taxable income is also very low.

11. SUMMARY AND CONCLUSION

Guam is faced with an economic survival cross-road. It is imperative that a solution, aside from tourism and the military, needs to be found. Should Guam achieve 2 million tourist arrivals or increase its population by 50 percent, all residents would have a comfortable life here. We should work on both goals. Increasing the population seems to be a subject very difficult to achieve. But by introducing the tax haven idea, this goal might be achieved sooner. We are talking about increasing quality residents, not poor immigrants.

The relative tax haven is comprised of a **Low Flat Tax of 12 percent** proposal. The flat tax is simple, fair and pro-growth and fits Guam very well. Implementation of the flat tax structure would bring more businesses and quality residents into Guam's market therefore bringing in fresh money. A flat tax would eventually increase tax revenues for Guam. When implemented with other tax incentives, improved business climate and other living conditions, a flat tax would really have a huge impact on Guam's future.

There is a concern among some politicians that adopting this flat tax would lose tax revenues. However, according to our rough calculations, the current tax receipts are about 12% to 15% of the total taxable income (We assume Guam will use the taxable income as a base for the flat tax). Therefore the loss of tax revenues as a result of a flat tax should not be a big concern.

The conclusion of this paper is this: The relative tax haven and the flat tax idea is worth looking into. We should not look at it only from the point of arguing whether flat tax is good or not, but from the point of whether it creates something attractive for Guam. We should view this as a concept so we can package a good deal to sell. The author acknowledges that it is not easy to implement this idea. This is only for discussion purposes with the hope that more studies would be done on this idea.

References:

"The Flat Tax: Restoring Freedom and Fairness to Federal Taxation." By Rep. Richard Armey. Published from the **National Public Accountant**, Jan-Feb 1998 v43 nl p7(2)

"Flat Taxes and Effective Tax Planning." By Mr. Michael Calegari. Published from **National Tax Journal,** Dec 1998 v51 i4 p689(1)

"The Flat Tax and the Real Estate Markets". By Mr. John S. Barry. Published from **Real Estate Financial Journal,** Fall 1996 v12 n2 p75(5)

"The Long Run Dynamics of the Fundamental Tax Reform". By Mr. Dale W. Jorgenson and Mr. Peter J. Wilcoxen. Published from **American Economic Review**, May 1997 v87 n2 p126(7)

"The Flat Tax in Theory and Practice; Simple, Effective, Fair. Or is it?" By Mr. William G. Gale. Published from **Brookings Review,** summer 1998 v16 n3 p40(5)

INTERNET ECONOMY AND ITS IMPACT TO GUAM[2]

The Internet has changed the way people live and work - people in Guam have gradually felt the impact of the Internet on the economy, from small retail business owners to University of Guam students; from government employees to travel agencies.

Reaching out and touching someone-instantly and almost anywhere-has never been easier or less expensive than the Internet, a place where literally millions of people gather to trade, debate, preach, get information or just leave a group message for anyone who cares about the same goods, subjects or services.

To assist the business community in Guam in recognizing the implications of the Internet, the Economic Research Center provides the following research results for our readers.

DISTRIBUTION CHANNELS AND THE INTERNET ECONOMY

Two areas have been identified here: the distribution of goods and the distribution of information (provisions of services). Viewed from a microeconomic standpoint, a key I-ECON issue that deserves serious attention is the determination of the pattern and pace of migration from traditional to Internet distribution of specific products and services.

DISTRIBUTION OF GOODS

Figure 1 illustrates the basic differences between two traditional production and distribution channels (columns IA and IB), vis-à-vis two Internet alternatives shown in Figure 2, columns II

[2] By Economic Research Center

and III. In both of the traditional channels shown in column I, end users get the goods they want from retailers. Some retailers order their goods directly from producers, while others operate at the end of a distribution chain, which includes one or more layers of wholesalers and/or regional distribution centers. Also, some industries have sales-driven distribution patterns (e.g. clothing, soft lines); others, such as the auto industry, are basically production driven, with sales forces with incentives to move products to consumers, via retail outlets, to clear out whatever their factories produce.

By way of contrast, the nascent Internet commerce sector appears to be employing two major alternative production/distribution models. The first, shown in column II (figure 2), is characterized as Amazonic Distribution (named after amazon.com). In this model, the end user orders products (e.g. books) directly from a distributor that maintains a warehouse inventory of products. Those products are ordered and reordered from producers, in response to sales, usually via wholesale-level Internet or private Intranet transactions. The end user gets the product directly from the distributor. This channel bypasses retailers and thereby undermines the retailer's business.

Column III of Figure 2, characterized as Dellphic Distribution (named after dell.com), involves direct contact between end users and producers in which there is no inventory of finished products anywhere in the distribution channel. In this model, end users respond directly to producers' promotional efforts by ordering custom-made products (telephonically or via the Web), which are then produced and shipped directly to the buyer.

SERVICES AND THE INTERNET

Many of the most publicly visible inroads of Internet commerce are in the service area, and most of them are Dellphic in nature. Airlines provide a good example. The industry has mounted intense efforts to migrate customers from traditional purchase methods (via travel agents or telephonic contacts) to direct electronic purchases. Incentives so far have been limited to offering frequent flyer bonus miles and spot discounts on approaching flights with unbooked space. But it may not be long before airlines introduce yet another layer of price segmentation into their fare structure by offering across-the-board discounts to Internet buyers. As a result, except for travelers who seek a complicated set of travel services, direct Internet purchases will undoubtedly continue to siphon market share away from traditional travel agents in the airline ticketing business. The same goes for booking cruises, hotels, tours etc.

Financial services is another area undergoing rapid change. While depository institutions have been moving in the direction of Dellphic service delivery for years, most early efforts were devoted to building proprietary platforms. That approach is now evolving toward using the Internet as the communication platform.

The biggest jump in recent years, however, has been seen in the trading of stocks, bonds and other financial instruments. Many large firms now offer on-line trading which, as in the case of the airline industry, bypasses the human contact normally involved in such transactions. Some traditional securities firms have also attempted to maintain their client base by building brand identification into their own Internet product (e.g.,discoverbroker.com of Morgan Stanley). The most intense threat to the traditional stock broker, however, is coming from a growing cadre of new companies (e.g., e-trade.com). with no visibility other than their web site, which compete solely on the basis of price and execution quality. And they are clearly forcing the old line companies (e.g., Merrill Lynch) to compete on the net or lose market share.

MOVING REAL ASSETS VIA THE INTERNET

In addition to marketing services, the Internet also has facilitated the introduction of a wider range of active secondary markets for various real assets. This development is fascinating in that many kinds of real assets have customarily lacked liquidity because of poor or even nonexistent secondary markets. However, the Internet is now rapidly changing that situation via the introduction of world-wide auction markets for many kinds of existing real assets. The most well-know player, of course, is ebay.com, and its success is attracting competition. Amazon.com, for example, has recently announced that it will add an auction market to its web site. So far, this phenomenon has been limited mainly to auctioning consumer goods, but the next logical step, e.g., adding sites for auctioning and/or trading producer durable goods and residential real estate, is already underway.

FACTORS INFLUENCING THE SPEED OF CHANGE

Both of the I-ECON distribution models shown in Figure 1, as they become more widely adopted, will clearly reshape the microeconomic structure and operating characteristics of many American industries, particularly in the retail sector of the economy. However, the migration from the traditional mode to either Amazonic or Dellphic production and distribution models will clearly not proceed at the same pace in all industries. That raises the question of what factors are likely to determine the rate of potential market penetration, by Amazonic or Dellphic competitors, across various industries. This presents a summary of some obvious factors that are affecting the rate of migration toward Internet Commerce on an industry-by-industry basis.

Logically, some products and services are highly unlikely to be impacted by either Amazonic or Dellphic competition. Services provided by barbers, beauticians, masseurs and gardeners, for example, will naturally continue to be delivered in the traditional on-site manner, although they may be marketed and/or scheduled with the help of Internet communication systems. The same goes for most low value and highly perishable products, such as fast foods and ice cream, although even these product markets are being penetrated by on-line web grocery sites.

At the other extreme, such products and services as sales of personal computers and books, stock trading, and travel services are already migrating very rapidly toward Amazonic and /or Dellphic distribution models.

With respect to the consumer sector, producers and distributors of high value-to-weight and high value-to-volume products are already experiencing rapid growth of Internet driven sales. Personal computers and peripheral equipment, computer software, books, video discs and some traditional lines of catalog merchandise are examples of this phenomenon. On the services front, as noted earlier, migration to Internet-driven sales is also moving rapidly into such areas as stock and bond trading, booking and sales of travel packages, as well as the marketing of life, auto and other insurance products.

Various sectors of the transportation industry are also being impacted heavily by the migration toward E-Commerce. Thus, as consumers acquire more Internet purchased products via home delivery from producers, the U. S. Postal Service (USPS) is experiencing a surge in both the weight and volume of its business. And its unionized workers are responding by demanding relief from the growing physical burdens it places on them. In the same vein, stock analysts are beginning to notice that the growth prospects of private carriers competing with the USPS, e.g., United Parcel Service, Federal Express, etc., are also benefiting from the growth of Internet Commerce.

The health care industry, which now accounts for about one-eight of GDP, is also likely to move much of its very costly transactions processing business onto the Internet, once the needed infrastructure is constructed. The current leader in this field is Healtheon Corporation (HLTH on NASDAQ). If Healtheon and its competitors are successful in moving a wide range of health industry transactions onto the Internet, major cost savings vis-à-vis the industry's current paper-intensive transaction processing will result. Health-related transactions that will be processed on the Internet include medical record-keeping, health provider searches and appointments, health/medical information directories, insurance applications and payments, pharmaceutical orders and records, etc.

Finally, on the microeconomic front, even where traditional distribution channels continue to function effectively, the I-ECON is profoundly impacting the way those channels function above the level of the end user.

Major discount stores such as Wal-Mart, for example, will surely continue to deliver a wide range of products to end users who shop at their retail outlets. Nevertheless, economic transactions and communications between such retailers and the producers of the products of the products they distribute are rapidly migrating toward the Internet, via privately run data network channels called Intranets or VANS.

Figure 1

The Impact of Internet Commerce on Distribution Channels

A. Sales Driven	B. Producer Driven
Sales Force presells products Production follows Products flow to wholesalers or directly to distributors Retailers market products to end users End user gets product	Producers manufacture products Sales forces sell products to wholesalers or retailers Products flow through wholesalers or retailers Retailers market products to end users End user gets product

Figure 2

The Impact of Internet Commerce on Distribution Channels

II. Amazonic Distribution	III. Dellphic Distribution
End user orders product via Internet/Phone Amazonic distributors pre-stock products from manufacturers Producers fill Amazonic orders End users get products directly from Amazon	End user orders custom-made products directly from Dell via Internet/Phone Dell produces and ships orders directly to end users

ELECTRONIC COMMERCE AND GOVERNMENT TAX[3]

A DEFINITION OF ELECTRONIC COMMERCE

Electronic commerce can usefully be defined as "the use of computer networks to facilitate transactions involving the production, distribution, and sale and delivery of goods and services in the marketplace".

TYPES OF ELECTRONIC COMMERCE

One can distinguish several types of electronic commerce: commerce in digital content delivered over the Internet, including selling of information services; commerce in non-information services such as travel that are ordered, but not delivered, over the Internet; commerce in tangible products ordered over the Internet; telecommunications and Internet access; and financial services. This paper focuses on commerce in digital content, commerce in tangible products, and telecommunications and Internet access.

Digital Content. Online provision of digital content can be characterized as "pure" or "true" electronic commerce, because the product is delivered online, by downloading it from the worldwide web. Commonly the product is also ordered online and payment commonly occurs online, via credit or debit cards. Online delivery poses serious problems for tax administration and compliance in a system of sales taxation based on the destination of sales, because neither the vendor nor tax administrators may be able to determine the location of the buyer. Section 3.2 elaborates on the problem inherent in electronic commerce in digital content.

Electronic Selling. Use of the Internet to sell tangible products that must be delivered in non-electronic forms is an extension of direct marketing conducted by traditional means-by mail order and, more recently, by telemarketing and television shopping channels. Since electronic selling involves tangible products that must be sent to an identifiable shipping address, it does not exhibit the problems of tax administration and compliance that are unique to electronic commerce-or exhibits them only in markedly attenuated forms. The resemblance of electronic selling to traditional mail-order is crucial because mail-order provides the legal precedents for the taxation of electronic selling-and arguably for the taxation of electronic commerce in digital content. If those precedents, which reflect the irrationality of the state sales and use tax system, were not so illogical, the current discussion could focus on the problems that are unique to pure electronic commerce (that in digitized products) rather than on issues that have scarce little to do with pure electronic commerce.

Telecommunications/Internet Access. Telecommunications and Internet access are integral to the conduct of electronic commerce. Telecommunications facilities are used to carry Internet signals, including digital content, and providers of Internet access link users to the telecommunications backbone, and thus to each other. Because of the convergence of technology, the lines between previously identifiable industries are becoming blurred, and "plain old telephone service" is becoming a thing of the past. Telephone companies, cable television companies, companies providing direct broadcast of television programs via satellite, and providers of Internet access are all entering each other's markets, sometimes in cooperation with publishers of software and creators of content. Many providers of Internet access also sell digital content, often bundled with

[3] Data Research by Economic Research Center Guam Department of Commerce

access and not subject to separate charges. For these and other reasons explained below, special and discriminatory taxes on telecommunications are an anachronism.

WHO BUYS WHAT, AND HOW MUCH?

Some of the best-known and most dazzling examples of electronic commerce involve primarily sales to households: these include Amazon.com, the online bookseller that claims to be able to deliver 2.5 million titles, and the nascent market in CD quality music downloaded from the Internet. In fact, electronic commerce between businesses swamps electronic sales to households. It is estimated that electronic sales to other businesses in the United States will total some $300 billion by 2002. Since this figure represents only 3 percent of GDP, there seems to be substantial room for growth. By comparison, it is estimated that retail sales to households completed over the Internet will be a mere $7 billion by the year 2000. Electronic sales of tangible products to households are actually still miniscule, compared to sales via conventional direct marketing, estimated at between $71 and $155 billion in 1996. But it has been estimated that retail sales conducted over the Internet could grow to $115 billion in five to eight years. (These figures are from the U.S. Department of Commerce, 1998). These facts are of fundamental importance, since a substantial fraction of the sales tax base of most states consists of sales to business.

WHY TAXATION OF ELECTRONIC COMMERCE MATTERS

It is important to tax electronic commerce like other commerce. Most obviously, a significant and rapidly growing amount of revenue is at stake. Both horizontal and vertical equity are also implicated-the latter because the affluent are much more likely than the poor to be engaged in electronic commerce, and thus to benefit from any failure to tax electronic commerce. Perhaps more important, economic neutrality and fairness for local vendors requires equal taxation of electronic commerce. Research shows that sales over the Internet are quite responsive to failure to collect use tax. Exempting electronic commerce would be distortionary and grossly unfair to competitors on Main Street.

Internet at a Glance

Country	Users (millions)	Total Population (millions)	Percent
U.S.	90.0	272.4	33
Japan	14.5	125.9	12
Germany	11.5	82.0	14
U.K.	9.8	59.0	17
Canada	8.0	30.7	26
Australia	5.5	18.6	29
France	3.9	58.8	7
Sweden	3.3	8.9	37

Netherlands	3.3	15.7	21
Spain	2.7	39.1	7
Taiwan	2.6	21.9	12
China	2.5	1236.9	0.2
Italy	2.3	56.8	4
Finland	2.0	5.1	39

Number of Sessions per Week - 5
Number of Unique Sites Visited - 7
Time Spent per Site - 0:19:02
Page Views per Week - 102
Page Views per Surfing Session - 19
Time Spent per Week - 2:09:00
Time Spent per Surfing Session - 0:25:48
Duration of a Page Viewed - 0:01:21
Average Click Rate for Top Banners - 0.32

Household Penetration (%)

Households with a PC - 48
Households with a cellular phone - 42
Households online - 33
Households with high-speed access - 0.06
Households shopping online in last 3 months - 10
Households that bank or invest online - 3.7

Internet Business and Finance Trade Site Rankings

Rank	Site	Unique Visitors at Work Monthly (000)
1	Yahoo! Finance	2800
2	Quicken Financial Network	2008
3	AOL Personal Finance	1720
4	MSN's MoneyCentral	1157
5	CBS Marketwatch	891
6	CNNfn	885
7	E*Trade	744
8	Wall Street Journal Sites	613

9	Bloomberg	559
10	Motley Fool	558

RESIDENT POPULATION OF GUAM[4]

Guam's resident population in March 1999 is estimated to be 134,725 persons, living in 34,091 housing units with an average household size of 3.95 persons.

This report presents a demographic profile of the resident population of Guam. The resident population excludes active duty armed forces and their dependents, temporary workers on visa, undocumented aliens and persons living in institutions. The data are estimates based on a sample survey (the March 1999 Current Labor Force Survey conducted by the Guam Department of Labor) and are not based on a complete enumeration of the population. Therefore there may be some sampling variability.

PLACE OF BIRTH

Most of Guam's resident population was born on Guam, about 76,017 persons, or 56.4 percent; and about 43.6 percent immigrated from other areas. Major senders of resident population to Guam are the Philippines, (21.4 percent), the United States (8.3 percent), and the Federated States of Micronesia (5.0 percent).

In-migration is primarily among persons in older age groups. As a result, most persons under the age of 30 were born on Guam, while about 60 percent of those over age 30 were born elsewhere.

ETHNICITY

No single ethnic group represents the majority of ethnic groups in Guam's resident population. Guam's indigenous Chamorros are the single largest group, 62,292 persons, or 46.2 percent. Reflecting the large amount of immigration from the Philippines, Filipinos are Guam's second largest ethnic group (41,204 persons, or 30.6 percent). No other ethnic group reached at least 10 percent of the population, with 4.7 percent White, 6.2 percent ethnicities from the Federated States of Micronesia, and 4.0 percent various Asian groups including Japanese, Korean, Vietnamese, Thai, and Chinese.

AGE AND SEX

About one-half of the resident population was over the age of 27.5 in March 1999. Females were older than males, a median age of 29.1 years for females, compared to 25.9 years for males. Persons born on Guam were youngest, with a median age of 19.1 years, compared to 31.1 years for those born in the United States and 43.6 years for those born in the Philippines.

Despite the island's low death rate and high life expectancy, there were relatively few persons in the older age groups who were born on Guam; about 5,223 persons or 6.9 percent were 60 years

[4] By Susan Ham Bureau of Planning Government of Guam

and older. Persons born in the Philippines contained a larger number and a larger percentage of elderly (5,362 persons and 18.6 percent).

Overall, there were more males than females in the resident population, with a sex ratio of 104.1; for every 100 females in the population, there were 104.1 males.

DEPENDENCY RATIO

The dependency ratio measures the number of very young and very old per 100 persons who are between the ages 15 and 64, the most economically productive years. The dependency ratio impacts labor force participation,investments, savings, pensions and government expenditures. In under-developed economies with high birth rates, the dependency ratio is above 100, while in developed economies such as the United States, the dependency ratio is about 50.

In March 1999, Guam had a resident population of 42,065 persons under the age of 16, 84,352 persons aged 16 to 64, and 8,307 persons 65 years and over. This provides a dependency ratio of 59.7.

CITIZENSHIP STATUS

The immigration law of the United States applies to Guam. All persons born on Guam are automatically U.S. citizens, though some foreign nationals living temporarily on Guam may choose to claim own nationality for their children born on Guam. This is especially true of persons from Micronesia.

Persons who are not U.S. citizens are either immigrants or non-immigrants. An immigrant is a person of foreign nationality working toward eventual U.S. citizenship through naturalization. A nonimmigrant is a person admitted into the United States with a non-immigrant visa for a specific purpose and for a limited duration; this category also includes undocumented or "illegal" aliens.

Persons from Micronesia (the Federated States of Micronesia, the Republic of the Marshall Islands and the Republic of Palau) are a special category; through treaties with the U. S. government, persons from these islands are nonimmigrant aliens who are treated as immigrants in that they may live, work, and attend school in the United States indefinitely and without visa. They are not, however, working toward U. S. citizenship.

In Guam's resident population, nearly 83 percent are U. S. citizens, 12 percent are immigrant aliens, and about 5 percent are FSM, Marshalls, and Palau citizens (other non-immigrants aliens are excluded for the purpose of this study).

Of those born outside Guam and the United States, about 53 percent claim U. S. citizenship, either through naturalization or through birth to American parents overseas.

EDUCATIONAL ATTAINMENT OF PERSONS 25 YEARS AND OVER

Education on Guam is compulsory through the age of 16 years. By age 25, 80.2 percent of the resident population had a high school diploma. Females were less likely than males to finish high school; 21.8 percent of females did not have a high school diploma, compared to 17.6 percent of males.

Place of birth was an even greater determinant of educational attainment than was sex; about 12.9 percent of those born on Guam completed at least 4 years of college, compared to 39.2 percent of those born in the U. S. and 25.4 percent of those born elsewhere.

HOME OWNERSHIP

As people marry, they tend to become household heads in greater numbers than when they were single; of Guam's 34,091 resident households, 23,089 had a now-married head (67.8 percent), compared to 4,612 never-married, and 6,391 who were formerly married (separated, widowed or divorced).

Not only do people tend to become heads of households after they marry, they also tend to become homeowners. Guam's homeownership rate was 56.2 percent in March 1999, rising to 62.3 percent among married-couple householders.

Household heads born on Guam were more likely than others to be homeowners; 70.7 percent of household heads born on Guam owned the home they lived in, compared to 57.8 percent of those born in the Philippines, 38 percent of those born in the United States, and 31.4 percent of all others.

RESIDENT POPULATION OF GUAM
Mar-99

Age	Sex			Place of Birth			
	Total	Male	Female	Guam	Philippines	U.S.	Other
Total	134,725	68,738	65,987	75,989	28,895	11,141	18,671
0 to 9	27,339	14,837	12,503	22,422	1,111	1,556	2,223
10 to 19	24,867	13,197	11,669	17,143	2,806	2,112	2,806
20 to 29	20,199	10,280	9,919	11,002	3,890	1,778	3,529
30 to 39	19,616	9,697	9,919	8,391	5,112	1,973	4,140
40 to 49	17,004	8,301	8,613	7,002	5,307	1,973	2,723
50 - 59	13,058	6,279	6,779	4,807	5,307	1,056	1,889
60 to 69	7,502	3,612	3,890	2,945	3,056	556	945
70 to 79	4,223	2,084	2,139	1,695	2,028	139	361
80 and over	917	361	556	583	278	-	56
Median Age	27.5	29.1	25.9	19.1	43.6	31.1	31.8
Ethnic Origin							
Chamorro	62,292	31,563	30,729	56,540	333	3,667	1,750
Filipino	41,204	20,255	20,949	10,947	28,284	1,389	583

Caucasian	6,335	3,973	2,362	1,056	-	4,584	695
Palauan	2,639	1,445	1,195	1,195	28	-	1,417
FSM Micronesian	8,319	4,390	4,001	1,852	28	250	6,251
Asian	5,446	2,417	3,028	945	-	167	4,334
Other	8,419	4,668	3,751	3,473	223	1,084	3,640
Place of Birth							
Guam	76,017	39,092	36,925	76,017	-	-	-
Philippines	28,895	13,670	15,226	-	28,895	-	-
USA	11,141	6,752	4,390	-	-	11,141	-
FSM	6,752	3,473	3,279	-	-	-	6,752
Palau	1,361	667	695	-	-	-	1,361
CNMI	2,723	1,167	1,556	-	-	-	2,723
Asia	4,112	1,834	2,278	-	-	-	4,112
Other	3,723	2,056	1,667	-	-	-	3,723
Citizenship Status							
U.S. Citizen	111,497	57,874	53,623	75,378	18,365	10,836	6,918
Immigrant, non-US Citizen	16,115	7,029	9,085	167	10,530	250	5,168
FSM Citizen	6,112	3,251	2,862	445	-	56	5,612
Palau Citizen	750	389	361	-	-	-	750
RMI Citizen	250	167	83	28	-	-	222
Educational Attainment							
Total	72,572	35,091	37,481	30,785	23,200	6,807	11,780
Less Than High School	14,337	6,168	8,168	6,696	4,918	417	2,306
High School Graduate	30,757	15,003	15,754	16,615	6,779	2,167	5,196
Some College	11,919	6,140	5,779	3,473	4,668	1,556	2,223
College Graduate	11,058	5,140	5,918	3,001	5,195	1,361	1,500
Post Graduate	4,501	2,639	1,862	1,000	1,639	1,306	556
Tenure							

Total	34,092	25,284	8,808	14,142	9,808	4,390	5,751
Owned	19,143	14,948	4,195	10,002	5,668	1,667	1,806
Rented	14,948	10,336	4,612	4,140	4,140	2,723	3,945

Source: Bureau of Planning, Government of Guam

RESIDENT POPULATION OF GUAM
Mar-99
(Percent)

	Sex			Place of Birth			
Age	Total	Male	Female	Guam	Philippines	U.S.	Other
Total	100.0	100.0	100.0	100.0	100.0	100.0	100.0
0 to 9	20.3	21.6	18.9	29.5	3.8	14.0	11.9
10 to 19	18.5	19.2	17.7	22.6	9.7	19.0	15.0
20 to 29	15.0	15.0	15.0	14.5	13.5	16.0	18.9
30 to 39	14.6	14.1	15.0	11.0	17.7	17.7	22.2
40 to 49	12.6	12.2	13.1	9.2	18.4	17.7	14.6
50 - 59	9.7	9.1	10.3	6.3	18.4	9.5	10.1
60 to 69	5.6	5.3	5.9	3.9	10.6	5.0	5.1
70 to 79	3.1	3.0	3.2	2.2	7.0	1.2	1.9
80 and over	0.7	0.5	0.8	0.8	1.0	-	0.3
Ethnic Origin							
Chamorro	46.2	45.9	46.6	74.4	1.2	32.9	9.4
Filipino	30.6	29.5	31.7	14.4	97.9	12.5	3.1
Caucasian	4.7	5.8	3.6	1.4	-	41.1	3.7
Palauan	2.0	2.1	1.8	1.6	0.1	-	7.6
FSM Micronesian	6.2	6.4	6.1	2.5	0.1	2.2	33.5
Asian	4.0	3.5	4.6	1.2	-	1.5	23.2
Other	6.2	6.8	5.7	4.6	0.8	9.7	19.5
Place of Birth							
Guam	56.4	56.9	56.0	100.0	-	-	-

Philippines	21.4	19.9	23.1	-	100.0	-	-
USA	8.3	9.8	6.7	-	-	100.0	-
FSM	5.0	5.1	5.0	-	-	-	36.2
Palau	1.0	1.0	1.1	-	-	-	7.3
CNMI	2.0	1.7	2.4	-	-	-	14.6
Asia	3.1	2.7	3.5	-	-	-	22.0
Other	2.8	3.0	2.5	-	-	-	19.9
Citizenship Status							
U.S. Citizen	82.8	84.2	81.3	99.2	63.6	97.3	37.1
Immigrant, non-US Citizen	12.0	10.2	13.8	0.2	36.4	2.2	27.7
FSM Citizen	4.5	4.7	4.3	0.3	-	0.5	30.1
Palau Citizen	0.6	0.6	0.5	-	-	-	4.0
RMI Citizen	0.2	0.2	0.1	-	-	-	1.2
Educational Attainment							
Total	100.0	100.0	100.0	100.0	100.0	100.0	100.0
Less Than High School	19.8	17.6	21.8	21.8	21.2	6.1	19.6
High School Graduate	42.4	43.8	42.0	54.0	29.3	31.8	44.1
Some College	16.4	17.5	15.4	11.3	20.1	22.9	18.9
College Graduate	15.2	14.6	15.8	9.7	22.4	20.0	12.7
Post Graduate	6.2	7.5	5.0	3.2	7.1	19.2	4.7
Tenure							
Total	100.0	100.0	100.0	100.0	100.0	100.0	100.0
Owned	56.2	59.1	47.6	70.7	57.8	38.0	31.4
Rented	43.8	40.9	52.4	29.3	42.2	62.0	68.6

Source: Bureau of Planning, Government of Guam

INCOME AND YEN RATE IMPACT ON JAPANESE VISITOR ARRIVALS TO GUAM[5]

This research is geared towards determining whether there is a causal relationship between the following variables: a) the Japan National Nominal Income per capita and tourist arrivals from Japan, and b) the yen exchange rate and tourist arrivals from Japan.

INTRODUCTION

Tourism on Guam – Guam is an island with year-round sunshine and beautiful sandy beaches that attracts many foreign visitors. Located in the Western Pacific with a U.S. dollar based currency, Guam is the closest geographical U.S. possession to Asian countries like Japan, Korea and Taiwan. As a U.S. territory, Guam enjoys political stability stemming from its relationship with the U.S.

Guam's visitor industry started in 1967 when the first commercial flight, Pan American Airways arrived from Japan. Various agencies of the Government of Guam actively promote tourism, i.e., Guam Economic Development Authority (GEDA) introduced tax incentives for foreign investment and Guam Visitors Bureau (GVB) develops and implements aggressive tourism promotional campaigns. Many tourist attraction facilities have been constructed, the expansion of the Guam International Airport is in progress, Guam's infrastructure has been improving dramatically (new $150 million 80 megawatt power plant) and air carriers have increased their flights between Guam and countries of tourist origination. Additionally, over the past 25 to 30 years there has been a strong inflow of foreign and domestic capital investments from Japan, Hawaii, Taiwan and Korea. All this has contributed to the growth of Guam's visitor industry.

The decline in visitor arrivals for 1998, as compared to 1997, is attributed to the effects of the Asian "flu". The monthly declines are as follows:

September 1998 declined by 16%
October 1998 declined by 29%
November 1998 declined by 27%
December 1998 declined by 8%
January 1999 declined by 8%
February 1999 declined by 19%

This downturn in the economy is directly tied to the prolonged weakening of the yen/dollar exchange rate, the overall state of the Asian financial markets, and the impact from the Korean Airline crash in August 1997.

Despite the decline in tourism in recent months, tourism on Guam overall for the past decade has shown continual growth, with the number of tourist arrivals rising from 477,491 in 1987 to 1,137,026 in 1998, an increase of over 135% in eleven years. The 1998 breakdown of visitor arrivals on Guam was Japan; 86%, Korea; 1.8%, U.S. including Hawaii; 3.7%, Taiwan; 1.8%, and 6.7% from all other areas. For 1998, Japanese visitors continued to have the greatest impact on

[5] By Ying Fang and Angie Sharma Guam Power Authority and Union Bank of California

visitor arrivals as Guam's largest market, making up 86% of all visitor arrivals, for a total of 975,402.

According to the Japan Travel Bureau (JTB) 1997 report, Japanese outbound travelers have been steadily increasing as follows: +13.7% in 1994, +12.6% in 1995, +9.1% in 1996 and +3.4% in 1997. However, last year, Japan outbound travelers decreased by 6% compared to 1997, according to JTB figures released in January 1999. The decline was only the third annual decrease since 1964. Many of the Japanese visitors who come to Guam are repeat visitors, constituting 34% of Japan arrivals. Guam's market share on outbound travelers from Japan increased slightly from 6.5% in 1996 to 6.7% in 1998.

The top five preferred reasons for travel was first to enjoy nature and scenery, second to visit historical sites and architecture, third for local cuisine or favorite foods, fourth to rest and relax and fifth for shopping.

DATA COLLECTION

In conducting the research for income elasticity, 1993 to 1996 data was collected from the web address presented by the Japan Consulate. In conducting the research for the yen exchange rate to Japanese tourist arrivals, monthly data for the past 10 years was collected from the Union Bank of California Treasuries department and Guam Visitors Bureau.

The obstacles confronted while conducting the research were the lack of monthly data and the lack of recent data in determining the income elasticity. Therefore, our group proceeded to contact the Japan Consulate. However, the Japan Consulate was also unable to provide recent data as they are currently in the process of compilation.

The Guam Visitors Bureau is also one of the primary source of data collection. The assistance provided by the Guam Visitors Bureau is appreciated as they gathered 10 years of data on a monthly basis and also provided up-to-date figures.

METHODOLOGY

Identifying Variables – If Japanese visitor arrivals is the dependent variable (y), we can list several independent variables such as: income (I), price (p), distance (d), services (s), foreign exchange (r), other destination attractiveness (o), and so forth. The relationship can be formulized as: $Y = f(I,p,d,s,r,o\ldots)$

We chose income and exchange rates as independent variables for this study because these two variables are good indicators of the strength of the Japanese economy.

Methods Used in this Study – For long-range analysis, such as trend comparisons, we used regression and Arc elasticity. For the yen rate versus Japan visitor arrivals, we chose to use point elasticity and not regression analysis.

Income Elasticity – Income Arc Elasticity is used in this study to identify the relationship between Japanese yearly income and Japanese visitor arrivals on Guam. The formula used in this study is: *Ei = ^y/^I x i1+i2/y1+y2*

Where i_1 is previous year's income, i_2 is the current year's income. Similarly, y_1 is Japan visitor arrivals in the previous year and y_2 is Japan visitor arrivals in current year.

The reason for using Arc elasticity in this case is that the Japan national income is only available as yearly data. The percentage change is usually greater than 5%. Arc elasticity is more accurate in this case than point elasticity. Simple regression is used to study the trend for these two variables.

Yen Rate Elasticity – To study the relationship between the yen exchange rate and Japan visitor arrivals we used point elasticity and applied a lagging period to each case. We analyzed four cases of Japan visitor arrivals lagging with the yen rate in different time frames. They are:

1. No lag
2. One month lag
3. Two months lag
4. Three months lag

The formulas used in these cases are:

1. No lag
2. With lag

Where: **r2** is current month's Yen exchange rate, **r1** is the previous month's Yen exchange rate. **n** is the number of the lagging months. **Yn+2** is Japan visitor arrivals in the **n** month from the current. **Yn+1** is Japan visitor arrivals in the **n-1** months from the current.

After calculating lagging month elasticity, we add all elasticity results together and compare the total elasticity by different lagging period. The highest total elasticity should be the best lagging period we would predict.

ANALYSIS

Income Elasticity – The income elasticity bar chart over ten years is shown in Figure 1.

Figure 1

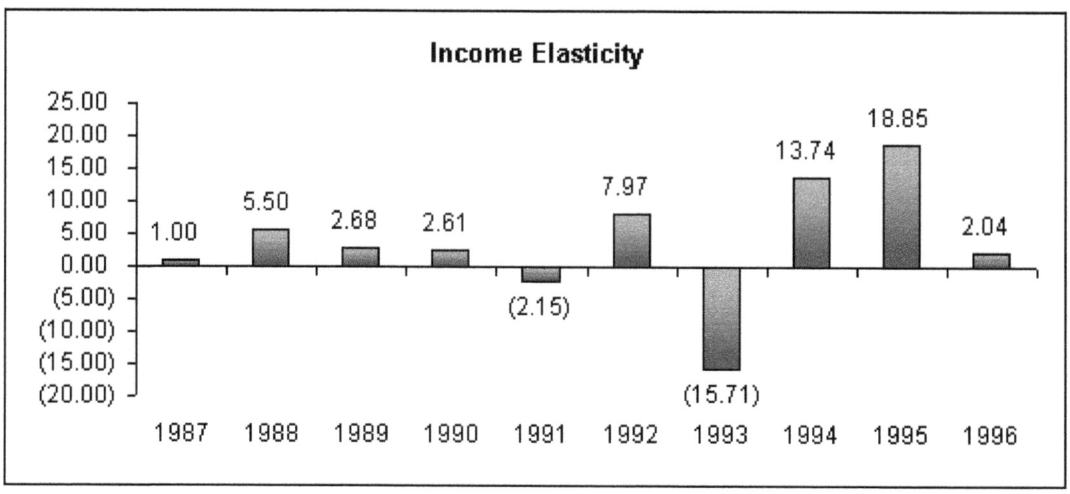

Except for years 1991 and 1993, all yearly income elasticity are greater than one, i.e: E1>1.

For goods having E1>1, demand is strongly affected by changing economic conditions [Hirschey: 202]. In other words, the higher the income, the higher demand for Japanese international travel. The recent Asian economic crisis strongly impacted the Japanese economy. We can predict that Japanese visitor arrivals will continually fall until there is a significant turn-around signal in the Japanese economy.

It is very clear that the two variables follow a similar trend. There are some deviations in years 1991 and 1993. The earthquake in 1993 caused a negative impact on tourist arrivals in spite of the strong Japan economy. In 1991, tourist arrivals decreased during February and March, although Japanese national income was growing during that period. What was taking place besides income variables to affect Japan visitor arrivals in 1991?

Yen Rate Elasticity – To find out what happened in early 1991 that caused Japan visitor arrivals to decrease significantly, we plotted the Yen exchange rate against Japanese arrivals in 1991. Interestingly, just before Japan visitor arrivals decreased the Yen fell from 137 to 129 within a month. This shows that the Yen exchange rate is another economic indicator that impacts visitor arrivals on Guam.

However, the Yen exchange rate cannot affect Japan visitors to Guam immediately for several reasons. First, people usually have to plan a trip in advance especially when they travel with their family. Second, Yen exchange rate is not predictable. No human actions can follow the Yen exchange rate without time delays.

There is a correlation between Japanese visitor arrivals and the Yen exchange rate. This correlation is strong except for a shift after 1993. This shift was caused by a massive reduction on tourist packages after the 8.1 earthquake.

During the period from 1993 to 1995 the data showed little correlation between Japanese visitor arrivals and the Yen rate for a variety of reasons that are beyond our scope in this paper. Japanese visitor arrivals follow the Yen rate change with some lagging period.

What is the lagging period we can predict based on Yen rate change? Figure 2 shows that a two-month lag has the highest overall elasticity.

Figure 2

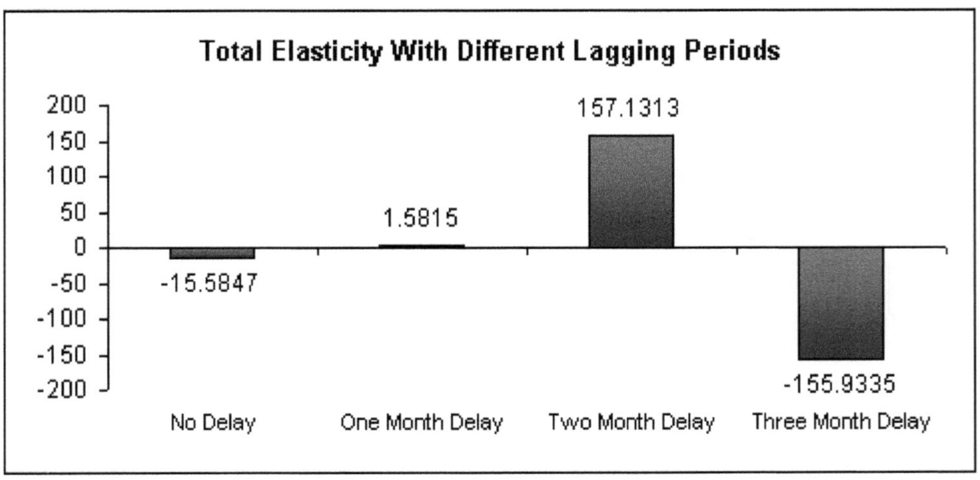

However, for more accurate results we need further study on multiple variables that might affect tourist arrivals on Guam.

Conclusion – Our research concludes that there is a causal relationship between: a) the Japan Nominal National Income per capita and tourist arrivals from Japan and b) the Yen exchange rate and tourist arrivals from Japan.

Our research further concluded that a lag period of two months exist when comparing the Yen exchange rate to tourist arrivals from Japan. This data will allow for future promotional planning.

It is further noted in our research that a turn-around in Guam's economy is directly tied to Japan's economy. Therefore, our assumption is that Japanese visitor arrivals will continually fall until there is a significant turn-around signal in Japan's economy.

References

1. Japan Travel Bureau (JTB) 1997 and 1998 Report. "All About Japanese Overseas Travelers".
2. GVB Visitor Statistics from January 1989 to February 1999.
3. Department of Commerce, "Guam Annual Economic Review". 1996 – 1997.
4. Japan Consulate – http://jin.jcic.or.ip/stat/stats/05ECN21.html.
5. Union Bank of California, N.A., Treasuries Department.
6. Hirschey, M. and Pappas, J. *Managerial Economics,* The Dryden Press 1996.

STRATEGIC AND PRACTICAL INFORMATION FOR CONDUCTING BUSINESS

GEOGRAPHY, TOPOGRAPHY & CLIMATE

For the adventurous investor looking for new and unexplored investment opportunities Guam, USA, offers unique advantages.

Our island's diverse geographic characteristics and ideal positioning within the Pacific basin, supportive business environment, stable political system, stewardship of the U.S. flag, and hospitable community are major pluses to put at the top of your list when considering investment on Guam.

Guam is the largest and southernmost island of the Marianas Islands chain. Formed through the fiery birth and re-birth of undersea volcanoes millions of years ago, Guam's topography boasts southern mountains and the high limestone northern plateau. Coral reefs are the foundation of a paradise 30 miles long with an overall land area of 212 square miles.

This geographic diversity is the basis for an island whose character ranges from the white sand beaches and limestone jungles of the north to volcanic mountains blanketed by sprawling savannas and tropical rain forests in the south. Our climate is tropical in nature and remains pleasantly warm throughout the year, with temperatures ranging from 75 to 86 degrees Fahrenheit.

Guam was the first Pacific island discovered by the western world. Then, as now, it served as the gateway to Asia, America and the Pacific region around it. Situated about three hours by plane from Tokyo and Manila, four hours from Hong Kong and Taipei, five to six hours from Seoul, Singapore, Bangkok and Australia, and only seven hours from Hawaii, Guam truly is the hub of the Western Pacific.

POLITICAL SYSTEM

The people of Guam enjoy the benefits of democratic self-government under the Organic Act of Guam, and the protection of rights under the

U.S. Constitution.

An unincorporated territory of the United States since 1950, the local government is organized into three branches — legislative, executive and judicial. Our system of checks and balances, the foundation of this form of democratic government, guarantees the protection of the inalienable rights of the people of Guam from intrusion by other individuals, groups and the state.

The legislative branch consists of a unicameral legislature of 15 senators elected for two-year terms. Empowered to make the laws that govern our society, the legislature is responsible for creating laws to protect the community, ensure its health and promote its development. It also provides a check on the other branches of government by its authority to approve or disapprove the policies of the Government of Guam pertaining to the use of funds held in the public trust.

Guam's judicial branch decides issues of constitutionality of local laws and interprets how these laws should be applied. The judiciary consists of two bodies, a Superior Court of Guam and the

Supreme Court. The lower court reviews and decides all issues of local law, while the Supreme Court primarily reviews lower-court decisions, providing additional opportunities to maintain the integrity of Guam's political system.

Finally, as the chief of the executive branch, the governor is tasked with implementing Guam's laws through the 73 departments, bureaus, committees and agencies making up the Government of Guam. The governor sets the tone, pace and direction in which the island progresses, especially in areas such as public health and safety, community development, management of Guam's natural resources, and economic development.

In addition to his role as chief executive, the governor provides an additional check for the people on the political system through his veto authority over all laws passed by the legislature.

When considering any type of investment in today's world, the careful investor should examine the political climate for stability and consistency, in order to ensure the security and safety of any investment. Guam's elected local government and United States territorial status offer investors a secure, stable and free political climate.

Guam Council on the Arts and Humanities Agency (KAHA) is also responsible for Guam's participation in the quadrennial Festival of Pacific Arts, sponsorship of local art shows, implementing legislation to provide local art at public places, the administration of grants and fellowship programs, etc.

Perhaps the most alluring gift Guam has to offer is the gentle spirit of her native people. As fierce warriors and hunters who lived in highly socialized villages in ancient times, the Chamorro people have built a proud heritage based on strong familial ties, a strong sense of sharing, commitment to hard work and religious faith that is still very much alive today.

ENVIRONMENT

A clean environment is one of Guam's most precious resources. During recent years, combined efforts between the local community, government, private businesses, and the U.S. military, have made a difference in providing a clean coastline for the island. Additionally, the annual Guam International Coastal Cleanup provides a long term benefit as a data collection tool, and a practical medium to educate school children on the problem of marine pollution.

The annual Beauty and the Beach Cleanup is another partnership event between the local government agencies and private businesses to clean up the beaches, followed by a time of celebration with food and entertainment for the participants.

The Guam Chamber of Commerce administers the "Chalan Mami" or "Our Street" program, whereby businesses have a mechanism to adopt and pay for the cleanup on a stretch of road, and at the same time provide fundraising opportunities for non-profit organizations.

EDUCATION

There are 37 public schools, 19 private schools (several of which include pre-K through high school), a community college and a four-year accredited university on Guam that are patterned after school systems in the continental United States. Public schools are accredited by the Western Association of Schools and Colleges.

POST SECONDARY LEVEL

Guam Community College (GCC): Established in 1977 and accredited by the Western Association of Schools and Colleges, GCC offers more than 40 courses of study.

By recognizing its role in the economic prosperity of the community and staying abreast of business trends, the college responds to the predominant training needs of the region by developing new and innovative educational programs.

Programs at the college are intended to meet the many educational needs and interests of the community and include: accounting, supervision and management, information systems, computer science, construction trades, architectural engineering technology, civil engineering technology, criminal justice, electro-mechanical trades, horticulture, early childhood education, cosmetology, sign language interpreting, marketing, automotive technology, food and beverage operations, hotel operations, travel agency management, tour operations management, waterworks technology and the apprenticeship training program for construction and hotel industries.

GCC also offers a variety of community service and special programs including English as a second language, adult basic education, general education development

preparation and testing, and an adult high school diploma program. The college runs a comprehensive vocational high school program on its campus and offers vocational classes in all of Guam's public high schools.

University of Guam (UOG): Founded as the Territorial College of Guam in 1952, this institution was granted its charter as the University of Guam in 1968. It is a land-grant institution accredited by the Western Association of Schools and Colleges.

The student body is made up of representatives from more than 40 countries in the Asia-Pacific Region and around the world. Enrollment in the five colleges, as well as specialized classes under the Center for Continuing Education and Outreach Program, is now more than 7,000 students and continues to grow.

The University's English Language Institute offers courses in English as a second language throughout the year, the primary purpose of which is to prepare non-English speakers to attend American universities.

There are five research units operating on campus. The Richard F. Taitano Micronesian Area Research Center houses the island's best source of photographs and thousands of documents from the Spanish era, and other regional sources. The Marine Laboratory is recognized internationally and holds a collection of more than 20,000 specimens. UOG's Water and Environmental Research Institute is considered by the U.S. government as one of the top five programs in the nation for work in this field. Finally, the Micronesian Language Institute is dedicated to the research, teaching and service of the indigenous languages of the region.

The University has established relations with institutions of higher learning to provide a forum for shared learning in Taiwan, China, Japan and Korea. UOG was the venue for the first-ever executive seminar for the Dun-Bu Insurance Co. of Korea, and the first-ever real estate seminar for executives from the Misawa Home Corp. in Tokyo. Students from Japan wishing to obtain U.S. Certified Public Accounts certifications come to UOG for the examinations. UOG also has a Master's program in Pohnpei and Saipan.

In addition, the university's spacious recreational complex (the University of Guam Fieldhouse) provides an excellent facility for indoor concerts, sports competitions, trade shows and other special events.

HEALTH CARE

Guam's health care system includes two major hospitals, a widespread clinic network, a broad selection of general and specializing physicians, and well-run medical evacuation operations to Hawaii, the U.S. mainland and the Philippines.

Guam's two hospital facilities are the Naval Regional Medical Center and the Guam Memorial Hospital. While the Naval hospital provides services to veterans, active-duty personnel and military dependents, Guam Memorial Hospital provides health care for the remainder of the general public. The Guam Memorial Hospital is a publicly-owned facility operated as part of the Government of Guam system.

The public hospital has a 192 bed capacity; 159 acute care beds and 33 long-term care beds. The hospital also has 16 newborn bassinets that accommodate more than 3,000 births per year. All customary acute care services (adult and pediatric medical services, neonatal, pediatric and adult intensive care services) and skilled nursing care are provided. Guam Memorial Hospital is capable of providing for the basic and specialized health needs of our community and the region.

The hospital provides a host of diagnostic and therapeutic services to both inpatients and outpatients, including:

laboratory and blood bank services
dietary services
radiology; nuclear medicine and CT scan diagnostic services
pharmaceutical services
respiratory care and cardiopulmonary services
hemodialysis
physical, occupational, recreational and speech therapy
pastoral care services
social services
patient education
24-hour emergency operation
cardiac catheterization lab
angiography suite

Guam has ten specialty and emergency care clinic systems, and as of May 2000, approximately 170 licensed physicians, 62 dentists, 532 registered nurses, 140 practical nurses, and 42 individual, marriage and family therapists. More than 28 pharmacies are available for prescription drug needs.

Recent additions to specialized healthcare facilities are the Cancer Institute of Guam and the Guam Radiology Consultants. They provide the latest state-of-the art technology and specialty cancer treatment, with American Board of Radiology certified physicians and ASRT certified radiation therapists. At the time of this publication, the Cancer Institute of Guam provides the only painless ultrasound prostate biopsy in the Western Pacific.

Just opened in 2000 and located one mile from the Guam Memorial Hospital is "Sagua Mañagu" or "Birthing Bay," the first privately owned and operated birthing center on Guam. The center is a spacious homelike facility, with seven labor/delivery/recovery rooms each fully equipped with amenities and accommodations for expectant mothers and families, such as kitchen facilities, large private bathrooms, TV & VCR, rocking chair, and rest areas for visitors.

HOUSING

Guam offers a wide variety of housing options, from ocean view villas and executive homes with top-of-the-line amenities to cozy condominiums, duplexes and homes well-suited for new and growing families. The 2000 Census recorded about 45,000 houses and apartments on island, an increase of about 15,000 from the 1990 Census.

Housing for purchase or lease on Guam is readily available. Construction costs range from $72 to $90 or more per square foot (depending on quality) giving an average three-bedroom house price of approximately $145,000 to $156,000. Mortgage loan funds are readily available from institutional lenders.

The rental market indices show two-bedroom units renting from $500 to $700 per month and three-bedroom units renting from $700 to $1,000 and up, depending on location and amenities.

RECREATION

Guam is a virtual tropical playground with recreational activities to suit every taste. In addition to a variety of international cuisines offered at local eateries and numerous formal dining establishments, Guam's dazzling hotel district features regular exhibitions, shows, concerts, carnivals and special events.

Each of Guam's villages hold a traditional "fiesta" celebration each year in honor of their patron saints. Fiestas are open to all, and feature outdoor feasts, music, dancing, and a chance to visit with friends and family.

of "things to do" can quickly fill an active social and recreational calendar:

golfing
parasailing
jet skiing
snorkeling and diving
beach resorts
water parks
dinner cruises
nature/hiking
dinner shows
night market
shopping
sightseeing
theme restaurants
aquarium
dolphin watching
underwater observation
museum

health spas
gun shooting
dog racing
helicopter tours

AMERICA IN ASIA

As the United States' westernmost territory, Guam is "Where America's Day Begins."

As a member of the American family, Guam is able to offer visitors a stable and secure environment. Federal law provides local self-government on Guam, U.S. citizenship for her people, and application of the U.S. Constitution to the island.

While maintaining its relationship with the United States, Guam also enjoys its strategic location as the gateway to Asia. It is 1,500 miles east of the Philippines, 1,500 miles southeast of Japan, and 3,100 miles northeast of Australia. This proximity makes travel to Guam quick and convenient.

GUAM, A MAJOR GATEWAY TO MICRONESIA AND THE FAR EAST.

Guam is serviced by several international, regional and inter-island carriers, including Continental Micronesia, Japan Airlines, Northwest Airlines, All Nippon Airways, Air Nauru, Asiana Airlines, China Airlines, Freedom Air and Pacific Island Aviation.

Under the Guam only visa waiver program, visitors from 16 countries are able to visit Guam for up to 15 days without a US visa. Please see Guam's Visa Waiver Program on page 35.

These airlines connect Guam via direct air service to major destinations in the United States, Asia and the Pacific. Flying time to Guam is about seven hours from Honolulu, and three to four hours from Tokyo, Manila, Taipei and Hong Kong. Average airline seat capacity is close to 2.3 million seats, with further increased seat capacity anticipated from all major origins.

BUSINESS CLIMATE

In addition to an enticing climate and prime location, Guam USA offers a strong business environment in which to develop and grow a successful company.

The proof of Guam's viability as a thriving commercial center is evidenced by the many U.S. and international companies who have already made Guam their home and the successful local companies who contribute to the strength of the the current port footprint to include new deep-water cargo piers, upgraded fisheries facilities, expanded container lay-down areas, and industrial park and cruise-ship facilities.

The Commercial Port currently maintains three containerized cargo berths with depths of 38 feet. To service these berths, the port utilizes three 40ton gantry cranes. For larger cargo items, a 150-ton heavy lift crane is used. Three fuel piers are available within the harbor, two for commercial use and one for the

Navy. To support its cargo activities, the port maintains a 26.5-acre container yard. In FY1999, more than 1.9 million revenue tons of cargo were moved through the port.

In addition to its current and expansion plans, the port has identified a waterfront location with a draft of 60 feet—an ideal candidate for installation of a deep-water pier with the most modern cargo equipment.

Plans are underway to expand the fisheries facilities to include the development of warehouses, ice plants, an auction house, net repair facilities and other support services for the fishing industry. In addition, modern passenger cruise ship facilities are also planned.

AIRPORT FACILITY

Guam's other port of entry is the Antonio B. Won Pat Guam International Air Terminal, which services more than eight international air carriers. More than 270 flights per week connect Guam to all major cities in the Pacific and Asia. In addition, the airport services nine air cargo carriers which moved more than 33,167 metric tons of cargo in 1999.

The terminal, built in 1982, experienced an increase in passenger traffic, peaking in 1995 at 1,653,327 passengers. In 1999, the airport handled approximately 1.3 million passengers. To meet Guam's current and projected needs, the island invested more than $240 million in an ambitious expansion and renovation program that tripled the airport's total area.

The net effect of this expansion increased passenger processing from its previous capacity of 1,500 passengers per hour to 5,000 passengers per hour, easily accommodating the growing arrival numbers.

In addition to the terminal expansion project, the conversion of the Naval Air Station, Agana, airfield facilities marked a major milestone for Guam and created a wealth of aviation-related opportunities. Among other facilities, the prime properties include:

207,212 sq. ft. of aircraft hangar space
92,120 sq. ft. of additional cargo and commuter terminal facilities
92,800 sq. ft. of warehouse space
67,006 sq. ft. of office space

The Airport Authority continues with capital improvement projects such as the extension of runways and upgrade of the Commuter Terminal Building to enhance its capacity and safety. Extended runways will provide the opportunity to expand air service to accommodate long haul trans-Pacific flights to the U.S. mainland for passenger and cargo aircraft.

The Guam International Airport Authority (GIAA) now oversees approximately 1,500 acres of land formerly held by the federal government. GIAA has successfully entered into sublease agreements with aviation-related commercial tenants such as the commuter service Freedom Air, and Continental Micronesia for which Guam serves as a regional hub.

POWER

Guam's public power system is managed by the Guam Power Authority (GPA), one of more than 2,000 public utilities in the United States. As a result of investments made in the creation of new generation facilities and the refurbishment of existing assets, Guam's current power generation capacity stands at 502 megawatts and provides power to more than 43,000 customers.

In addition to capital investments designed to expand the island's power assets, GPA has also implemented unique incentives to promote efficient use of power. One of these programs is the Guam Energy Sense incentive which offers up rebates through credits for power consumption, to commercil users who purchase and install energy efficient equipment. The energy-wise equipment also helps reduce utility bills and conserve power.

In order to build system reliability and accommodate growth on Guam, GPA has entered into twenty-year agreements with three Independent Power Producers to enhance generation capacities, increasing the island's generation by 120 megawatts.

HIGHWAY SYSTEM

Guam's modern system consists of a network of 961 miles (some with seven-lanes) of highways running from northern to southern Guam, supported by secondary highways and two-lane roads, connecting all points on the island. Guam continues to improve its highway infrastructure by consistently maintaining roads and highways, monitoring traffic patterns to identify and plan for future expansion of the system based on needs assessments. Funding for Guam's highway projects during 1995-1998 totaled approximately $155,925,019.

Two of the more significant projects just completed are Phase I of the Tumon Bay Beautification Project which upgraded all the infrastructure on the Pleasure Island section of San Vitores Road, the tourism center of Guam, and the completion of Guam's first Underpass/ Overpass structure located near the Guam International Airport.

TELECOMMUNICATIONS

Guam possesses the most advanced telecommunications infrastructure and systems in this region. The island sits at the nexus of the Pacific's underwater fiber optics cabling network, making Guam a telecommunications hub for numerous international providers.

The Guam Telephone Authority, or "GTA" as it is known locally, was created as an autonomous agency of the Government of Guam twenty-six years ago. With island wide fiber-optic trunking, GTA is currently the only local telephone service provider. GTA's system is implicitly redundant and provides alternate routing should damage occur to any part of the fiber-optic loop. Its services are at par with other U.S. areas and much cheaper than other similar sized service areas.

amount of usage, varying from $5 to $30 a month.

Guam's unique advantage is its connectivity in terms of fiberoptic cable and satellite. It's particular position on the globe allows data packets to make a single hop to be fiber-connected to the other part of the world. Guam's political and economic stability also provide an attractive environment for setting up call centers, sales centers and telecommunication gateways.

The educational system in Guam, from the public schools to the University, and innovative private enterprises are taking proactive steps to prepare an educated and tech-savvy workforce for the immediate and distant future.

All these initiatives are designed to further Guam's status as a full service telecommunications hub in the Pacific. While the island's advanced local telecommunications system provides the basis for international giants like MCI and AT&T to operate here already, there is plenty of room for expansion in this industry. With the rapid movement of major American companies into the

Pacific Rim areas (especially Vietnam, Malaysia, Indonesia, Philippines and China), Guam is the prime location for major firms who rely heavily on advanced telecommunications.

As Guam is included in the North American Numbering Plan, long distance rates to the

U.S. mainland now average between 5 cents and 30 cents per minute, depending on the time and day of the week. Due to increasing competition and the entrance of pre-paid calling cards, international rates are also much cheaper. Currently there are 7 companies that offer long distance service, and 2 main carriers of cellular service. Incentive plans are offered by some companies which provide consolidated services for land lines, mobile and the Internet. Half a dozen companies offer Internet access to local residents, with rates according to the

BANKING AND FINANCIAL SERVICES

There are more than 16 international and local banks, subsidiaries of "Big Eight" accounting firms, two international insurance fronting companies, a strong network of local insurance agents and stock brokers, and a substantive number of legal firms experienced in doing business with Asia. The Guam Department of Revenue & Taxation oversees the licensing and regulating of all these institutions. All national and local banks and savings & loans associations are insured by the Federal Deposit Insurance Corporation (FDIC).

All of the conveniences of modern banking are available to conduct financial transactions with virtually every corner of the globe. A number of banks and credit unions are now offering insurance to their customers. Several banks are also offering investment services and opening or strengthening their trust departments as a result of recent legislation that has attracted Guam-based trusts to be established on island.

POPULATION AND LABOR

Guam has a population of 159,827 (1998 estimate based on the latest available census in 1990) inclusive of the military.

Guam's labor laws are patterned after those of the U.S. and regulated by the Guam Department of Labor. The Governor of Guam is vested with the authority to issue temporary labor certifications on Guam if, after testing the local labor market, it is found that: qualified U.S. citizens or permanent residents are not available to perform the required services and that employment of a non-immigrant alien will not adversely affect the wages and working conditions of U.S. resident workers who are similarly employed on Guam. This temporary certification is issued by the Guam Department of Labor for a period of one year or less. Extensions may be granted for a period not to exceed three consecutive years. Minimum wage is set by the prevailing U.S. rates.

The diverse cultural composition of Guam's population provides a unique human resource for the specialized language, cultural and skilled needs of any regional operation.

GUAM'S TAX STRUCTURE

GENERAL

U.S. citizens file only one tax return to that jurisdiction (Guam or U.S.) in which they reside on the last day of the tax year. Pursuant to Section 32 of the Organic Act, Guam uses the income tax laws enforced in the United States. Income taxes applicable in Guam are determined by applying the U.S. tax law (Internal Revenue Code) and substituting the word "Guam" for the words "United States." The Department of Revenue and Taxation through its Taxpayer Assistance and Processing Branch issues official pamphlets with detailed income tax information and provides assistance to taxpayers.

Personal Income Tax

U.S. citizens residing in Guam on the last day of the year, unless exempt, are required to file a tax return (Guam Form 1040) with the Government of Guam reporting all world-wide income. Their personal income taxes must be paid into the Treasury of Guam.

Corporate Income Tax

Guam corporations unless exempt, are subject to income tax on their income from all sources. Other corporations doing business in Guam incur income tax liabilities to Guam for all Guam source income. Most Guam sourced income of alien corporations are subject to tax at the same rates as for U.S. corporations if "effectively connected" with the conduct of a Guam trade or business.

Local Tax

Guam has the usual range of local taxes found in the U.S. mainland, such as gasoline, real property, gross receipts, admissions, hotel, occupancy, etc. However, there is only one legal taxing authority. There are no separate municipal, county or district taxes. Other than admissions, use and hotel occupancy taxes, there is no general sales tax imposed directly on the consumer.

Gross Receipts Tax

Unless exempt by law, all persons (individual, professions, partnerships, corporations, etc.) doing business or performing services in Guam are subject to a 4% monthly privilege tax on their gross receipts or gross income. Banks and other lending institutions report their income on an annual basis and are taxed at the rate of 4% on their net income. In general, retailers must report quarterly and pay the tax required on the gross proceeds of sales on a monthly basis. Wholesale sales, although generally exempt from Gross Receipts Tax, need to be reported quarterly. Petroleum and alcoholic beverages manufactured on Guam are exempt.

Use Tax

All personal property imported into Guam for use or consumption by the person importing it is subject to a 4% tax on the landed cost, payable upon importation. The tax does not apply to property having previous substantial use by the person bringing it into Guam or to certain other property specifically exempt. No tax is imposed when the total value of all property imported by any one person in any one calendar month is $1,000 or less, not to exceed $5,000 in any calendar year. Purchase of personal property in Guam from a person not liable for the gross receipts tax is also subject to the 4% use tax. A Use Tax return is due quarterly.

Real Property Tax

A real property tax is levied upon land and/or improvements and is significantly lower than similar taxes encountered in the United States.

The rates are: one half of one percent of the assessed value of the land and one percent of the assessed value of the improvements on the land. The assessed value is 35% of the appraised value. Typically a tax of $600 in California would be equivalent to a tax of $90 in Guam.

OTHER TAXES

Guam has an Alcoholic Beverage Tax, Tobacco Tax, Liquid Fuel Tax, Admission Tax, Amusement Tax, Recreation Tax, Facilities Tax, Hotel Occupancy Tax and Vehicle Transfer Tax.

STARTING A BUSINESS

GENERAL INFORMATION

On Guam, as in all states of the United States, there are many laws, rules and regulations governing business activities. Guam has adopted the provisions of the Uniform Commercial Code. Most of the laws and procedures encountered in transacting business on Guam are similar to those in the United States.

REGISTRATION OF A BUSINESS

All corporations, partnerships, joint ventures, and associations must register with the Business License Branch of the Department of Revenue and Taxation, located in Tiyan. Their mailing address is: Bldg. 13-2, Mariner Avenue, Tiyan,

Guam 96913. Registration must take place prior to the issuance of any business license.

All trade names or DBA's (doing business as) to be used in conjunction with a business (whether proprietary, partnership, corporate, or other forms) must be registered with the same branch.

LICENSING A BUSINESS

The Government of Guam requires all businesses to have a license, whether a corporation, partnership, sole proprietor, or other form. To ensure that efficient and adequate assistance and support are made available to all prospective businesses, the Government of Guam has established the One Stop Building and Business License Service Center, at 855 W. Marine Drive, where application forms may be picked up and the applicant will be advised of the required clearances depending on the type of license to be obtained. Licenses are renewable every June. General qualifications are: applicant must be at least 18 years of age, owe no taxes and be of good moral character. Questions regarding the various processes & fee schedules involved regarding permitting and licensing should be sent to:

One Stop Service Center P.O. Box 2950 Hagåtña, Guam 96910 Telephone (671) 475-4530/31 Fax: (671) 472-2128. For additional information, please visit: http://www.gov.gu/government.html

Below are the Government of Guam's requirements that you must be aware of prior to starting your business. Also, a listing of the available applications and forms needed to fulfill these requirements are provided below. To obtain these applications and forms, you can visit our offces at the former Pricesmart Building below Barrigada Heights or at our website and related links at ww.guamtax.com. If you have an existing business, you should be familiar with these requirements.

1. Business License Requirements:

Generally, all persons or business entities doing business on Guam are required to be licensed with the Department of Revenue and Taxation's (DRT) General Licensing and Registration Branch. An exception to this general rule is permitted in the case of Professionals such as Certified Public Accountants, Attorneys, and

Medical Practitioners. These Professionals are subject to the rules and regulations of the applicable regulating

Agency or Board. However, if you are a domestic or foreign Corporation, Partership, Limited Liability

Corporation (LLC) or Limited Liability Partership (LLP), you wil be required to first register your Corporation,

Partership, LLC, or LLP with the Department of Revenue and Taxation's (DRT) General Licensing and Registration Branch. Registration wil require notarized or certified copies of the business Articles of

Incorporation, Corporate By-Laws, Partnership Agreements, the appropriately filled applications, etc... Depending on the tye of business you wil be conducting, you wil be required to obtain clearances from various government agencies. For example, if you were to convert your home to rental propert, you wil be required to obtain clearances from the Department of Land Management and the Departent of Public Works (DPW). For your convenience, all clearances may be obtained at the One Stop Building located at DPW. Keep in mind that in order to obtain the clearances, some agencies wil require site inspections, and presentation of documentation relative to the business license application. Upon approval of the Business License, you wil be issued a Gross

Receipts Tax (GRT) Account Number for purposes of fiing and paying your GRT.

II. Business Privilege Tax Requirements:

Section 26201, Article 2, Chapter 26 of Title 11, of the Guam Code Annotated (GCA), states there is hereby levied and shall be assessed and collected monthly privilege taxes against the persons on account of their businesses and other activities in Guam measured by the application of rates against values, gross proceeds of sales or gross income as the case may be. Under this local law, you are required to fie a monthly or a quarterly Gross Receipts Tax Return based on the period the income was received or accrued (depending on your accounting method).

The method of reporting and the applicable percentage has changed in recent years:

From October 01. 1997 to March 31. 2003, the tax rate was four percent (4%). The filing requirement was changed to a quarterly basis, with the return (Form BRQ) due at the last day of the month following the end of the quarter. For example, the return for the fourth quarter (October, November, and December) of 1997 was

due on January 31, 1998. Deposits of the tax, however, were required monthly. For example, a deposit for October 1997 was due November 15, 1997. From April 04. 2003 to March 31. 2004, the tax rate was increased to six percent (6%). The return (Form BRQ) was stil required to be filed quarterly and the deposits made monthly (same requirements as above).

From April 01. 2004 to Present, the tax rate decreased to four percent (4%). The fiing requirements also changed. The return (Form GRT) is required to be fied on a monthly basis and is due on the twentieth (20th) day of the following month, even if no taxes are due. The payment of the tax is also due on the twentieth (20th) of the following month. For example, the return and the payment of tax for the month of April 2004 wil be due on May 20, 2004. For more details, please refer to the "IMPORTANT INORMATION AND INSTRUCTION" section of Form BRQ and Form GRT (whichever is applicable).

The Business Privilege Tax laws provide for certain exemptions for purposes of computing the taxable amount of income for Gross Receipts Taxes purposes. For more information on "Exemptions" please refer to §26203, Article 2, Chapter 26, Division 2, Title 11 of the GCA.

II. Use Tax Requirements:

Business owners or entities may also be responsible for paying a Use Tax. Guam's Use Tax Laws may be applicable if you import any tangible personal propert (i.e. equipment) to be used or consumed by your business operations. As per §28103, Chapter 28, Title 11 of the GCA, there is hereby a levy and shall be paid and collected at the times, and by the persons, hereinafter provided an excise tax upon the use or consumption of all property in Guam unless said equipment is to be exported upon completion of the project. The Use Tax is payable upon the importation of any propert not held for resale.

iv. Pavroll Tax Requirements:

If your business is a corporation or partnership or if you should have employees, you wil be required to obtain an

Employer Identification Number (EIN) for your business. To apply for an EIN, simply go to ww.Irs.org or ww.Irs.gov to apply online. If you do not apply online, you may apply by telephone, fax or mail to obtain an EIN (Please refer to the instrctions for Form SS-4, "Application for Employer Identification Number"). If Business owners or entities have employees, they are required to fie a quarterly return, Form W-i, "Employer's Quarterly Guam Tax Return" to report salary and wage withholding taxes on Guam to DRT, and are required to deposit the withholding taxes monthly using Form 500, "Guam Depository Receipt" with the Government of

Guam. Pursuant to the United States Internal Revenue Code Section 7651, the income tax laws in effect in the United States are the same as the income tax laws in Guam. Therefore, Income Taxes and Wage and Withholding on Guam earned income wil be paid to the Treasurer of Guam. However, Social Security Taxes/FICA Taxes

(Form 941SS) wil be paid to the Treasury of the United States.

v. Corporate Income Tax Requirements: Guam has its own terrtorial income tax system based on the Internal Revenue Code, except that the words "United States" are replaced with "Guam" where appropriate. This mirror system of taxation remains in effect until an implementation agreement between Guam and the United States goes into force. As an owner or entity doing business on Guam, you are required report and fie a Guam Terrtorial Income tax Return. If you are a the Territory of Guam, you are required to fie Form 1120.(domestic) corporation incorporated under the laws

If you are Foreign (not incorporated under Guam laws) corporation registered with DRT, you are required to fie Form 1 120F to report your Guam-sourced income and expenses.

V1. RefJortinJ! Cash Pavments or

Over $10,000 Requirement:

Title 26 and Title 31 of the Guam Territorial Income Tax Code require that you fie Form 8300, "Report of Cash Payments Over $10,000 Received in a Trade or Business", if your business receives more than $10,000 in cash

from one buyer as a result of a single transaction or two or more related transactions. Dual reporting of this information wil now be made to both DRT and the U.S. Treasury Department's Financial Crimes Enforcement Network (FinCEN). For more information regarding Form 8300, visit the IRS website at ww.lrs.gov.

A listing of the applications and forms is summarized below necessary to meet your requirements to the Government of Guam. I hope that this wil help answer some of your questions. If you have any questions, you may contact the Department of Revenue and Taxation at the following telephone numbers:

General Licensing Branch (671) 635-1826/7/8

Business Privilege Tax Branch (671) 635-1835/6 Income Tax Processing Branch (671) 635-1840/1

STARTING YOUR BUSINESS ON GUAM FORMS/APPLICATIONS/E-SERVICES

To obtain Forms and Applications, please visit our offices located at the former Pricesmart Building, or visit our website at www.guamtax.com for applicable links. You can also file certain forms online at www.guamtax.com, and make online tax payments at www.guampay.com. These online services are specified below, where applicable.

I. Business Registration Requirements:

A. You MAY need to first register your company with our General Licensing Branch as:

Form Description	
Domestic or Foreign Corporation	govguamdocs.com
Domestic or Foreign Limited Liability Partnership	govguamdocs.com
Domestic or Foreign Limited Liability Company	govguamdocs.com

B. If you are not required to be licensed by the Guam Contractors License Board, you WILL need to apply for a business license:

Form Description

II.

Business Privilege Tax Requirements:

A.

Upon issuance of your business license you must then obtain a Gross Receipts Tax Account Number from our Business Privilege Tax Branch.

Applicable Period	Percentage	Form Description	Download	E-File	E-Pay
10/1/97 to 3/31/03	4%	BRQ (Revised Oct.1997)	govguamdocs.com	N/A	guampay.com
04/1/03 to 3/31/04	6%	BRQ (Revised Dec.2003)	govguamdocs.com	N/A	N/A
10/1/97 to 3/31/04		BMD (Guam Business Monthly Deposit)	govguamdocs.com	N/A	N/A
4/1/04 to Present	4%	GRT (Revised Apr. 2004)	govguamdocs.com	guamtax.com	guampay.com

NOTE: Use of online services requires online registration. Certain transactions on guampay.com may require applying for a Taxpayer PIN.

III. **Income Tax Requirements:**

A. At the end of your tax year, you are required to file an Income Tax Return by the 15th day of the third month following the close of your tax year.

B. You are also required to deposit Wage Withholding Taxes on a monthly basis and file quarterly returns with DRT.

Name	Form Description	Download
Form 1120	US Corporation Income Tax Return	www.irs.gov
Form 1120F	US Income Tax Return of a Foreign Corporation	www.irs.gov
Form 1065	US Return of Partnership Income	www.irs.gov

Note: Tax instructions can be downloaded from the IRS website (www.irs.gov).

Name	Form Description	Download	E-File	E-Pay
Form 500	Guam Depository Receipt	govguamdocs.com	N/A	guampay.com
Form W-1	Employer's Quarterly Guam Tax Return	govguamdocs.com	N/A	guampay.com
Form SW-2	Employer Quarterly State Wage Report	govguamdocs.com	guamtax.com	N/A
Form W-2GU	Guam Wage & Tax Statement	www.irs.gov	N/A	guampay.com
Form W-3SS	Transmittal of Wage & Tax Statements	www.irs.gov	N/A	guampay.com

Post Office Box 23607, Guam Main Facility, Guam 96921 • Tel. / Telifon: (671) 635-7699 • Fax / Faks: (671) 633-2643

BUSINESS STRUCTURE

The Civil Code of Guam governs all corporations, whether profit or non-profit, stock or non-stock. The basic types of corporations authorized to transact business on Guam are as follows:

DOMESTIC CORPORATION

Domestic corporations are those formed in Guam by the voluntary association of three or more persons in the manner prescribed for any lawful purpose. Articles of Incorporation must be filed with the Business License Branch, setting forth the name, purpose, place of the principal office in Guam, term (not to exceed 50 years), names and residences of incorporators, the number of its directors (not less than 3 nor more than 7), amount of capital stock, etc. The Articles must be accompanied by the statement of the corporation's treasurer showing that at least 20% of the entire capital stock has been subscribed and at least 25% of that subscription has been paid. The secretary or treasurer of a domestic corporation must be a resident of Guam. Foreign Sales Corporations are considered domestic as defined in Sec. 922(a) of the Internal Revenue Code and Sec. 278 of the Civil Code of Guam.

LIMITED LIABILITY CORPORATIONS & LIMITED LIABILITY PARTNERSHIPS

P.L. 23-65 and P.L. 23-125 allow Guam to recognize Limited Liability Partnerships (LLP's) and Limited Liaiblity Corporations (LLC's) business structures that deliver the key advantages of "pass-through taxation" and limited liability for its owners and permit them to operate with less formality. Professionals still remain liable for their professional performance. Pursuant to P.L. 24103, LLP's and LLC's are eligible to apply for benefits under the GEDA Qualifying Certificate program.

FOREIGN CORPORATIONS

All off-island corporations are considered foreign. A foreign corporation must obtain a Foreign Corporation License and a Certificate of Registration before being permitted to transact business on Guam. The managing agent of the corporation must file a notarized statement including the name, purpose, location of home office, capital stock, net assets, resident agent of Guam, accompanied by a certified copy of the Articles of Incorporation and a certificate that the corporation has been established according to the laws of the place of incorporation. A Certificate of Good Standing, usually prepared by the Secretary of State must also be furnished. In the case of other foreign (alien) corporations, it must be issued by a U.S. Consul.

SPECIFIC BUSINESS ACTIVITIES

Certain laws, rules, and procedures have been established for specific professions, businesses and trades. Standards are established by various boards, administrators, commissions, etc. as specified by various sections of the Government Code of Guam.

ALCOHOLIC BEVERAGE CONTROL

The sale, import or manufacture of alcoholic beverages in Guam is subject to the Alcoholic Beverage Control Act. The Alcoholic Beverage Control Board is authorized to issue licenses for wholesale, retail and manufacture of alcohol, and to agents, clubs, etc. Individuals or partners applying for a license must have resided in Guam for at least one year at the time of application.

If the applicant is a corporation, the majority of the members of the Board of Directors must be Guam residents for at least one year.

Attorneys

The District Court of Guam may admit persons who have been certified by the committee of examiners of the Judicial Council to practice law. In addition to passing the Guam Bar Exam, applicants must meet residency and educational requirements. The Attorneys Act specifies regulations on duties, discipline, disbarment, etc.

Banking

Applications by new banks are made to the Commissioner of Banking (Director of Revenue and Taxation). Banks incorporated in a foreign country may maintain a branch office in Guam, but shall not conduct a domestic banking business.

Building

The Building Law provides detailed standards and requirements for the location, design, construction, repair, use, occupancy, removal, etc. of building and structures. It is administered by the Director of Public Works. All buildings must follow the Uniform Building Code, National Electrical Code and Uniform Plumbing Code, which are the acceptable standards used on the

U.S. mainland.

Certified Public Accountancy

Annual permits to practice as Certified Public Accountants are issued by the Director of Revenue and Taxation to holders of certificates which are granted by the Territorial Board of Public Accountancy to persons who have passed the examination and met the other requirements of the Territorial Board of Public Accountancy.

Contractor

Application for a Contractor's License shall be made with the Guam Contractors Licensing Board. Applicants must meet statutory requirements, pass an examination and obtain clearance from the Departments of Revenue and Taxation, Land Management, Labor, and Public Works.

Consumer Credit

The Uniform Consumer Credit Code governs credit transactions such as retail installment sales, consumer credit, small loans and usury. It is administered by the Savings and Loans Commissioner (Director of Revenue and Taxation) and is applicable to all businesses extending credit to customers.

Cosmetology

The Cosmetology Law requires registration and licensing of cosmetologists, electrologists, manicurists and cosmetology instructors. A Board of Cosmetology administers the rules and regulations prescribed by this law.

ENGINEERS, ARCHITECTS, LAND SURVEYORS

Application for registration is made to the Board of Engineering and Architectural Examiners (Department of Public Works). The Board issues a certificate of registration, renewable annually, to applicants who meet all the requirements. Firms may obtain a permit for a regular business license after registration of members.

INSURANCE UNDERWRITERS

An individual, partnership or corporation desiring to transact business in Guam as an insurer must first be admitted and may transact only those classes of insurance specifically authorized in the Certificate of Authority issued by the Commissioner of Insurance. Applications are filed with the Commissioner of Insurance at the Guam Department of Revenue & Taxation.

SAVINGS AND LOAN

The Savings and Loan Commissioner (Director of Revenue and Tax) administers and enforces the Savings and Loan Association Act. Savings and loan associations require a certificate of approval from the Commissioner and a business license.

SECURITIES

Application for registration as a broker-dealer, agent, or investment advisor is made to the securities administrator (Director of Revenue and Taxation). Securities sold in Guam must be registered unless specifically exempt.

TRADE PRACTICES

The Trade Practices and Consumer Protection Law defines and prohibits unfair methods of competition and unfair or deceptive practices such as false advertising, false origin of goods, misrepresentation, etc. It applies to all businesses in trade and commerce.

TRUST COMPANIES

Application is filed with the Commissioner of Banking at the Guam Department of Revenue and Taxation, pursuant to the Guam Trust Companies Act.

OTHERS

Other local laws and requirements of interest to certain businesses include Zoning, Subdivision, Vehicle Code, Workmen's Compensation, Fair Labor Standards, etc. Establishing a new business in Guam or maintaining and expanding an established business require compliance with applicable laws and requirements (including payment of applicable fees).

OBTAINING A LICENCE

Individuals and firms who are interested in engaging in business in Guam must obtain a business license prior to starting their business operations. Most licensing transactions can be processed and approved at a single location, the Government of Guam's ONE STOP LICENSING CENTER located at 542 N. Marine Drive, Tamuning, Guam 96913, Telephone No. (671) 646-3259 or

Facsimile No. (671) 649-6178. Hours of operation for the center are from 8:00am to 5:00pm, Monday through Friday, except legal holidays.

The One Stop Center provides the convenience of processing most business license applications at one location within one day. Exceptions to this process are for those individuals or entities that are applying for professional services licenses in health (all disciplines), cosmetologists, contractors, Attorney, Certified Public Accountant, insurance, real estate, securities, engineers, architects, surveyors who must have their licenses approved and issued by their respective professional boards in Guam.

- The license will be issued after all clearances are completed. Applicable fees are made payable to the Treasurer of Guam.
- There is no citizenship requirement for the application of a business license.
- Forms available at http://www.govguamdocs.com/index.htm
- For questions please access http://www.guamtax.com/

CATEGORIES OF BUSINESS LICENSES

1. Wholesale: The sale of tangible goods for resale by a licensed retailer.
2. Retail: The sale of tangible goods to the ultimate consumer or end user.
3. Service: Performing or providing a service for others (e.g. house rental, cleaning service, travel agency, etc.)
4. Other: Banking, Home Industry, Hand Manufacture, Coin Vending, etc.

DOCUMENTS REQUIRED FOR A BUSINESS LICENSE APPLICATION

1. Application
2. Character questionnaire
3. Certificate of Transacting Business under a Fictitious Name (if applicable)
4. Registration with the Dept. of Rev. &Tax

ADDITIONAL INFORMATION REQUIREMENTS

1. Social Security no. or passport no.
2. Legal description of business location (block, lot no., and municipality)
3. Indicate the type of firm (please see - Firm Classification).
4. Indicate type of business activity
   (please see - Categories of Business Licenses).

REQUIREMENTS FOR ALCOHOLIC BEVERAGE CONTROL LICENSES

1. Individuals applying for an Alcoholic Beverage Control license must have resided on Guam for at least one year at the time of application.
2. If the applicant is a partnership, then each partner must satisfy the same requirement.
3. If the applicant is a corporation, the majority of the members of the Board of Directors must meet this requirement.
4. General On-Sale and General Off-Sale licenses are issued on a municipality basis. One of each license per one thousand persons or fraction thereof is issued. However, a special

provisions of the law allows application for a license if the establishment is a hotel with at least twenty rooms or if it is a public restaurant where the investment in the building is not less than $50,000.

GUAM BUSINESS LICENSE FEES

BUSINESS LICENSE BRANCH FEES

Tobacco License	
Retail Tobacco License	
Wholesale Tobacco License	$
Coin Vending Tobacco License	
Penalty for failure to renew license on June 30th - $50 plus $1.00 for each day until July 31st	
Penalty for violation of Tobacco products not accessible to minors	
Reproduction of Documents & Records	
Copy of each business license	
Certificate of Existence	
Certificate of Good Standing	
Certificate of Exemption	
Authentication/Certification fee documents filed at General Licensing	
Copy of each page of any document filed with General Licensing Br.	
Replacement of Corporate Certificate	
Copy of any Compliance, Regulatory Testing or study guide pamphlet	
Wholesale Licenses (Annual)	
$1.00 to $100,000.00	
$100,001.00 to $500,000	
$500,001.00 to $1,000,000.00	
$1,000,001.00 to $2,000,000.00	
Exceeding $2,000,000.00	$
Retail Licenses (Annual)	
$1.00 to $250,000.00	
$250,001.00 to $500,000.00	
$500,001.00 to $1,000,000.00	
$1,000,001.00 to $2,000,000.00	
Exceeding $2,000,000.00	$
Each Coin Vending Machine for printed materials	
Manufacturer's License	
a) Hand	
b) Machine	
Service business or calling non-professional activities	
Rental (1) unit residential real property	
Rental unimproved real property	
Rental multiple residential units	
Basic $25.00 or $5.00 for each additional unit whichever is greater	
Rental of each commercial office unit	
Rental of hotel or motel	
$5 for each unit	
Rental warehouse storage space	
Registration of Corporation & Other Entity	
Domestic Corporation (Guam) - Articles of Incorporation	
Article of Non-Profit Corporation/Association/Organization	

Filing of Corporate By-Laws
Filing of By-Laws - Non-Profit Corporation
File amended Article of Incorporation
File amended By-Laws
Filing fee voluntary corporate dissolution
File Service of process on domestic corporation
Off-island plus additional cost incurred
Foreign corporation
Filing Articles of merger
Dissolution of partnership
Registration of limited liability partnership $250 each partner not to exceed $1000 if partners are more than fou
Foreign partnership, designate agent for service of process or serve process on Director
Pawnshop

Alcohol Beverage Control Fees

Wholesaler	$1,000.00
On-Sale Beer	$300.00
General On Sale	$1,000.00
On Sale Wine	$300.00
Waiter/Waitresses	$15.00
Managers/assistant Managers	$25.00
Off Sale Beer	$200.00
General Off Sale	$1,000.00
Special Alcoholic	$25.00
Temporary Beer (Charge Per Event) $20 per day not to exceed $100.00	$100.00
Public Warehouseman's	$50.00
Club	$500.00
Temporary General License	$100.00
$50.00 per day not to exceed $100.00	
Mobile Limousine Service	$750.00
Mobile charter Van 10 passengers	$500.00
Mobile Charter Van plus 10 passengers	$750.00
Mobile - buses	$1,000.00
Mobile License - general on sale	
License only	

Penalty for Violation of Alcoholic Beverage Control Act	
First Offense	$750.00
Second Offense	$1,500.00
Third Offense	$2,500.00
Fourth Offense	$3,500.00
Fifth Offense & a 48 hour suspension ABC Board may revoke license	$4,500.00
Occupational Licenses Greyhound ID	$15.00

IMPOSITION AMUSEMENT DEVICES	
Pinball	$100.00
Pachinko, or similar machines	$100.00
Multiple-Coin Pinball	$500.00

Coin activated phonograph/music producing machine plus 15.00 each coin slot in excess of one	$40.00
Coin activated Kiddie rides	$50.00
Video Horse/Greyhound race machine	$1,250.00
Video type amusement machine	
• Symbolic	$500.00
• Liberty	$500.00
• Others	$500.00
Each coin slot on any amusement machine in excess of one	$25.00
Each coin activated video amusement device for use of children	$50.00
Bowling Alleys (Per Lane)	$50.00
Penalty for nonregistration of revenue generating amusement device	$5,000.00

IMPOSITION RECREATIONAL FACILITY	
Each bowling alley	$50.00
Regulation Golf Course per 9 holes or a fraction thereof	$500.00
Each golf driving range or miniature golf course	$200.00
Each pool or billiard table	$25.00
Each shooting range/gallery	$250.00
Each game room	$200.00
Each go-cart facility	$200.00
Each off-track racing park	$250.00
Paint Ball Gun Facility	$100.00
Shuffle Boards	$100.00
Each coin operated pool table	$50.00
Each mahjong table	$100.00
Baseball Batting Cage	$50.00
Each water park	$200.00
Sling Shot/Bungy	$200.00
Any recreational facility not substantially similar to the items above	$200.00

Insurance, Securities and Banking Fees

INSURANCE	
Ceritificate of Authority New	$900.0C
Renewal of Certificate of Authority	$500.0C
Filing of any other certificate, statement, paper or exhibit required by insurance law	$20.0C
Filing of new application after refusal to issue original Certificate of Authority	$900.0C
Filing of application for Certificate of Authority after revocation or expiration	$900.0C
Filing of application for withdrawal	$200.0C
Furnishing copies of papers filed per page	$1.0C
Certifying copies of paper filed, per document	$25.0C
Penalty for transacting insurance business in Guam without insurer's license no more than $5,000.00	$5,000.0C
Filing fee for Annual Statement domestic insurers	$50.0C
Penalty for failure to file annual statement on or before April 1st of each year	$500.0C
Penalty after May 15th, additional late filing fee of $100 per day	$100.0C
Penalty for any person violating the provisions on domestic insurers shall be fined no more than $5000.00	$5,000.0C
Filing fee for Annual Statement foreign insurers	$50.0C
Penalty for failure to file annual statement on or before April 1st of each year	$500.0C
Penalty after May 15th, additional late filing fee of $100 per day	$100.0C
Filing fee for Annual Statement for alien insurers	$50.0C

Penalty for failure to file annual statement on or before April 1st of each year	$50
Penalty after May 15th, additional late filing fee of $100 per day	$10
License for persons selling insurance:	
Broker	$10
General Agent	$10
Subagent	$2
Nonresident producer	$2
Solicitor	$2
Insurance Adjuster	$5
Penalty for violating provisions relating to agents, brokers, solicitors and adjusters not more than $5,000	$5,00
Surplus Lines Broker	$10
Form Filing	$2
Rate Filing	$20
Penalty for using rates not filed and not approved by the commissioner not more than $5,000.00	$5,00

BANKING

Uniform Commercial Code
Original Financing Statement per document
Amendment or continuation per document
Termination of financing statement per document
Release of financing statement
Statement of Assignment
Information from Filing Officer
Copy of Filed Financing Statement $1 for first page & $.50 for each add. Page
Bulk Sales Filing Fee

Uniform Consumer Credit Code
Notification by Persons subject to regulated lending for consumer sales, leases or loans basic fee
Additional fee for consumer sales, leases & loans for each $100,000 or fraction of $100,000 of original unpaid b
Additional fee for assignees of consumer sales, lease or loans for each $100,000 or fraction of $100,000 of unp

BANKS	
Main Office ,includes Main Branch of national banks, out-of-state and alien banks	$1.000.00
Assessment on Total Assets($0.022/$1,000) $0.022	
Other Lending Institutions	$500.00
Foreign Exchange License	$500.00
Agent of Foreign Exchange License	$50.00

SECURITIES

Broker-dealer
Investment Advisor
Agent of Securities Broker - dealer
Securities Registration Statement by qualification minimum of $200.00 of offering price times one fifth of one pe
(0.2%) not to exceed $2,500

REAL ESTATE

Trust Accounts: Penalty $100 for each violation for failure to deposit into trust account, any down payment, ear

Original Broker's License - 2 Years
Restricted Broker's License - one (1) year
Renewal Broker's License - 4 years
Original Salesman's License - 2 years
Restricted Salesman's License -one (1) yr
Renewal Salesman's License - 4 yrs
Limited Salesman's License -120 day pd.
Branch Office Broker's License
Change of Name or Address
Salesman's License Transfer
Duplicate License
Reinstatement of License

REAL ESTATE APPRAISER:	
License and Renewal	
Certified Appraiser - 2 years	$200.00
Licensed appraiser - 2 years	$200.00
Non-resident certified or licensed appraiser	$200.00
Non-resident temporary certified or licensed appraiser	$100.00
Trainee appraiser	$200.00

INCOME TAX BRANCH FEES

INCOME TAX SERVICE FEES
For each page
W-1 Duplication Fee
Certification Notice to Taxpayer
Form F-500 Duplication Fee
SWICA Duplication Fee
Tax Preparer Examination Fee
Annual Fees - Tax Preparers
Registration
Location Fee
Additional Location fee
Employee/partner/Officer Fee
• 2 - 49 employees
• 50 - 99 employees
• 100 - 499 employees
• 500 or more employees
REVENUE RULING
Revenue Ruling except when a different fee is identified and assessed by the Internal Revenue Code
CHANGES IN THE DAVE SANTOS ACT
§ 26203(k) (9),(28 - (32) are amended. The Fifty Thousand Dollars ($50,000) exemptions in the above code sections ($50,000) effective May 18, 2007.
Visible GRT REPEALED
§26201(b),(c)&(d) of 11 GCA repealed. These sectioins pertained to the visible GRT that were enacted to provide ar

FIRM CLASSIFICATION

1. Sole Proprietorship: Single business owner.

2. Partnership: An association of two or more persons to carry on as co-owners of a business for profit. Guam law also allows for the formation of Limited Liability Partnerships (LLP's). A LLP is a general partnership in which the personal liability of each partner is limited to the amount invested by that partner.
3. Corporation: Artificial being created by law, having the rights of succession and the powers, attributes and properties expressly authorized by law or incident to its existence. Please note that all corporations must be registered with the Department of Revenue and Taxation prior to applying for a business license.
4. Limited Liability Company (LLC): A company that is organized for the sole and specific purpose of rendering professional service and that has as its members only individuals licensed or otherwise authorized within Guam to render the same professional service as the limited liability company. Neither partners nor managers are personally responsible for the obligations of an LLC.

BUSINESS PRIVILEDGE TAX (Gross Receipts Tax GRT)

Upon receiving the business license, you will receive an explanation on Guam's Business Priveledge Tax filing. More commonly referred to as the Gross Receipts Taxes (GRT), this tax is to be filed quarterly and is based on gross receipts (revenues) of the business. The GRT is due between the 1st and 20th of each month and should be paid at the Department of Revenue and Taxation.

CONTRACTORS DOING BUSINESS WITH THE FEDERAL GOVERNMENT

On behalf of the people of Guam, we would like to congratulate you on your successful bid for a contract on Guam with

the Federal Government. Below are the Government of Guam's requirements you must be aware of

prior to starting your project. Also, a listing of the necessary applications and forms you wil need to fulfill these requirements are provided below. If you are a domestic contractor, you should be familiar with these requirements.

i. Registration and Business License Requirements:

Generally, all contractors doing business on Guam are required to be licensed with the Guam Contractors License

Board. An exception to this general rule is permitted in the case of a foreign or an off-island contractor doing

work exclusively on military installations. The Guam Attorney General's opinion CLB 93-0543, dated June 17, 1993 states that with the exception of domestic contractors, contractors with contracts exclusively on military installations are not required to obtain a contractor's license with the Guam Contractors License Board. However, if you are a foreign or off-island corporation (whether or not you wil be performing work exclusively on military installations), you wil be required to first register or apply for a Certificate of Authority with the Department of Revenue and Taxation's (DRT) General Licensing and Registration Branch. If you are a contractor who is not required to obtain a contractor's license under the above exception, you are required to obtain a business license from DRT's General Licensing Branch before you begin your project. Please note that if you later decide to expand your contracting business to the local community (outside military installations), you would then be required to obtain a contractor's license from the Guam Contractors License Board.

II. Business Privilege Tax Requirements:

Section 26201, Aricle 2, Chapter 26 of Title 11, of the Guam Code Annotated (GCA), states there is hereby levied and shall be assessed and collected monthly privilege taxes against the persons on account of their businesses and other activities in Guam measured by the application of rates against values, gross proceeds of sales or gross income as the case may be. Under this 10ca11aw, you are required to file a monthly or a quarterly

Gross Receipts Tax Return based on the period the income was received or accrued (depending on your accounting method).

The method of reporting and the applicable percentage has changed in recent years:

From October 01, 1997 to March 31. 2003, the tax rate was four percent (4%). The fiing requirement was changed to a quarterly basis, with the return (Form BRQ) due at the last day of the month following the end of the quarter. For example, the return for the fourth quarter (October, November, and December) of 1997 was due on January 31, 1998. Deposits of the tax, however, were required monthly. For example, a deposit for

October 1997 was due November 15, 1997. From April 04, 2003 to March 31. 2004, the tax rate was increased to six percent (6%). The return (Form BRQ) was stil required to be fied quarterly and the deposits made monthly (same requirements as above). From April 01. 2004 to Present, the tax rate decreased to four percent (4%). The filing requirements also changed. The return (Form GRT) is required to be fied on a monthly basis and is due on the twentieth (20th) day of the following month. The payment of the tax is also due on the twentieth (20th) of the following month. For example, the return and the payment of tax for the month of Apri12004 wil be due on May 20,2004. For more details, please refer to the "IMPORTANT INORMATION AND INSTRUCTION" section of Form BRQ and Form GRT (whichever is applicable).

For purposes of computing the Gross Receipts Tax as a contractor, amounts paid to a subcontractor may be deducted from gross income in determining the Gross Receipts Tax liability. Section 26202(e), Article 2, Chapter 26, Division 2, Title 11 of the GCA (**Tax on Contractors**) was repealed and reenacted to state that there shall be levied, assessed and collected a tax rate of four percent (4%) measured against the gross income of any contractor; *provided*, that there shall be deducted from the gross income of the taxpayer so much thereof as has been included in the measure of tax levied under this Subsection on another taxpayer who is a contractor, as defined in §26101(b); *provided*, that any person claiming a deduction under this Subsection shall be required to show in the person's return either the name and contractor's license number or the registration number for a professional engineer, architect or land surveyor or the Certificate of Authorization (COA) number for a business authorized to provide engineering, architecture or land surveying services by the Guam Board of Registration for Professional Engineers, Architects, Land Surveyors of the person paying the tax on the amount deducted by the person.

The Business Privilege Tax laws also provide for other exemptions for purposes of computing the taxable amount of income for Gross Receipts Taxes purposes. For more information on **"Exemptions"** please refer to §26203, Article 2, Chapter 26, Division 2, Title 11 of the GCA.

Use Tax Requirements:

Contractors may also be responsible for paying a Use Tax. Guam's Use Tax Laws may be applicable if you import any tangible personal property (i.e. equipment) to be used or consumed by you in the performance of your contract or brought for the exclusive use on the military installation. As per §28103, Chapter 28, Title 11 of the GCA, there is hereby a levy and shall be paid and collected at the times, and by the persons, hereinafter provided an excise tax upon the use or consumption of all property in Guam unless said equipment is to be exported upon completion of the project. The Use Tax is payable upon the importation of any property not held for resale.

Payroll Tax Requirements:

Contractors are also required to file a quarterly return, Form W-1, "Employer's Quarterly Guam Tax Return" to report salary and wage withholding taxes on Guam to DRT, and are required to deposit the withholding taxes monthly using Form 500, "Guam Depository Receipt" with the Government of Guam. Pursuant to the United States Internal Revenue Code Section 7651, the income tax laws in effect in the United States are the same as the income tax laws in Guam. Therefore, Income Taxes and Wage and Withholding on Guam earned income will be paid to the Treasurer of Guam. **However, Social Security Taxes/FICA Taxes (Form 941) will be paid to the Treasury of the United States.**

Corporate Income Tax Requirements:

Guam has its own territorial income tax system based on the Internal Revenue Code, except that the words "United States" are replaced with "Guam" where appropriate. This mirror system of taxation remains in effect until an implementation agreement between Guam and the United States goes into force. As a contractor doing business on Guam, you are required report and file a Guam Territorial Income tax Return. If you are a (domestic) corporation incorporated under the laws of the Territory of Guam, you are required to file Form 1120. If you are Foreign (not incorporated under Guam laws) corporation registered with DRT, you are required to file Form 1120F to report your Guam-sourced income and expenses.

Reporting Cash Payments of Over $10,000 Requirement:

Title 26 and Title 31 of the Guam Territorial Income Tax Code require that you file Form 8300, "Report of Cash Payments Over $10,000 Received in a Trade or Business", if your business receives more than $10,000 in cash from one buyer as a result of a single transaction or two or more related transactions. Dual reporting of this information will now be made to both DRT and the U.S. Treasury Department's Financial Crimes Enforcement Network (FinCEN). For more information regarding Form 8300, visit the IRS website at www.irs.gov.

VII. BOS Contractor Requirements: Public Law 27-103, the "Guam Competitiveness Act of 2004" aims to increase the competitiveness of Guam-based businesses when they bid for contracts and subcontracts driven by the A-76 effort to outsource major functions on Guam military bases. The law offers tax incentives to Base Operating Service (BOS) contractors and subcontractors to help them obtain price competitiveness when bidding against larger off-island companies for military contracts.

Specifically, the law provides:

1. Rebates of up to one-hundred percent (100%) of income taxes paid to the government of Guam, on income received exclusively from BOS contract operations, for the period covered under the BOS contract or such independent contract as the entity may have.

2. An abatement of one-hundred percent (100%) of Business Privilege (Gross Receipts) Taxes assessed on amounts received by businesses operating as BOS contractors or subcontractors for the period covered under the BOS contract or such independent contract as the entity may have.

The law however, requires the Guam Economic Development and Commerce Authority (GEDCA) to verify the following when considering any application for Qualifying Certificate (Q.C.) benefits by a Contractor or Subcontractor:

1. The Contractor/Subcontractor give first consideration for employment to former civil service

employees employed in those activities taken over by the BOS Contractor, and that their salaries shall be consistent with the United States wages in the same positions;

2. The Contractor/Subcontractor avoid utilizing extraneous capacity in competition with Guam businesses or with Guam public utilities;

3. The Contractor/Subcontractor require all employees and persons working on the project, including its subcontractors and their employees, to be U.S. citizens or resident aliens; and

4. The Contractor/Subcontractor require at least seventy-five percent (75%) of the BOS Contractor and its Subcontractors to be former civil service employees employed in full-time positions in those activities taken over by the BOS Contractor.

In addition to the abovementioned conditions, the Q.c. Law requires that, to be deemed eligible, beneficiaries must create new jobs, and one or more of

the following:

1. Replacement of imports
2. Reduction of consumer prices; or

1. Creation of affordable housing or vitally needed facilities; or
2. Creation of economic activity of value to the territory

The next step in this process is to submit an application for Qualifying Certificate, along with the application fee of $750 to GEDCA. In addition to the required forms, the application should include a market analysis and a comprehensive business plan that details your company's contracting efforts, employee information, and other relevant company information. The subsequent underwriting process, performed by GEDCA's Industr Development Division, wil include a staff review of your application packet, statutorily required notices and public hearing, and reporting on their review to the GEDCA Board of Directors. Should the GEDCA Board of

Directors recommend approval of your request, the Q.C. document wil be forwarded to the Governor for approval and signature.

GEDCA welcomes interest in the QC program, and would consider requests for benefits given the above-mentioned eligibility criteria. For further information on the Q.c. application process, please do not hesitate to contact GEDCA's Industr Development Division directly at 647-4332.

Enclosed are general instructions and related forms necessary to meet your requirements to the Government of Guam. I hope that this wil help answer some of your questions. If you have any questions, you may contact the Department of Revenue and Taxation at the following telephone numbers:

General Licensing Branch (671) 635-1826/7/8

Business Privilege Tax Branch (671) 635-1835/6 Income Tax Processing Branch (671) 635-1840/1 Sincerely,

Department of Revenue & Taxation

Contractors Doing Business with the Federal Government Forms/Applications/E-Services

To obtain Forms and Applications, please visit our offices located at the former Pricesmart Building, or visit our website at www.guamtax.com for applicable links. You can also file certain forms online at www.guamtax.com, and make online tax payments at www.guampay.com. These online services are specified below, where applicable.

I. Business Registration Requirements:

A. You MAY need to first register your company with our General Licensing Branch as:

Form Description	
Domestic or Foreign Corporation	govguamdocs.com
Domestic or Foreign Limited Liability Partnership	govguamdocs.com
Domestic or Foreign Limited Liability Company	govguamdocs.com

B. If you are not required to be licensed by the Guam Contractors License Board, you WILL need to apply for a business license:

Form Description	
Business License Application	govguamdocs.com

Business Privilege Tax Requirements:

A. Upon issuance of your business license you must then obtain a Gross Receipts Tax Account Number from our Business Privilege Tax Branch.

Applicable Period	Percentage	Form Description	Download	E-File	E-Pay
10/1/97 to 3/31/03	4%	BRQ (Revised Oct.1997)	govguamdocs.com	N/A	guampay.com
04/1/03 to 3/31/04	6%	BRQ (Revised Dec.2003)	govguamdocs.com	N/A	N/A

10/1/97 to 3/31/04		BMD (Guam Business Monthly Deposit)	govguamdocs.com	N/A	N/A
4/1/04 to Present	4%	GRT (Revised Apr. 2004)	govguamdocs.com	guamtax.com	guampay.com

NOTE: Use of online services requires online registration. Certain transactions on guampay.com may require applying for a Taxpayer PIN.

Income Tax Requirements:

A. At the end of your tax year, you are required to file an Income Tax Return by the 15th day of the third month following the close of your tax year.

B.You are also required to deposit Wage Withholding Taxes on a monthly basis and file quarterly returns with DRT.

Name	Form Description	Download
Form 1120	US Corporation Income Tax Return	www.irs.gov
Form 1120F	US Income Tax Return of a Foreign Corporation	www.irs.gov
Form 1065	US Return of Partnership Income	www.irs.gov

Note: Tax instructions can be downloaded from the IRS website (www.irs.gov).

Name	Form Description	Download	E-File	E-Pay
Form 500	Guam Depository Receipt	govguamdocs.com	N/A	guampay.com
Form W-1	Employer's Quarterly Guam Tax Return	govguamdocs.com	N/A	guampay.com
Form SW-2	Employer Quarterly State Wage Report	govguamdocs.com	guamtax.com	N/A
Form W-2GU	Guam Wage & Tax Statement	www.irs.gov	N/A	guampay.com
Form W-3SS	Transmittal of Wage & Tax Statements	www.irs.gov	N/A	guampay.com

Post Office Box 23607, Guam Main Facility, Guam 96921 • Tel. / Telifon: (671) 635-7699 • Fax / Faks: (671) 633-2643

COST OF DOING BUSINESS

AVERAGE POWER RATES

For residential services, the monthly service charge is $5.21. The first 500 kilowatt hours are $.03354 each per month, and over 500 kilowatt hours the rate increases to $.07950 each.

For General Service, power rates run $.18916 per kilowatt hour for the first 200 used each month, and $.17198 thereafter.

For Large Power Service (demand in excess of 200 kilowatts per day) the cost ranges between $.17917 and $.22797 per kilowatt hour.

AVERAGE WATER & SEWER RATES

Water Rates are based on meter sizes, and are as follows:

Base rate of $6 plus:

For Residential $2.40 per 1,000 gallons

For Commercial $3.00 per 1,000 gallons

For Irrigation $1.00 per 1,000 gallons

For Livestock $1.00 per 1,000 gallons

Sewer rates are as follows:

Residential $20

Commercial rates are calculated by multiplying $0.80 by total water consumption billed at the rate per 1,000 gallons.

Additional information may be obtained by contacting Guam Waterworks Authority at:

jhjohn@ite.net

Telephone Rates Residential: Installation per line Monthly fee for basic service Commercial: Installation per line Monthly fee for basic service	$35 per jack $18.50 $60 per jack $43.00

Facsimile installation is the same as for a regular phone line. Custom calling features are also available at additional cost.

Detailed and current information regarding services and fees may be obtained by contacting: gta@kuentos.guam.net

AVERAGE LONG DISTANCE RATES

Rates for direct dial and operator-assisted calls vary between 5 cents and 30 cents per minute, depending on the time and day of the week and the destination called. Pre-paid calling cards offer rates as low as 3 cents per minute to the U.S. mainland, and at comparable savings to other destinations around the globe.

Internet Rates vary from $5 to $30 per month, depending on the amount of usage.

APPROXIMATE FUEL COSTS

Fuel Type	Full Service	Self Service
High Octane Unleaded	$2.18	$1.97
Regular Unleaded	$2.08	$1.86
Diesel	—	$1.86

Volume discounts can be negotiated, and incentive programs for customer loyalty provide a variety of choices for the consumer.

POSTAL SERVICES AND RATES

The U.S. Postal Service is the main air and surface parcel carrier on island with numerous satellite offices. Guam is within the domestic area of the U.S. postal system, so standard U.S. domestic fees apply. A one oz. letter requires 33 cents to mail to a U.S. destination. International rates apply to other destinations around the world. (Private courier services are also available for off-island deliveries.)

Air Freight Rates depend upon the origin and destination of the shipment. Prices are very competitive and may be negotiable and vary according to the type of commodity. Generally, the rates for outbound packages to the U.S. are considerably cheaper than inbound packages. Most courier companies are open for business 6 days a week. Overnight service is available to Asia, and packages to the U.S. normally take 2-3 days.

Ladera Tower, Village of Mangilao

TOURISM FINANCIAL SERVICES FISHERIES TELECOMMUNICATIONS FILM PRODUCTION LAND OPPORTUNITIES

Governor Carl T.C. Cutierrez on a trade mission to Ireland

INVESTMENT OPPORTUNITIES

Coconot Oil Mill and Soap Factory, Pre World War II

TOURISM: GUAM'S NUMBER ONE INDUSTRY

EARLY YEARS AND CURRENT TRENDS

Guam's visitor industry has grown dramatically since its inception more than 30 years ago to become the most significant sector today of the island's economy.

Despite its relatively brief history, tourism clearly is Guam's number one industry, accounting for up to 60% of the government's annual revenues and providing more than 20,000 direct and indirect jobs. With local government and industry leaders aiming for 2 million visitors by the year 2005, tourism on Guam will remain the cornerstone of the island's economy, with ever-increasing opportunities to meet our visitors' needs.

In the first year of tourism on Guam (1967), approximately 6,600 visitors came to experience this island paradise. Since then, Guam's tourism industry has grown with great magnitude and importance in this U.S. territory, with rising statistics attesting to the industry's success.

In 1994 Guam joined the elite club of tourism destinations in the region when it recorded for the first time ever, more than 1 million visitors selecting Guam as their destination of choice. In 1995 visitor arrival growth, as compared with the previous year was registered at 25%, climbing steadily to almost 1.4 million tourists in 1997, when a fatal Korean Air Line crash suddenly brought to a halt the momentum of Guam's 2nd strongest market. The economic uncertainties in the region also impacted Guam.

Despite these external factors, Guam made a dramatic rebound with an intense rebuilding period after Supertyphoon Paka in December 1997. To mitigate downside effects, the government and private sectors joined to augment promotional efforts in Japan, Korea, and other target markets. With the gradual recovery of Guam's major markets, the lifeline of the island's economy managed to survive with more than a million visitors in each of the following years, and visitor arrivals have steadily increased since June 1999 to 738,594 during the first seven months in 2000.

The hotel room inventory saw a significant increase in the last two years with the opening of the Outrigger Guam Resort, Pacific Islands Club expansion, Royal Orchid, Guam Garden Villa, Hotel Accion, and The New Century Hotel. To accommodate Guam's goal of 2 million visitors by the year 2005, the Governor's Vision 2005 Task Force aims to increase airline seat capacity from an annual 2.5 million to 3.6 million.

Although the weakened Asian economies brought a dip in visitor arrivals throughout the region, the hotel occupancy rate in Guam bottomed at around 59% in December 1997, and has climbed to an average of 70% despite a 25% increase in the island's hotel room inventory. Currently, available hotel rooms number at around 10,000 and the average room rates range from $40 - $195 per night. There are a variety of hotel establishments on Guam, ranging from exclusive five-star level resorts to mid-range facilities to family-style accommodations.

GUAM'S MARKETS

Visitors from Japan historically have dominated the island's market mix, with the latest figures showing that 83% of visitors to Guam came from that country.

Guam's market share of Japanese outbound travelers for 1999 was 5.77%, with a projection of 6.51% for 2000, according to Japan's Ministry of Justice. The robust recovery of the visitor arrivals from Korea can be attributed to Guam's aggressive marketing efforts to rebuild the market, the nation's economic recovery and strengthening of the Korean won. Korea National Tourist Organization reports that Korean outbound travelers increased by 42% in 1999. Guam's market share was 1.37% during the 1st quarter of 2000.

The Guam Visitors Bureau continues to maintain an aggressive marketing campaign in Japan, Korea and Taiwan. In all, more than90% of all visitors hail from Asia, with the balance comprised of visitors from the United States, neighboring islands or other areas.

The island's marketing focus includes incorporating the senior citizens of Japan's population as it is the fastest growing segment with greater disposable income. Activities and special programs are also offered to attract family travelers. Another target market is the incentive traveler and regional conferences.

Other than as a golfing mecca, Guam's reputation as a honeymoon destination has stimulated the recent growth of the wedding industry. There are 3 major wedding companies on island working with at least 7 hotels with wedding facilities, to provide the couples with everything from a standard wedding service to a complete wedding package including gown and tuxedo rental, limousine and escort services.

Recent changes in international affairs have heightened the strategic importance of Guam in the Asia Pacific region. In 1999, Guam was the location for Operation Tandem Thrust, a joint military exercise bringing 12,000 men and women from countries such as Australia, Japan, South Korea, Singapore, Canada and the United States. Through the joint efforts of the Guam Chamber of

Commerce, the U.S. military, government and community leaders, Guam is again playing an increasingly major role as training grounds and a rest & relaxation port for the armed forces of the U.S.

Guam Visitors Bureau The Guam Visitors Bureau (GVB) is the island's tourism development and promotion organization. Formally created in 1970, the bureau's mission is to promote and develop Guam as a safe and satisfying destination for visitors, while providing opportunities for the benefit of the people of Guam. As a governmental entity, GVB is defined as a public, non-profit membership corporation that receives 80% of its funding from the government and the remaining 20% from membership dues and in-kind contributions. The bureau's organizational setup fosters the important and thriving working relationship between the island's public and private sectors for tourism's success.

Short-term, well-defined fiscal year marketing plans consisting of advertising and promotional activities for Japan, Korea, Taiwan, Hong Kong, the Philippines and North America help guide the bureau in accomplishing its marketing goals.

Operating on a fiscal year basis, GVB's most recent budget is $15 million, with close to $10 million allocated for marketing programs as appropriated by the Guam Legislature. Additionally, a separate annual appropriation to GVB is made for investments to the island's visitor industry, beautification and landscaping efforts, and other special projects.

The Tourist Attraction Fund (TAF) consists of funds derived from hotel occupancy taxes, currently assessed at 11% of the room rate. The TAF has been identified for funding direct or related tourism projects, such as streetlight improvements, additional beautification efforts, and tourism education programs.

Extensive research studies conducted by GVB on Guam's major markets provide a wealth of information on visitor demographics, behavior, satisfaction and expenditures, which greatly assist in the island's overall marketing efforts. Public and private sector industry leaders now rely extensively on the exit surveys conducted by GVB's research department.

GUAM'S VISA WAIVER PROGRAM

The implementation of Guam-only visa waivers by the United States federal government allows for more convenient travel to the territory. The program provides for visa-free entry to Guam for a period of up to 15 days for business or pleasure. First introduced in 1988, with subsequent additions in 1990 and 1993, countries eligible for the program include Japan, Korea, Taiwan, Australia, Brunei, Burma, Indonesia, Malaysia, Nauru, New Zealand, Papua New Guinea, Singapore, Solomon Islands, United Kingdom (including Hong Kong*), Vanuatu and Western Samoa.

* HK British Citizen (BC) and British National Overseas (BNO) passport bearers only

OPTIONAL TOURS

Guam's visitor attractions encompass a wide range of activities. While "beautiful seas",

"relaxation", and "shopping" remain at the top of the list in surveys determining travel motivation, a variety of optional tours are available, including golfing, jet skiing, scuba diving, parasailing, beach resorts, night market, nature hiking, and island sight-seeing. Guam's year-round tropical weather sets the perfect stage for these activities. For visitors with a penchant for enjoying

Guam's waters without getting wet, deep sea fishing, dolphin watching, underwater submersibles and an underwater observatory and the world's largest walk-through tunnel aquarium of Underwater World at Pleasure Island top the list.

Guam boasts a total of ten premier golf courses, a growing number of water parks, world class theme restaurants, dinner shows and cruises.

For investors considering the tourism market on Guam, it may be helpful to note that the top four attractions visitors from Japan, Korea, and Taiwan would most like to see are:

Japan Korea Taiwan Theme Park 60% 35% 45% Archaeological

Site Visit 23% 37% Village Fiesta 21% 29% 36% Nature/Hiking Trail 13% 37% Botanical Garden 15% Micronesian Cultural Center 22%

Source: GVB Exit Surveys (April and May 2000)

Several informational notes on these attractions may be considered:

> The Underwater World, several underwater submersibles and an underwater observatory are the results of the preferences indicated by the island's visitors.
> July 2, 1999 marked the grand opening of Pleasure Island, a complex of internationally renown entertainment facilities in the heart of Tumon, designed to market Guam.
> The development of "retailtainment" (integration of retail and entertainment) became the theme of major retail establishments, such as DFS Galleria, Micronesia Mall, the Guam Premium Outlets with their 10-screen and 14screen theaters, respectively, and restaurants like Hard Rock Café, Planet Hollywood, TGIF, etc.

Bolstered by a strong partnership between the public and private sectors and marked by continuous growth, Guam's tourism industry aims for 2 million visitors by the year 2005.

In order to accommodate this increase, Guam is aggressively pursuing hotels and resort developments and additional tourist attractions that are culturally sensitive and environmentally sound.

Although the majority of hotels are located on Tumon Bay, the heart of tourism activity, pristine areas in other parts of the island have been identified for viable ecotourist hotels and resorts and attractions that would respect the traditions and cultures of the people, preserve the environment, while educating and welcoming visitors. A theme amusement park and convention center (with conference and cultural and performing arts facilities) are high in priority to create new markets for Guam.

Guam has developed into a major tourist destination, an industry that provides the bulk of the island's non-government income. Approximately 1.2 million tourists arrive in Guam each year generating approximately $1.35 billion revenues with visitors from Japan continuing to provide 80% of the tourist market. Although the number of Guam's visitors fell slightly after several disastrous world events, visitor arrivals have been steadily increasing.

Core Components of Guam's Economy

Major Revenue Source in the 1960s:
Tourism: 20% Military/Federal: 75% Other: 5%

Major Revenue Source in 2003:
Tourism: 60% Military/Federal: 30% Other: 10%

Guam's Hospitality Industry

- Hotel Inventory as of January 2007 – 6,798 rooms for 25 hotel properties
- Capacity in room nights: 223,231 (GHRA)
- Employee-room ration: 0.66 (employee to 1 room)

Guam's Airline Partners - provide seat Capacity of 1,581,874 (February 2007)

- Continental Micronesia
- Northwest Airlines
- All Nippon Airways
- China Airlines
- Japan Airlines
- Korean Air
- Asiana Airlines
- Philippine Airlines

Guam Visitor Arrivals 1998-2006

1998: 1,137,026
1999: 1,161,849
2000: 1,286,807
2001: 1,159,071
2002: 1,058,704
2003: 909,506 (an anomalous year)
2004: 1,156,199
2005: 1,210,147
2006: 1,217,111

Tourism Highlights

- In 1995 Guam hit its 1 million visitor arrival mark and has consistently achieves this record for the past 10 years
- In 1996 Japan visitors alone reach 1 million

  - Japan, Korea, Taiwan, Hong Kong, Philippines, U.S. are main markets for Guam.

  - Guam-only visa waiver program for core markets contributes to the consistent hiah visitor arrivals from these countries

- $272 million spent to upgrade Guam International Airport Terminal
- $52.9 million Tumon Redevelopment Project - Infrastructure changes to roadways, beautification in our primary tourist economic zone

Tourism 2007-2011 Goals

- Increase total annual visitor arrivals to 1,530,000
- Increase Japan & Korean visitors to 1,101,600 and 290,700 respectively
- Increase length of stay from 3 nights to 4+ nights by 13% for Japanese visitors and nights to 5+ nights by 6% for Korean visitors
- Increase the hotel inventory
- Increase airline seat capacity
- Set quality standards
- Protect our natural surroundings
- Build up the visitor experience
- Exceed visitor expectations
- Replenish the marketing war chest

Desired Attractions

Potential investment opportunities based on Visitor Exit Surveys:

- Theme Park
- Sports Tourism
- Micronesian Cultural/Visual/Performing Arts Center
- Tumon Boardwalk
- Botanical Garden
- Village Fiesta/Tumon Night Market
- Guam Museum
- Guam Music & Film Fests
- More family-oriented attractions & activities
- Sea Life Park
- Chamorro Food/Chamorro Village

Contact Information:
Guam Visitor's Bureau
401 Pale San Vitores Road
Tumon, Guam 96913
Tel: (671) 646-5278

Fax: (671) 646-8861
Website: http://www.visitguam.org

Guam Hotel and Restaurant Association
P.O. Box 8565
Tamuning, Guam 96931
Tel: (671) 649-1447
Fax: (671) 649-8565
Email: ghra@ghra.org
Website: http://www.ghra.org

FINANCIAL SERVICES

FOREIGN SALES CORPORATION

With the enactment of the U.S. Tax Reform Act of 1984, Guam was the first eligible jurisdiction to provide financial incentives for the establishment of a Foreign Sales Corporation, (FSC), through a Guam law known as the Export Incentive Act. The federal law allows a U.S. exporter with an FSC to receive a 30% to 35% reduction on its federal income tax, provided the goods exported have a minimum of 50% U.S. content. Guam FSCs may be exempt from the Territorial Income Tax on the following income:

(1)foreign trade income; (2) investment income;
(3)carrying charges; and (4) gross income derived from sources outside of Guam. To the extent that any of this income should become non-exempt, a Guam FSC may apply for a special Qualifying Certificate to expire December 31, 2026 which would allow for the rebate of all such income taxes paid to the government of Guam. FSCs are foreign incorporated subsidiaries of U.S. parent corporations engaged in export transactions which qualify them for partial U.S. tax exemptions, provided they maintain certain processes.

FSCs can be formed by manufacturers or export groups, such as export trading companies, and other non-manufacturers. An FSC can function as a principal, buying and selling for its own account, or as a commission agent. It can be related to a manufacturing parent company or an independent merchant or broker.

Companies such as Boeing, Chevron, Hallmark, Mobil, Tektronix, and Weyerhaeuser are among the 146 currently licensed FSCs in Guam.

INSURANCE

Several laws have been passed to encourage the location of insurance underwriters on Guam, to further expand the finance and investment sectors of the island economy towards making Guam a center for financial investment domicile.

Spurred by increasing inquiries from underwriters throughout the world about Guam's potential as an insurance center, our government and private sectors joined forces to actively pursue incentives for this industry. Under current law, insurance issuers, including reinsurers, commercial insurers, or captive insurers whose headquarters are located in Guam, may enjoy the following benefits:

100% abatement of gross receipts taxes on insurance premiums and other revenues;

Rebate of all income taxes resulting from the operation of an insurance underwriting entity.
100% rebate of income tax withheld from shareholders on dividends from the insurance underwriting business.

WHAT IS A CAPTIVE?

Captive insurance refers to a subsidiary corporation established to provide insurance to the parent company and its affiliates not primarily engaged in the business of insurance. A captive may be a single-parent shareholder (pure captive), or a group of shareholders with similar captive risks (group captives). As the name implies, all or a significant portion of the risks written are "captive," related in some way to the risks of shareholders, or third-party risks which the shareholders control.

This approach provides an option for many corporations and groups who wish to take financial control and manage risks by underwriting their own insurance rather than paying premiums to third-party insurers. A captive may underwrite

U.S. risks, foreign risks, or both. The coverage may include workers' compensation, property, liability, employee benefits or malpractice.

WHY FORM A CAPTIVE?

There are numerous advantages to forming a captive, however a company should conduct a feasibility study to determine whether a captive is the best means for the company to achieve its risk management objectives and other goals.

Captives are formed to provide necessary coverage at acceptable prices and for various good economic reasons that include the following:

Tailored coverage to a company's specific needs
Reduction of operating costs

Improved cash flow
Accumulated investment income to fund losses
Increased coverage and capacity for risks uninsurable in conventional markets
Direct access to wholesale reinsurance markets

GUAM'S CAPTIVE INSURANCE LAW

Guam's captive insurance law was created through the enactment of the Captive Insurance Companies Law in Chapter 23, Title 22, Guam Code Annotated. This law was amended in 1997 in order to make easier the formation of a captive in Guam and to create the environment conducive to captive companies. Public Law 23-109 authorizes the Guam Economic Development Authority (GEDA) to offer tax incentives to the insurance industry through its Qualifying Certificate program. A qualifying certificate is a contract issued by the Governor of Guam on the recommendation of GEDA and grants abatements and rebates of all Guam taxes for periods not to exceed twenty (20) years; provided, that the entity remains in good standing under the laws of Guam and GEDA's rules and regulations. Beneficiaries may apply for an extension of the certificate for an additional twenty (20) years.

The major provisions of the Amended Captive Insurance Law are as follows:

The law redefines captive insurance and affiliated companies.
No captive insurance company may directly insure any risks arising in Guam.
Pure captives are required a minimum of $50,000 capital and $100,000 of surplus.
Group captive companies incorporated as a stock insurer are required $100,000 capital and $150,000 surplus.
Incorporated industrial insured captives are required $150,000 capital and $200,000 surplus.
Capital must be in the form of cash deposited in a member bank of the Federal Reserve System licensed to do business in Guam and approved by the

Commissioner.

Surplus may be in the form of cash or an irrevocable letter of credit (LOC). The form of the LOC, or any other form of surplus, must be approved by the Insurance Commissioner.
All information pertaining to Guam captive insurance companies are deemed proprietorial and confidential.

THE LICENSING PROCESS

The initial step in forming a captive in Guam involves an introductory meeting of the applicant and a representative of the Insurance Branch to discuss the captive insurance application process.

Once the application has been completed entirely as instructed by the Insurance Branch with payment of a non-refundable application fee of $200, it can then be submitted. The application will then be forwarded to an independent risk consultant for review, and within 28 calendar days, the applicant will receive

BENEFITS FOR CHOOSING GUAM AS A DOMICILE ~ INSURANCE

100% tax rebates for commercial and captive insurers and reinsurers
100% abatement of all gross receipts taxes on all insurance underwriting income
Established financial services community with FDIC Guarantee
Guam does not require an annual board of directors meeting in the domicile
There is no requirement for proof of necessity
Insurance risks are generally allowed (writing direct Guam risks is prohibited)
Reinsurance business is allowed in Guam
Start up costs include a minimal application fee of $200 and a $2500 licensing fee
Foreign tax credit eligibility in certain cases for

U.S. companies

• Details of captive insurance companies on Guam are kept confidential notification from the Insurance Commissioner. Once the application has been approved and the company has been incorporated and funded, the applicant has 30 days following approval to submit the license fee to the Insurance Branch.

It is strongly suggested that companies seeking to form captives in Guam solicit professional assistance of risk consultants, and supporting professionals who are knowledgeable and familiar with Guam's captive insurance law and the application process in order to facilitate a successful application.

Applications for a Special QC for a captive insurance company or a Guam-based trust receive priority processing, provided all required documents are submitted. More detailed information is available in GEDA's publications booklets on QC's for Insurance and Guam-based Trusts.

Guam Captive Insurance Association

The Guam Captive Insurance Association Corporation (GCIA) was formally organized in 1997. GCIA was formed to support, promote, foster, and market Guam as an attractive and competitive captive insurance domicile; to assist and advise the Insurance Commissioner regarding matters affecting captive insurance companies in Guam; and to support Guam's captive insurance industry with respect to legislative, regulatory and other matters which affect formation or operation of captive insurance companies.

Membership

Membership in GCIA is open to all captive insurance companies licensed in Guam and to all individuals and entities with a bona fide interest consistent with the positive promotion, development and maintenance of captive insurance in Guam. Annual dues are $500 per Corporate member and are not prorated. Two current members of GCIA are needed to sponsor prospective members.

In addition to Guam's Insurance Commissioner (an ex-officio member), plus captives licensed in Guam, GCIA members include captive managers, brokers, financial institutions, accounting firms, legal firms, actuary/risk consultants, insurance companies, and claims administrators, all of whom are either directly involved in captives and/or support the development of a quality captive environment in Guam.

Membership Benefits

- Opportunity to participate in Guam/GCIA promotional events
- Organization/Name listing in captive insurance literature for prospective captive companies
- Annual update of captive insurers
- Opportunity to participate in GCIA's recommendations to the Guam Legislature and other regulatory bodies
- Participation in educational workshops
- Notices of GCIA meetings
- Each member will have one vote in GCIA

Association Committees

Membership/Education Committee: Members in this Committee are responsible for matters relating to membership requirements, fees, and ongoing education.

Legislation/Tax/Accounting Committee: This Committee shall propose and/or review legislative, regulatory, and administrative bills, proposals, and other initiatives which affect the formation and maintenance of captive insurance companies in Guam, and to make recommendations to the GCIA Board regarding same. When appropriate and necessary, the committee shall assist in the drafting of legislative, regulatory and other administrative initiatives which would improve the climate for the formation and maintenance of captives domiciled in Guam.

Marketing Committee: Members in this Committee are responsible for matters relating to marketing Guam as a captive domicile. Conference Committee: This Committee is responsible for planning, organizing, and overseeing annual insurance related conferences to be held in Guam and sponsored in-part by the corporation.

Benefits For Choosing Guam As A Domicile Guam-based Trusts

100% rebate of income tax paid to the government of Guam.
100% rebate of taxes withheld from payments to non-resident beneficiaries of a Guam-based trust.
For trusts originating from the U.S., Guam-based trusts are considered U.S. domestic trust pursuant to Treasury Regulation §301.7701-7(c)(4)(ii)(D)
For trusts originating from foreign sources, Guam offers the stability of the U.S. flag, court system, and dollar-based economy
Guam is not a "tax haven" because taxes are paid prior to their rebate; there is transparency in money transactions; Guam's financial services system, in particular local banks, are regulated by both federal and local law.

Guam-based Trusts

Recent laws also authorize similar tax incentives for Guam-based trusts. These incentives are available through the Qualifying Certificate Program of the Guam Economic Development Authority. Beneficiaries enjoy rebates for a period of twenty years, which may be extended for an additional twenty years if in good standing under the laws of Guam and under the rules and regulations of the Authority.

The major provisions of Guam's trust legislation are:

100% rebate of all income tax paid by a Guam-based trust on all its earning from either inside or outside of Guam, provided administration of the trust is in Guam.
100% rebate of income tax withheld from the non-resident beneficiaries of a Guam-based trust on the payments or distributions made to such beneficiaries from such a Guam-based trust.

Summary

Guam seeks to follow a Bermuda-type model for the development of its financial services industry. Just as Bermuda has become a financial capitol in the Atlantic over the last fifteen years with its financial services industry employing more than 17,000 and generating more than $18 billion per year, Guam is now poised to serve as the financial hub of the Pacific for companies seeking a domicile where they can enjoy attractive tax benefits on worldwide income.

A prosperous international insurance market and trust industry on Guam will also drive additional growth which broadens the island's economic base. Support services like accounting, legal and courier, office supply, and telecommunications are just a few business sectors which grow in connection with the insurance and trust industries. In addition, the deposit of collected premiums and trust corpora in local banks and financial services institutions will significantly broaden the availability of capital, and can stimulate additional investment through convenient, local financing in areas such as hotels, residential homes, and other vitally needed facilities.

For the keen insurance investor, Guam offers the opportunity to operate aggressively in worldwide markets without local taxes, while enjoying the advantages of the stability of U.S. soil, location in a modern island paradise community, state-of-the-art communications, and access to American courts, schools, and health care.

FISHERIES

Transshipment Facilities and Ocean Resources

Fisheries is a leading money-producing industry on Guam, bringing in around $150 million of direct expenditures in 1999. Approximately 9,900 tons of fish valued at more than $99 million were processed through Guam, providing jobs for more than 200 island residents. According to the Western Pacific Regional Fishery Management Council, the port in Guam ranked among the top 10 in the United States ports in terms of the value of fish landing on Guam, at approximately $90 million in 1999.

Prior to 1986 Guam's large-scale offshore fisheries consisted mainly of purse-seiner tuna transshipment. Currently, most of the purse-seiners home porting in Guam are from Korea & Taiwan. Most of the cargo is shipped or transshipped to canneries in Bangkok, Thailand and Korea, with five agents providing services such as fueling provision, equipment and net repairs to these vessels.

Foreign longline fisheries on Guam grew from five vessels in late 1986 to 328 vessels in 1990. During FY1999, longliners made more than 1,661 port calls to the island. Longline transshipment fisheries on Guam consist mainly of Japanese and Taiwanese vessels.

Longline vessels, which fish mainly in the waters of the Federated States of Micronesia, offload their catch (consisting mainly of yellowfin and big-eye tuna) at the commercial port on Guam, where the fish is processed for transshipment by air to Japan for the sashimi markets. Tuna portions that do not meet the required

standards are frozen for container transshipment to canneries or processed locally. Several spin-off industries have resulted from processing nonsashimi-grade tuna, including tuna jerky products, tuna loins and other value-added products. Tests in the export markets in the U.S. mainland and Europe show very good reception to the quality of commercial tuna available out of Guam.

The primary destination of the tuna transshipped is bound for Narita since refrigerated trucking is available to all parts of Japan, but additional markets are found in the cities of Osaka and Nagoya in Japan.

There are currently 13 local agents handling fishing vessels at the port. These agents organize and facilitate procedures involving entry into the commercial port, customs and immigration clearances; purchasing of fuel, water and ship's chandlery; and payments for port call services. These agents also handle the dockside off-loading, inspection, packaging and shipping of the fish.

Lower fuel costs, rest and recreation facilities for ships' crew, medical facilities, modern communications provisioning, equipment and ship repair services are among the factors that attract vessels to Guam. The availability of live bait fish also will increase Guam's attractiveness as a base port for fishing vessels. Bait fish is a particularly marketable item because large tuna fleets are finding that live bait, usually milkfish, is three to five times more effective in increasing the catch rate than dead bait. Obtaining live bait on Guam would save three to four weeks in fishing time, which translates into a savings in ship operating expenses.

Some of Guam's transshipping agents provide live milkfish bait to the tuna longline vessels they service. Live bait farming activities make up a major component of the $2 - $5 million annual local production.

Guam continues to experience growth unmatched by any island or community of its size and population. The success of Guam's fishing industry is proof of Guam's maritime advantages; our natural deep-water seaport and modern airport facilities, our advanced transshipment facilities like modern highways and state-of-the-art storage facilities and the managed resources of the Pacific Ocean are tried and true advantages. Add to these planned improvements and expansion of Guam's port facilities and you have the foundation for lucrative investment opportunities in the maritime industry.

Another major component of Guam's fishery industry is sport-fishing and subsistence fleet, with approximately 300 fishing boats. Approximately 15% of these cater to the tourist market, employing close to 150 residents. Catch from the rest of these boats provide most of the fresh seafood for the resident market and support a $1.3 million fishermen's cooperative.

Aquaculture

Currently Guam imports $7 million worth of seafood annually, to supplement the $2 to $5 million annual local production. The main species grown on Guam are both fresh and saltwater shrimp, milk fish, tilapia, catfish, eels, and ornamental (aquarium) fish. There is great potential if current imports can be substituted with local production.

The University of Guam College of Agriculture and Live Sciences and the Guam Department of Agriculture support the efforts of the farmers by providing specialized training and technical assistance.

There are currently over 100 acres of fish farms in operation on Guam. Because of the island's proximity to the Japanese market, a European fish farm group has seen the viability of growing seafood on Guam and is proposing a $30 million investment to start a salt water salmon farm. Such a project would create about 100 jobs for island residents.

The government of Guam is negotiating with investors in the development and operation of Hotel Wharf at Guam's port. The proposed facility, to include cold storage facilities, auction house and recreational facilities for visiting crews, is designed to make Guam a major fishing hub in Micronesia.

TELECOMMUNICATIONS

Privatization of Guam Telephone Authority (GTA)

The Guam Telephone Authority (GTA) is Guam's exclusive local exchange carrier, with about 40% of the local cellular telephone market. As a result of the Telecommunications Act of 1996 that deregulated the telecommunications industry, GTA is now seeking proposals for privatization. According to a Coopers and Lybrand study, GTA is assessed at a value of $20 to $60 million.

New and Emerging Technologies

The introduction of digital technology has radio systems will also be turned into a digital system, with a new technology known as Integrated Dispatch Enhanced Network (iDEN).

The merger of a cable TV company with an Internet provider will be offering cable modem Internet service to Guam customers, so that accessing the Internet will be as simple as turning on a television set. Digital technology will also facilitate the convergence of data and voice. One company with 71 IP (Internet Protocol) gateways throughout the world, including Guam, is working on a combination of the Internet and voice (VoIP), making Guam the Asia Pacific centerpoint of their managed VoIP network.

Call centers on Guam could take advantage of the island's location for warehousing goods for transshipment into Asia in e-commerce by reducing the delivery time required.

Guam is considered the telecommunications hub of the Western Pacific, all transpacific undersea cables pass through Guam to and from Asia. Guam has a telecommunications infrastructure in place far exceeding most communities with equivalent population. Guam's fixed line, mobile, cable and satellite communications infrastructure support a full range of domestic and international services encompassing voice, video, data, internet and other advance communication services.

The enactment of the (U.S. Congress) Telecommunications Act of 1996 ("Telecom Act") resulted in Guam becoming a part of the North American Numbering Plan and changed its country code to an area code to an area code (671) of the U.S. affording residents with inexpensive communication to the U.S. U.S. toll free service (800, 888, 877 and 866 prefixes) is also accessible from Guam.

GTA is Guam's local exchange carrier and serves over 70,000 subscribers on the island-wide underground fiber optic rings its infrastructure and is built to withstand a Category 5 typhoon. Services include ISDN and T1 networks and for small businesses, the basic rate interface offers multiple channels for data transfer and can run a couple of applications simultaneously. For larger organizations, primary rate interface has as many as 30 channels operating at 2 MB per second to operate a number of applications at once. With a local business line, GTA will set up the phone system and provide monthly inside wire maintenance. For an additional low monthly fee, they also offer useful services such as caller id, call forwarding, and 3-way conference calling.

Basic Monthly Phone Service Rates:	
Residential – single line	$14.00
Security Deposit – one time charge	$35.00
Business – single line	$36.00
Business – rotary line	$39.00
Business – truck line	$49.00
Security Deposit – one time charge	$90.00

The Telecom Act also changed the status of Guam from an international location between the U.S. to a domestic location. This change applied rate integration to Guam, requiring carriers to provide interstate rates between Guam and the US that are comparable to the rates they charge in the rest of the nation.

Long distance and wireless plans to fit a companies unique requirements are offered by a number of companies in Guam – GTA, GuamCell Communications, IT&E Overseas, Inc., Verizon, Pacific Telecom, Inc. (PTI), TelePacific Network, Inc. (TNI), Hafa Tel and I Connect under TDMA and/or GSM mobile network.

Average Long Distance Service Rates:	(per minute)
U.S.A, Puerto Rico, USVI	$0.10
CNMI	$0.10
Hong Kong	$0.17
South Korea	$0.17
Taiwan	$0.17
China	$0.17
Australia	$0.17
Canada	$0.20
Japan	$0.20
Philippines	$0.21
Singapore	$0.25
American Samoa	$0.30
Palau	$0.40
Micronesia	$0.65

Internet connectively through either ISP dial-up or DSL is provided by MCV Kuentos, IT&E, GuamCell, PTI and GTA's Spyder integrated Internet service.

Internet Service Rates: (monthly)	
Dial-up	$13.95 to $34.00
High speed DSL	$44.95 to $45.95
CableNet	$34.95 to $62.45

The U.S. Federal Communications Commission (FCC) regulates all interstate and international telecommunications facilities and services in Guam.

Media

Guam is served by four (4) English-language newspapers, the Pacific Daily News, the Marianas Variety, the Marianas Business Journal and the Pacific Navigator. The Pacific Daily News is

Guam's primary newspaper with a circulation of 26,000. It focuses mainly on the issues that affect local residents. The Marianas Variety and the Marianas Business Journal are wider in scope covering the Marianas chain of islands. The Pacific Navigator is centered on military events and is published by the US Navy in Guam.

Guam has fifteen (15) radio stations and four (4) local TV stations (KUAM, KGTF, Pacific News Center and the Marianas Cable Vision). The Marianas Cable Vision is also the island's sole provider of digital cable service.

Media Links:

- Pacific Daily News - http://www.guampdn.com
- Marianas Variety - http://www.mvariety.com
- KUAM - http://www.kuam.com
- Pacific News Center - http://www.pacificnewscenter.com

FILM INDUSTRY

Vision 2005 has identified film festivals as a desirable attraction to showcase the film productions of our neighboring countries. U.S. Hollywood-based and Japanese film producing companies have both expressed interest in Guam as a potential site for shooting a full length film. Another Hollywood-based production group is proposing to bring the most technically advanced equipment to establish a sound studio on Guam with a post production facility. Their plans are to make Guam a center point where film groups can rent or purchase this equipment for their regional film production.

LAND OPPORTUNITIES

Excess Federal Lands

Nestled in the middle of Guam is a military base the U.S. Navy used during the first half of the 20th century. As part of the Base Realignment and Closure decision of the

U.S. Congress in 1993, the U.S. Navy terminated its operation in the Naval Air Station in Agana. To counterbalance the significant economic impact on Guam caused by the closing of the former Naval Air Station, now known as "Tiyan," GEDA has developed a re-use plan aimed to provide opportunities to stimulate Guam's economy, creating long-term employment and maximizing financial returns to the investor as well as to the original Tiyan landowners.

In September 2000, the U.S. Navy conveyed a total of 1,800+ acres of excess federal lands via quitclaim deeds to the Government of Guam, the single largest land transfer since 1950. Plans for the property deeded to GEDA for economic development purposes include a free trade zone (89 acres), commercial plaza (49 acres), government center (66 acres), and industrial park (31 acres).

Located atop the Tiyan Bluff in central Guam, the Tiyan Economic Development Zone is situated within the most heavily populated areas and within a two mile radius of the majority of the island's business and tourist destinations. It is close to the international airport, Guam's main post office, and the main thoroughfares that traverse the island. Commercial, industrial and warehouse facilities and land in the area are adequately serviced by water, sewer, and supportive infrastructure.

Projected growth will occur as a result of increased local demand, development of the islands in Micronesia and expansion of the Asia-Pacific markets. GEDA will be recruiting qualified investors through the issuance of requests for proposals for the development and economic use of these facilities. To receive such requests for proposals, interested parties may contact GEDA at the addresses shown below:

Guam Economic Development Authority Suite 511, ITC Building 590 S. Marine Drive Tamuning, Guam 96911 Tel: (671) 647-4332 Fax: (671) 649-4146 Email: investguam@geda.guam.net

The local government is fully committed to promoting the viability of businesses and welcomes foreign investment. A public-private partnership to develop the Tiyan Economic Development Zone will foster profitability while allowing the Government of Guam to achieve its developmental, employment and modernization goals.

Private Lands for Development

There are privately owned lands that are available for sale, lease or development under a joint venture. More information regarding these properties can be obtained by contacting the Guam Board of Realtors at http://www.guamrealtors.com. GEDA's website at http://www.investGuam.com also contains a Land Information System (LIS) describing government and privately-owned properties for development.

Tax incentives ~ Qualifying Certificate Program ~ Special Qualifying Certificate for Insurance Companies ~ Special Qualifying Certificate for Guam-based Trusts

Trade Incentives ~ Headnote 3(a) ~ Generalized System of Preferences ~ Other Incentives ~ Guam Product Seal

Financial Assistance Programs

Investor Services ~ Customized Government-to-Business Services ~ Land Information System ~ Guam Investor Guest Book ~ World Wide Web

TAX INCENTIVES

Firms licensed to do business on Guam pay a territorial income tax based on sections of the

U.S. Internal Revenue Code applicable to Guam; however, they do not pay federal income taxes.

Interest earned by a bank through the operation of an off-shore lending facility in Guam is not treated as a Guam source income for tax purposes.

Qualifying Certificate Program

The Government of Guam, through the Guam Economic Development Authority, is authorized by law to allow tax rebates to qualified investors. Qualifying Certificates for tax incentives are granted on the basis of investment commitment as well as the potential for creating new employment and expanding the base of the island's industry. These incentives are aimed primarily at manufacturers, insurance companies, trusts, commercial fishing companies, corporate headquarters, specialized medical facilities, high technology, agricultural and tourism development firms.

Qualified firms may be granted up to 100% income tax rebates for a maximum of 20 years; 100% abatement on real property tax for a maximum of 10 years; up to 75% rebate on corporate dividend tax for a maximum of 5 years; and abatement on gross receipts tax on petroleum and alcoholic beverages made in Guam for a maximum of 10 years.

Public Laws 23-135 and 24-266 allow developers of qualified hotels and tourist facilities to provide funds needed to "jump start" the construction of affordable housing on Guam, in exchange for enlarged tax benefits.

These two laws also provide a two-year period (extendible for another two years at the discretion of the GEDA Board) whereby eligible developers of hotels and tourist facilities may apply for these benefits under GEDA's Qualifying Certificate program. These expanded benefits include:

Exemption of Gross Receipts Taxes for suppliers of building materials & supplies, contractors for labor/supervision furnished for a qualified project.
Exemption of Use Tax by the owner of the hotel/tourist facilities.
Rebate of Rental Income, up to 50% for the first 5 years and up to 25% for the next 5 years, to the lessor of land, buildings, machinery/equipment to QC holder for hotel/ tourist facilities.
Rebate of Capital Gains, up to 50%, to the seller of land and other real property to hotel/ tourist facility of affordable housing developer.

Special Qualifying Certificates for Insurance Companies

Insurance issuers – whether reinsurers, commercial insurers or captive insurers – whose headquarters are located in Guam, may enjoy the following benefits:

100% abatement of gross receipts tax on insurance premiums.
100% rebate of income taxes resulting from the operation of an insurance underwriting entity.
100% rebate of income tax withheld from shareholders of an insurance underwriting business on the dividends from such business.

Special Qualifying Certificate for Guam-based Trusts

Guam-based trusts may receive the following benefits:

100% rebate of income tax paid to the government of Guam.
100% rebate of taxes withheld from payments to non-resident beneficiaries of a Guam-based trust.

These incentives are made available through the Qualifying Certificate program of the Guam Economic Development Authority. Beneficiaries of the qualifying certificate may enjoy the abatements or rebates for a period of up to 20 years, which may be renewed for additional periods of 20 years so long as they remain in good standing under the laws of Guam and under the rules and regulations of the Authority.

TRADE INCENTIVES

Headnote 3(A)

The General Headnote 3(a) program of the Tariff Schedules of the United States (TSUS) allows duty-free entry into the U.S. Customs Territory for those items manufactured or assembled in Guam that meet certain requirements that enable Guam to be considered the "country of origin." Manufacturers may import foreign raw materials or component parts, to which at least 30% (in some cases, 50%) of the value of the finished product must be added on Guam. These items must undergo a "substantial transformation" in order to benefit from the duty free provision of this program. It is advisable for an exporter to obtain a binding ruling as to whether the specific article meets the criteria for a duty-free (in certain cases, quota free) entry in the

U.S. Customs Territory, by writing to the director, classification and value division, U.S. Customs Service, 1301 Constitution Avenue, N.W., Washington, D.C. 20229.

Generalized System of Preferences

Another trade incentive program allows products manufactured in Guam to be imported by participating nations at a reduced tariff rate. Guam is the beneficiary of the following countries: Japan, Australia and the European Common Market nations. Requirements of each participant vary, so interested exporters should contact the appropriate trade office of the particular country of destination.

OTHER INCENTIVES

Guam Product Seal

To help promote products made on Guam for the tourism industry and to enhance export potential, Public Law 18-42 created the Guam Product Seal to identify products manufactured on Guam. To be eligible, a manufacturer must:

Possess a valid Guam business license
Substantially transform the material(s) so that the final product is converted into "a different and distinguishable commercial use or character" when completed
Must add value of at least 50 percent of the production cost on Guam

Financial Assistance Programs

GEDA administers several loan programs to assist local businesses with financing for startup and expansion. The Guam Development Fund Act (GDFA) provides financing in areas of agriculture, aquaculture, manufacturing, tourism, commercial support industries and any other industry that GEDA's board of directors determines will improve the island's economy. The Agriculutural Development Fund offers low interest loans to bonafide commercial farmers and agricultural related businesses. The Chamorro Heritage Foundation Program provides loans or grants for activities that preserve, develop and enhance the Chamorro culture and heritage of the indigenous people of Guam.

For loans under the GDFA, applicants must demonstrate that they have sought and were declined financial assistance under reasonable terms and conditions from at least three private lenders on island. Following are other prerequisites applicants must meet: 1) If a sole proprietorship, the owner must be a resident of Guam and either a U.S. citizen or permanent resident alien; 2) If a partnership or corporation, the entity must be registered with the Government of Guam's Department of Revenue and Taxation; 3) All applicants must be licensed to do business on Guam.

INVESTOR SERVICES

Customized Government-to-business Services

For qualified projects, the Guam Economic Development Authority provides individually designed assistance to the serious prospective investor. Friendly and competent services by industry specialists range from initial consultations, in person or by mail, to arranging meetings with pertinent authorities and facilitation during the licensing process.

Land information system

The Guam Economic Development Authority maintains an inventory of government and private lands that are available for development. The information can be accessed via the Internet at http://geda.guam.org:591. Interested investors may obtain additional information by contacting GEDA by telephone at (671) 647-4332; by facsimile at (671) 649-4146; by email at investGuam@geda.guam.net. The Land Information System is provided as a public service by the Guam Economic Development Authority.

Guam Investor Guest Book

A new component of GEDA's website at http:// www.investguam.com is the Investor Guest Book, designed to facilitate contact between investors and entreprenuers seeking investment capital for Guam-based projects. Those who wish to post investment opportunities for Guam-based projects may do so on-line at http://www.investguam.com> or by filling out the Investor Guest Book form directly with the Authority.

World Wide Web

For updated information on current developments, please visit GEDA's webpage at www.investGuam.com. We also welcome your comments, suggestions and individual inquiries.

ECONOMIC DEVELOPMENT AUTHORITY

Guam Economic Development Authority Suite 511 ITC Building • 590 South Marine Drive, Tamuning, Guam 96911 Telephone: (671)647-4332 • Facsimile: (671)649-4146 Internet: www.investGuam.com • Email: investGuam@geda.guam.net © 2000 Guam Economic Development Authority

INVESTMENT AND BUSINESS CLIMATE

For the adventurous investor looking for new and unexplored investment opportunities Guam, USA, offers unique advantages.

Our island's diverse geographic characteristics and ideal positioning within the Pacific basin, supportive business environment, stable and permanent political system, stewardship of the U.S. flag, and hospitable community are major pluses to put at the top of your list when considering investment on Guam. Guam is the largest and southernmost island of the Marianas Islands chain. Formed through the fiery birth and re-birth of undersea volcanoes millions of years ago, Guam's topography boasts southern mountains and the high limestone northern plateau. Coral reefs are the foundation of a paradise 30 miles long with an overall land area of 212 square miles. This geographic diversity is the basis for an island whose character ranges from the white sand beaches and limestone jungles of the north to volcanic mountains blanketed by sprawling savannas and tropical rain forests in the south. Our climate is tropical in nature and remains pleasantly warm throughout the year, with temperatures ranging from 75 to 86 degrees farenheit.

Guam was the first Pacific island discovered by the western world. Then, as now, it served as the gateway to Asia, America and the Pacific region around it.

Situated only three hours by plane from Tokyo and Manila, four hours from Hong Kong and Taipei, five to six hours from Seoul, Singapore, Bangkok and Australia, and only seven hours from Hawaii, Guam truly is the hub of the Western Pacific.

For more information on Guam's Geography, Topography and Climate, visit the official Guam, USA website: www.gov.gu .

BUSINESS CLIMATE

In addition to an enticing climate and prime location, Guam USA offers a strong business environment in which to develop and grow a successful company.

The proof of Guam's viability as a thriving commercial center is evidenced by the many international companies who have already made Guam their home and the successful local companies who contribute to the strength of the business community. A quick glance through the Guam Chamber of Commerce membership directory will reveal names of world renowned hotels such as Hilton, Hyatt, Nikko, Westin, Sherwood, and Outrigger; international financial institutions like Bank of Hawaii and Hongkong Bank, and international retailers such as Duty Free, K-Mart, Liberty House, Chanel, Gucci, United Colors of Benneton, and Esprit. Restaurant chains including Sizzler, Pizza Hut, Maxim's, Jolly Bee, Burger King, McDonald's, Wendy's, Lone Star, Tony Roma's and Denny's can be found throughout the island. Tumon is also the home of TGI Friday's, Hard Rock Cafe and the Planet Hollywood Restaurant. Guam invites you to discover the lucrative results companies such as these derive through their operations on Guam.

INFRASTRUCTURE

During the late 1980's and early 1990's Guam reaped the economic benefits created by astounding growth in its tourism industry. The increased government revenues generated by this growth allowed for a community investment into the expansion and enhancement of our island's infrastructure.

POWER

Guam's public power system is managed by the Guam Power Authority (GPA), one of over 2,000 public utilities in the United States. As a result of investments made in the creation of new generation facilities and the refurbishment of existing assets, Guam's current power generation capacity stands at 502 megawatts and provides power to more than 42,000 customers.

In addition to capital investments designed to expand the island's power assets, GPA has also implemented unique incentives to promote efficient use of power. One of these programs is the Guam Energy Sense incentive which offers up to $25,000 in rebates to commercial users who purchase and install energy efficient equipment. The energy-wise equipment also helps reduce utility bills and conserve power.

In order to build system reliability and accommodate growth on Guam, GPA has entered into twenty-year agreements with three Independent Power Producers to enhance generation capacities. Two of these are already in place and another scheduled to be online as early as the first part of 1999.

POPULATION AND LABOR

Guam has a population of 159,827 inclusive of the military.

Guam's labor laws are patterned after those of the U.S. and regulated by the Guam Department of Labor. The Governor of Guam is vested with the authority to issue temporary labor certifications on Guam if, after testing the local labor market, it is found that: qualified U.S. Citizens or permanent residents are not available to perform the required services and that employment of a non-immigrant alien will not adversely affect the wages and working conditions of U.S. resident workers who are similarly employed on Guam. This temporary certification is issued by the Guam Department of Labor for a period of one year or less. Extensions may be granted for a period not to exceed three consecutive years. Minimum wage is set by the prevailing U.S. rates.

EMPLOYMENT BY INDUSTRY	
INDUSTRY	JUNE
Agriculture	300
Construction	6,350
Manufacturing	1,770
Transportation and Utilities	5,600
Wholesale Trade	2,170
Retail Trade	12,520
Finance, Insurance and Real Estate	2,720
Services	14,880
Federal Government	5,000
Government of Guam	16,980 *
TOTAL	66,380
* Includes 3,070 disaster recovery & summer youth under AHRD	

AVERAGE HOURLY WAGES		
BUSINESS SECTOR	AVERAGE EARNINGS PER HOUR	AVERAGE HOURS PAID PER WEEK
Agriculture	$7.99	29.10
Construction	$11.99	44.00
Manufacturing	$11.63	38.80
Transportation & Public Utilities	$14.24	33.30
Wholesale Trade	$11.75	40.00
Retail Trade	$8.62	34.40
Finance, Insurance & Real Estate	$10.89	38.20

Services	$8.23	36.20

The diverse cultural composition of Guam's population provides a unique human resource for the specialized language, cultural and skilled needs of any regional operation.

INVESTMENT INCENTIVES

The Guam Economic Development and Authority (GEDA) is a public corporation and an agency of the government of Guam, created to assist in the implementation of an integrated program for the economic development of Guam.

GEDA promotes the investment of entrepreneurial capital by developing and maintaining facilities for lease or sale, providing incentives for the establishments and/or expansion of targeted industries and facilities through financial assistance (direct and guaranteed loans) and various incentive tools (see Qualifying Certificate Program).

GEDA Business Development and Marketing Division provides assistance to prospective investors with certain development requirements such as licensing, site identification and/or acquisition, and obtaining land use permits. The Public Finance Division markets and manages the island's bond issuances to increase the supply of money and provides financing for projects approved by the Guam Legislature.

For the keen investor, Guam offers the opportunity to operate aggressively in worldwide markets without local taxes, while enjoying the advantages of the stability under the U.S. flag, location in a modern island paradise community, state-of-the-art communications, and access to American courts, schools and health care.

QUALIFYING CERTIFICATE PROGRAM

The government of Guam, through GEDA, is authorized by law to allow a variety of tax incentives to encourage new investment by qualified investors to Guam. GEDA grants Qualifying Certificates to investors on the basis of investment commitment, potential for creating employment and expanding the base of the island's economy. These incentives are intended primarily for the businesses engaging in tourism, manufacturing, agriculture, commercial fishing, insurance, and facilities and services deemed vital to Guams economic growth.

Tax incentives for qualified firms may include:

Up to 75% in corporate income tax rebates (up to 20 years)
100% abatement on real property tax (up to 10 years) (fee simple ownership only) ß A maximum of 75% rebate on corporate dividend tax (up to five years)
100% abatement on business privelage receipts tax on petroleum and alcoholic beverages (up to 10 years)

Special Qualifying Certificates for Financial Services Industries: Spurred by increasing inquiries from insurance underwriters throughout the world, Public Law 23-109 was enacted to provide for 100% abatement of business privelage taxes on insurance premiums and other revenues and 100% rebates on all income taxes of an insurance underwriting entity domiciled on Guam. Beneficiaries can enjoy rebates for a period of twenty (20) years, which may be extended for an additional twenty years if in good standing under the laws of Guam and GEDA rules and regulations.

Guam-based Trusts: Guam law also authorize similar tax incentives for Guam-based trusts through the Qualifying Certificate program. Benefits for choosing Guam as a domicile for Guam-based trusts include 100% rebate of income tax paid to the government of Guam by a Guam-based trust on all its earning from either inside or outside of Guam, provided administration of the trust is in Guam, and 100% rebate of income tax withheld from the non-resident beneficiaries of a Guam-based trust on the payments or distributions made to such beneficiaries from such a Guam-based trust.Beneficiaries can enjoy rebates for a period of twenty years, which may be extended for an additional twenty years if in good standing under the laws of Guam and GEDA rules and regulations.

Telecommunications: Tax benefits are available for e-commerce and Internet systems to include rebate of a percentage of income tax and shareholders dividends tax and an abatement of real property tax under GEDA's primary QC program.

ADDITIONAL FINANCIAL SERVICES INCENTIVE

Offshore Banking: The absence of federal income taxes, and the fact that interest earned by banks through the operation of an offshore lending facility in Guam is not treated as a Guam-source income for tax purposes are also powerful incentives for investment.

MANUFACTURING AND TRADE INCENTIVES

General Headnote 3(a): The General Headnote 3(a) program of the Tariff Schedules of the United States allows duty-free entry into the United States on most exports for those items manufactured and assembled in Guam. Certain requirements enable Guam to be considered the "country of origin." Manufacturers may import foreign raw materials or component parts, to which at least 50% of the value of the finished product must be added on Guam. These items must undergo a "substantial transformation" in order to benefit from the duty-free provision of this program.

Generalized System of Preferences: Another trade incentive program allows products manufactured in Guam to be imported by participating nations at a reduced tariff rate. Guam currently has arangements with the following countries: Japan, Australia, and the European Common Market nations. Requirements of each participant vary and interested exporters should contact the appropriate trade office of the particular country of destination.

TOURISM, IMMIGRATION AND FOREIGN INVESTMENT

Guam Immigrant Investor Visa Program: The EB-5 Investor Visa was created under the Immigration Act of 1990. This visa category allows qualified applicants to obtain lawful Permanent Resident Status (Green Cards) through investment in a U.S. enterprise. Ten thousand (10,000) Immigrant Visas are available each year to foreign investors establishing a "new commercial enterprise" or is actively in the process of investing in the enterprise in Guam.

A "new commercial enterprise" is any lawful, for-profit business established after November 29, 1990. Both the creation of a new business, and the purchase and re-capitalization or reorganization of an existing business is allowed.

Minimum investment in the fifty US States is $1,000,000, however Guam has been granted an exemption by the US Citizenship & Immigration Services reducing the minimum investment requirement to $500,000.

Guam Visa Waiver Program: This program allows residents of 36 nations to travel to Guam, as tourists or to conduct business, for a maximum stay of 15 days without having to obtain a visa. Countries currently covered by this program include: Andorra, Australia, Austria, Belgium, Brunei, Denmark, Finland, France, Germany, Iceland, Ireland, Italy, Japan, Liechtenstein, Luxemburg, Monaco, the Netherlands, New Zealand, Norway, Portugal, San Marino, Singapore, Slovenia, Spain, Sweden, Switzerland, United Kingdom, Indonesia, Republic of South Korea, Malaysia, Nauru, Papua New Guinea, Solomon Islands, Taiwan, Vanuatu and Western Samoa. All other visitors must conform to U.S. passport and visa requirements.

For more information, please contact: The Guam Economic Development Authority
ITC Building, Suite 511
Tel: (671) 647-4332 590 South Marine Corps Drive
Fax: (671) 649-4146 Tamuning, Guam 96913
e-mail: help@investguam.com
or visit www.investguam.com as of 6/2009

STARTING BUSINESS: GENERAL INFORMATION

On Guam, as in all states of the United States, there are many laws, rules and regulations governing business activities. Guam has adopted the provisions of the Uniform Commercial Code. Most of the laws and procedures encountered in transacting business on Guam are similar to those in the United States.

REGISTRATION OF A BUSINESS

All corporations, partnerships, joint ventures, and associations must register with the Business License Branch of the Department of Revenue and Taxation, located in Tiyan. Their mailing address is: Bldg. 13-1 2nd Floor, Mariner Drive, Tiyan, Guam 96913. Registration must take place prior to the issuance of any business license. All trade names or DBA's (doing business as) to be used in conjunction with a business (whether proprietary, partnership, corporate, or other forms) must be registered with the same branch.

LICENSING A BUSINESS

The Government of Guam requires all businesses to have a license, whether a corporation, partnership, sole proprietor, or other form. To ensure that efficient and adequate assistance and support are made available to all prospective businesses, the Government of Guam has established the One Stop Building and Business License Service Center, where application forms may be picked up and the applicant will be advised of the required clearances depending on the type of license to be obtained. Licenses are renewable every June. General qualifications are: applicant must be at least 18 years of age, owe no taxes and be of good moral character. Questions regarding the various processes & fee schedules involved regarding permitting and licensing should be sent to:

One Stop Service Center
P.O. Box 2950
Hagatna (Agana), Guam 96910

Telephone (671) 472-7867, 475-4540
Fax: (671) 472-2128.

BUSINESS STRUCTURE

The Civil Code of Guam governs all corporations, whether profit or non-profit, stock or non-stock. There are two basic types of corporations authorized to transact business on Guam:

DOMESTIC CORPORATION

Domestic corporations are those formed in Guam by the voluntary association of three or more persons in the manner prescribed for any lawful purpose. Articles of Incorporation must be filed with the Business License Branch at Department of Revenue and Taxation, setting forth the name, purpose, place of the principal office in Guam, term not to exceed 50 years, names and residences of incorporators, the number of its directors (not less than 3 nor more than 7), amount of capital stock, etc. The Articles must be accompanied by the statement of the Treasurer showing that at least 20% of the entire capital stock has been subscribed and at least 25% of that subscription has been paid. The secretary or treasurer of a domestic corporation must be a resident of Guam. Foreign Sales Corporations are considered domestic as defined in Sec. 922(a) of the Internal Revenue Code and Sec. 278 of the Civil Code of Guam.

LIMITED LIABILITY CORPORATIONS & LIMITED LIABILITY PARTNERSHIPS

P.L. 23-65 and P.L. 23-125 allow Guam to recognize Limited Liability Partnerships (LLP's) and Limited Liaiblity Corporations (LLC's) which deliver the key advantages of "pass-through taxation" and limited liability for its owners and permit them to operate with less formality. Professionals still remain liable for their professional performance. Pursuant to P.L. 24-103, LLP's and LLC's are eligible to apply for benefits under the GEDA Qualifying Certificate program.

FOREIGN CORPORATIONS

All off-island corporations are considered foreign. A foreign corporation must obtain a Foreign Corporation License and a Certificate of Registration before being permitted to transact business on Guam. The managing agent of the corporation must file a notarized statement including the name, purpose, location of home office, capital stock, net assets, resident agent of Guam, accompanied by a certified copy of the Articles of Incorporation and a certificate that the corporation has been established according to the laws of the place of incorporation. A Certificate of Good Standing, usually prepared by the Secretary of State must also be furnished. In the case of other foreign (alien) corporations, it must be issued by a U.S. Consul.

SPECIFIC BUSINESS ACTIVITIES

Certain laws, rules, and procedures have been established for specific professions, businesses and trades. Standards are established by various boards, administrators, commissions, etc. as specified by various sections of the Government Code of Guam.

ALCOHOLIC BEVERAGE CONTROL

The sale, import or manufacture of alcoholic beverages in Guam is subject to the Alcoholic Beverage Control Act. The Alcoholic Beverage Control Board is authorized to issue licenses for wholesale, retail and manufacture of alcohol, agents, clubs, etc. Individuals or partners applying for a license must have resided in Guam for at least one year at the time of application. If the applicant is a corporation, the majority of the members of the Board of Directors must be Guam residents for at least one year.

ATTORNEYS

The District Court of Guam may admit persons who have been certified by the committee of examiners of the Judicial Council to practice law. In addition to passing the Guam Bar Exam, applicants must meet residency and educational requirements. The Attorneys Act specifies regulations on duties, discipline, disbarment, etc.

BANKING

Applications by new banks are made to the Commissioner of Banking (Director of Revenue and Taxation). Banks incorporated in a foreign country may maintain a branch office in Guam, but shall not conduct a domestic banking business.

BUILDING

The Building Law provides detailed standards and requirements for the location, design, construction, repair, use, occupancy, removal, etc. of building and structures. It is administered by the Director of Public Works. All buildings must follow the Uniform Building Code, National Electrical Code and Uniform Plumbing Code, which are the acceptable standards used on the U.S. mainland.

CERTIFIED PUBLIC ACCOUNTANCY

Annual permits to practice as Certified Public Accountants are issued by the Director of Revenue and Taxation to holders of certificates which are granted by the Territorial Board of Public Accountancy to persons who have passed the examination and met the other requirements of the Territorial Board of Public Accountancy.

CONTRACTOR

Application for a Contractor's License shall be made with the Guam Contractors Licensing Board. Applicants must meet statutory requirements, pass an examination and obtain clearance from the Departments of Revenue and Taxation, Land Management, Labor and Public Works.

CONSUMER CREDIT

The Uniform Consumer Credit Code governs credit transactions such as retail installment sales, consumer credit, small loans and usury. It is administered by the Savings and Loans Commissioner (Director of Revenue and Taxation) and is applicable to all businesses extending credit to customers.

COSMETOLOGY

The Cosmetology Law requires registration and licensing of cosmetologists, electrologists, manicurists and cosmetology instructors. A Board of Cosmetology administers the rules and regulations prescribed by this law.

ENGINEERS, ARCHITECTS, LAND SURVEYORS

Application for registration as one of these professionals is made to the Board of Engineering and Architectural Examiners (Department of Public Works). The Board issues a certificate of registration, renewable annually, to applicants who meet all the requirements. Firms may obtain a permit for a regular business license after registration of members.

INSURANCE UNDERWRITERS

An individual, partnership or corporation desiring to transact business in Guam as an insurer must first be admitted and may transact only those classes of insurance specifically authorized in the Certificate of Authority issued by the Commissioner of Insurance. Applications are filed with the Commissioner of Insurance at the Guam Department of Revenue & Taxation.

SAVINGS AND LOAN

The Savings and Loan Commissioner (Director of Revenue and Tax) administers and enforces the Savings and Loan Association Act. Savings and loan associations require a certificate of approval from the Commissioner and a business license.

SECURITIES

Application for registration as a broker-dealer, agent, or investment advisor is made to the securities administrator (Director of Revenue and Taxation). Securities sold in Guam must be registered unless specifically exempt.

TRADE PRACTICES

The Trade Practices and Consumer Protection Law defines and prohibits unfair methods of competition and unfair or deceptive practices such as false advertising, false origin of goods, misrepresentation, etc. It applies to all businesses in trade and commerce.

OTHERS

Other local laws and requirements which are of interest to certain businesses include Zoning, Subdivision, Vehicle Code, Workmen's Compensation, Fair Labor Standards, etc. Establishing a new business in Guam or maintaining and expanding an established business require compliance with applicable laws and requirements (including payment of applicable fees).

COSTS OF DOING BUSINESS

AVERAGE ELECTRICITY RATES

For residential services, the monthly service charge is $5.21. The first 500 kilowatt hours are $.03354 each per month, and over 500 kilowatt hours increases to $.07950 each.
For General Service, power rates run $.18916 per kilowatt hour for the first 200 used each month, and $.17198 thereafter.
For Large Power Service (demand in excess of 200 kilowatts per day) the cost ranges between $.17917 and $.22797 per kilowatt hour.

SHIPPING

For general cargo and merchandise, a general listing of rates is as follows:		
Destination	Out Bound Rate	Incoming Rate
Manila	$1,779.10	$1,950.00
HongKong	$1,779.10	$1,950.00
Taiwan	$1,779.10	$1,950.00
Japan	$2,093.00	$2,099.60
Korea	$2,093.00	$2,099.60
U.S. - East	$2,750.00*	**
U.S. - West	$2,190.00*	$2,700.00*
*Freight of all kinds (Not including port fees and agent charges).		
** Depends on type of commodities		

AIR FREIGHT

Air Freight Rates depend upon the origin and destination of the shipment. Prices may be negotiable and vary according to the type of commodity.		
AVERAGE AIR FARES TO SELECTED DESTINATIONS		
(does not include special rates, promotions, etc.)		
Destination	R/T - Excursion	R/T - Business
Japan	$473.00	$875.00
Philippines	$460.00	$1,016.00
Hong Kong	$751.00	$1,141.00
Taiwan	$551.00	$790.00
Hawaii	$933.00	$2,300.00
U.S. - West Coast	$1,133.00	$3,100.00
Korea	$603.00	$881.00
Australia	$1,396.00	$4,692.00

APPROXIMATE FUEL COSTS

Fuel Type	Full Service	Self Service
High Octane Unleaded	$1.869	$1.689
Regular Unleaded	$1.769	$1.549
Diesel	$1.670	$1.670

Approximate Cable Television Costs	
Cable Options	Monthly Cost
Basic Cable (45 channels)	$29.95 per month
Home Box Office	$11.95 per month
Cinemax	$11.95 per month
Showtime, Sundance, Movie Channel	$14.95 Pkg/per month
Additional Outlets	$5.00 per month
Note: discounts available if more than one premium service is requested	
Installation: $25.95	

U.S. POSTAL RATES (DOMESTIC)

First Class Mail	Letter Rates	First Ounce $0.33	Each Additional Ounce* $0.23
	Card Rates	Single Postal Cards = $0.20	Double Postal Cards = $0.38
Second Class Mail	Regular and preferred second-class rates are available to newspapers and periodicals that have been authorized second-class mail privileges.		
Third Class Mail	Circulars, books, catalogs and other items weighing less than 16 ounces.		
Ounces*	Rates	Ounces*	Rates
1	$0.32	7	$1.70
2	$0.55	8	$1.93
3	$0.78	9	$2.16
4	$1.01	10	$2.39
5	$1.24	11	$2.62
6	$1.47	13	$2.90
*For items in excess of 13 but less than 16 ounces - $2.95			

Advertising Costs - Average Costs By Form Of Advertising	
Form of Advertising	Rate
Newspaper	$21.25/column inch
Radio	$50-$80/30 seconds

Television	$112.50/30 seconds, prime time

STARTIGN BUSINESS IN GUAM BASICS

NON-PROFIT ASSOCIATION/ORGANIZATION

Guidelines to follow for registering a Constitiution and By-Laws as a NON-PROFIT ASSOCIATION/ORGANIZATION.

Both documents must be filed with a fee of **$2.00** ($1.00 each).

I. CONSTITUTION

The Name of Association
The Objectives for which the Association is formed
The Location of the principal place of business
Names of the Officers, Title and Residence Address
Filing of Amendments requirements
Must be signed by the Officers and notarized by a Notary Public

II. BY-LAWS

Requirements of Membership and Termination
Requirements on dues
Activities and Functions of the Association
Functions or Duties of the Association
Requirements in setting for meetings
Requirements in collecting and disbursing of dues
Requirements Termination/Dissolution
Must be signed by the Officers and notarized by a Notary Public

NOTE: You may apply for **T A X E X E M P T I O N** at Business Privilege Tax Branch

Requirements for registering a NON PROFIT CORPORATION

CODE PROVISIONS REQUIREMENTS C.C., Section 650.7 1) The **NAME** of the Corporation 2) The **PURPOSE** for which it is formed 3) **LOCATION** of its principal office must be in GUAM 4) The **NAME** and **RESIDENCE ADDRESS** of the DIRECTORS 5) **TERMS** of **EXISTENCE** - must not exceed fifty (50) years 6) Directors must not be less than three (3) nor more than seven (7)

Corporation formed by the voluntary association of three or more persons.

Payment of filing fee of **$50.00** Articles and **$10.00** By-Laws.

Directors named must sign Articles and Acknowledge such execution before a person authorized by law to administer oaths.

C.C., Section 290A **THE** filing of Articles (requires) (does

not require)
the attachment of Certificate of Approval from the Governor as the Corporation will (conduct) (not conduct)
business as executor, administrator, guardian of estates, assignee, receiver, depository or trustee.

C.C., Section 295 **THE** name of the corporation (is) (is not) or (resembles)
(does not resembles) closely that of a domestic or Foreign Corporation that is likely to mislead or tend to deceive the public. It also provides that if the words "Trust" or "Trustee" appear, a certificate
of approval from the Governor must first be obtained.

C.C., Section 308 **THE** Secretary of Treasurer of the Corporation must
be a resident of Guam.

Treasurer must prepare an affidavit that he or she was duly elected Treasurer of this non-stock, non-profit corporation. (This is needed for
we need to know who to contact for the annual report)

NOTE: Public Law 19-10 requires that Articles of Incorporation and
By-Laws are to be prepared by **Attorneys.**

REQUIREMENTS FOR REGISTERING A DOMESTIC CORPORATION IN GUAM

CODE PROVISIONS	REQUIREMENTS
C.C., Section 290	1) **NAME** of the Corporation
	2) **PURPOSE**
	3) **LOCATION** of its principal office - must be in **GUAM**
	4) **NAMES** and **RESIDENCES** of the incorporators
	5) **TERMS** of existence - must not exceed fifty (50) years
	6) **DIRECTORS** must not be less than three (3) nor more than seven (7)
	7) **AMOUNT** of its capital stock in U.S. Currency and number of shares into which it is divided
	8) The amount of **CAPITAL STOCK** actually subscribed, the names and residence of the person subscribing, the amount subscribed by each, and the sum paid by each on his subscription

C.C., Section 285 — Corporation formed by the voluntary association of three (3) or more persons

C.C., Section 290 — Payment of filing fee of **$50.00** (articles) **$10.00**(by-laws)

C.C., Section 290A — The filing of the Articles (requires) (does not requre) the attachment of Certificate of approval from the Governor as the corporation will (conduct) (not conduct) business as executor, administrator, guardian of estates, assignee, receiver, depository or trustee.

C.C., Section 292 — Directors named must sign articles and acknowledged such execution before a person authorized by law to administer oaths

C.C., Section 293 — **Sworn statemnet of Treasurer showing that at least 20 per centum of the entire capital stock has been subscribed and at least 25 per centum of the subscription has been paid to him for the benefit and to credit of the corporation

C.C., Section 295 — The name of the Corporation (is) (is not) or (resembles) (does not resembles) closely that of a Domestic or Foreign corporation that it is likely to mislead or tend to deceive the public. It also provides that if the words "Trust" or "Trustee" appear, a certificate of approval from the Governor must first be obtained

C.C., Section 306 — Every Director own in his own right at least one share of the capital stock of the stock corporation of which he is director

C.C., Section 308 — **The Secretary or Treasurer of the corporation must be a resident of **GUAM**

I. APPLICATION FOR BUSINESS LICENSE

WHERE AN APPLICANT CONDUCTS BUSINESSES IN TWO OR THREE LOCATIONS, HE IS REQUIRED TO OBTAIN A LICENSE FOR EACH LOCATION.

(A) PREPARE IN TRIPLICATE, PRINT OR TYPEWRITE. (B) EXPLANATION OF ITEMS.

FULL NAME OF APPLICANT, PROPRIETOR, PARTNERSHIP NAME, OR CORPORATE NAME. BUSINESS OR TRADE OR FICTITIOUS NAME, IF DIFFERENT FROM 1. BUSINESS MAILING ADDRESS, STATE POST OFFICE BOX NUMBER, IF ANY. TYPE OF LICENSE, CHECK ONLY ONE. A SEPARATE APPLICATION MUST BE FILED FOR EACH LICENSE. SIGNATURE MUST BE SIGNED BY PROPRIETOR, PARTNER, OR AUTHORIZED REPRESENTATIVE. TITLE OR CAPACITY OF PERSON SIGNING SHOULD BE STATED. AUTHORIZED REPRESENTATIVE MUST FURNISH EVIDENCE OF AUTHORITY.

II. GENERAL REQUIREMENTS:

EACH APPLICANT FOR ANY CLASS OR LICENSE MUST:

(A) CLEAR WITH BUSINESS PRIVILEGE TAX(GRT) THAT HE OWES NO OBLIGATION WHICH IS DUE AND OR DELINQUENT TO THE GOVERNMENT OF GUAM.

(B) COMPLETE QUESTIONNAIRE FOR EVIDENCE OF GOOD MORAL CHARACTER, INTEGRITY AND GENERAL REPUTE.

III. ENDORSEMENT:

ENDORSEMENT FOR CERTAIN TYPES OF BUSINESS ACTIVITIES MUST BE OBTAINED FROM COGNIZANT DEPARTMENTS BEFORE A LICENSE CAN BE ISSUED TO DETERMINE THE ENDORSEMENTS REQUIRED, FIND UNDER COLUMN 1 BELOW THE ACTIVITY FOR WHICH LICENSE IS REQUIRED.

(2) ENDORSEMENTS (3) TYPE OF ENDORSEMENTS (1) TYPE OF BUSINESS ACTIVITY REQUIRED (A) HEALTH CERTIFICATE FROM DEPT. OF MEDICAL FOOD PREPARATION AND DISPENSING_____(A) (B) SERVICES FOR EACH PERSON HANDLING FOOD. LIQUID FUEL VENDING_________________(C) (B) HEALTH AND SANITATION CERTIFICATE FROM DEPT. OF MEDICAL SERVICES COVERING PREMISES FIREARM AND AMMUNITION VENDING______(C) WHERE BUSINESS IS TO BE CONDUCTED. BARBER SHOP__________________________(B) (B) (C) SAFETY AND RESPONSIBILITY CERTIFICATE FROM GUAM POLICE DEPT.(RECORDS). BEAUTY SHOP__________________________(A) (B) (D) QUALIFICATION CERTIFICATE FROM DEPT. OF TATTOO ARTIST_______________________(A) (B) PUBLIC WORKS/GUAM BOARD OF CONTRACTORS. PLACE OF AMUSEMENTS_________________(B) (C) (E) QUALIFICATION CERTIFICATE FROM DEPT. OF EDUCATION/U.O.G./G.C.C. ELECTRICIAN_________________________(D) (F) CERTIFICATE FROM DEPT. OF REV. & TAX SHOW- PLUMBER_____________________________(D) ING THAT APPLICANT HAS LEGALLY PROVIDED FOR SERVICE OF PROCESS TO BE MADE UPON HIM BY CONTRACTOR__________________________(D) SERVICE UPON THE DIRECTOR OF REV & TAX IN THE EVENT SUCH PERSON CANNOT PERSONALLY BE PRIVATE SCHOOL______________________(B) (E) SERVED IN GUAM. AGENT AND ITINERANT SALESMAN________(F) (G) (G) CERTIFICATE FROM DEPT. OF LAW SHOWING THAT

APPLICANT HAS PRODUCED EVIDENCE THAT HE IS THE DULY RECOGNIZED REPRESENTATIVE OF THE SUPPLIER OF EACH OF HIS PRODUCTS.

MARRIAGE LICENSE REQUIREMENTS:

PURSUANT TO SECTION 60, VOL. I, ARTICLE II OF THE CIVIL CODE OF GUAM AND PUBLIC LAW 16-73, THE FOLLOWING MUST BE COMPLIED WITH BEFORE THE ISSUANCE OF ANY MARRIAGE LICENSE:

1. **BOTH APPLICANTS** must be present at the time of submission of this application.

2. **BIRTH CERTIFICATES:** Both applicants must present their Birth Certficates issued by the Office of Vital Statistics or Registrar. **Baptismal or Hospital Certificates are not acceptable.** Birth Certificates in Foreign Languages must be translated by an Official Translator.

3. **ADOPTION:** If either applicant was adopted, Adoption Papers must be presented.

4. **NATURALIZED CITIZENS:** If either applicant is a Naturalized Citizen, a Naturalization Certficate or Certificate of Citizenship must be presented; and/or accompanied by a U.S. Passport.

5. **FOREIGN COUNTRY:** If either applicant was born abroad (foreign country) to U.S. Citizens/Parents, be it on military installations/other, a Certificate Abroad or Certificate of Birth must be presented.

6. **ALIEN:** If either applicant is an alien or of foreign descent, it is mandatory that he or she present their BIRTH CERTIFICATES, dully translated into English, and their respective COUNTRY'S CURRENT PASSPORT. AFFIDAVITS are required from Aliens (whether Resident Alien of Non-Immigrant Alien) applicants must make out a written statement containing YOUR correct full name; date and place of birth; where presently residing; parents complete names (living and deceased) presently residing at; whether or not you have been previously married. This AFFIDAVIT must be notarized.

7. **PREVIOUS MARRIAGE:** In case of termination of previous marriage by Divorce, Death, or Annulment, the applicant must furnish an **Original Certified Sealed Copy** of the **Final Divorce Decree, Death Certificate and/or Annulment Document**. Please Note:**MUST FURNISH MEANS TO KEEP!** Photo or Xerox copies are **NOT ACCEPTABLE. (CC Vol. I Sec. 69(d) and Attorney General Memo, Ref. 81-0292, dated July 7, 1981).**

8. **RETENTION OF MAIDEN NAME: If a female applicant desires to maintain her maiden name after marriage, she must prepare / attach an affidavit in triplicate stating the fact that she elects to keep her maiden name after marriage and the reason. HYPHENATION: No hyphenation may be used for last name after marriage(ULLOA-CRUZ) until a court order has been obtained and filed at Office of Vital Statistics, Public Health.**

9. **FEE: A fee of $15.00 is required upon filing of this application and is not refundable if the license is not issued or used. (CC Vol. I, Sec. 69(i) Amd. 16-73, Sec. 11).**

10. **WAITING PERIOD. No license shall be issued / released until after the expiration of five(5) days after the filing of the application. Such waiting period may be waived for good cause shown. An additional fee of Ten Dollars ($10.00) will be assessed for the waiver if approved.**

11. MINORS: Applicants under the age of (18) must obtain a COURT ORDER to marry and MUST BE ACCOMPANIED by a parent or guardian giving consent upon filing this application.

INVESTMENT OPPORTUNITIES

Nestled in the middle of the Western Pacific lies the largest, natural deep water seaport in this part of the world.

Tracing its history from the days of Pan Am's China Clippers that brought passengers from the United States, Apra Harbor has served as an important stopover en route to the population centers and markets of Asia. Later, Apra Harbor served the United States Navy as a ship repair and re-supply point for the Seventh Fleet operating in the Pacific and Indian Oceans.

Today, Apra Harbor continues to satisfy military logistic needs and has evolved into a bustling transshipment, cargo, fishing and tourist seaport operated by the civilian Government of Guam with the potential to become a significant hub for cargo ships plying the waters in Micronesia and between Asia and the United States.

Projected growth in Apra Harbor will occur as a result of increased local demand, development of the islands in Micronesia and expansion of Asia-Pacific markets. In anticipation of this growth, the Government of Guam expects to receive up to 3,700 acres of Navy property over the long term as a result of the 1995 decision of the Base Realignment and Closure Commission, as approved by the U.S. President and Congress, to make available to the Government of Guam significant seaport facilities no longer needed by the U.S. military.

Availability of these properties will allow for civilian use of fully developed Navy waterfront assets creating an economic investment opportunity unparalleled in Guam's history.

Navy land in Apra Harbor is fully developed with almost 4.6 million square feet of warehouse space, 16,500 linear feet of wharf space, 1.3 million square yards of paved open storage areas complete with infrastructure, utilities, and support equipment. The inner harbor area has a depth of 28 to 37 feet and the addition of Navy wharfage will result in a 400% increase in available berthing space.

During the next two years, the Government of Guam will receive 100 acres of waterfront property, with 78 buildings valued in excess of $90 million, specifically designed to perform all facets of ship repair.More than $20 million in plant equipment and at least 3,200 linear feet of wharf space with full utilities are expected to be transferred for civilian use. This transfer of property includes the island's only foundry, Guam's largest motor rewind facility, environmentally controlled sandblasting facilities, painting and corrosion control facilities and a fully certified dry dock.

The U.S. Navy is outsourcing those functions and activities performed by the former Fleet Industrial Supply Center (FISC), under the Base Operations Support (BOS) contract. As an added incentive to reduce costs, Public Law 24-295 provides income tax rebates from 25%-100%, for a maximum of 20 years, to private companies that take over these Navy support jobs.

The Navy's industrial supply center offers 37 buildings with 2.4 million square feet of space, 6,600 linear feet of berthing space, 1.4 million barrels of fuel storage capacity, 1.2 million square yards of cargo staging area, and 42,000 square feet of cold storage on 1,400 acres of land. As the closest U.S. resupply center, provisioning support will continue to be needed throughout the South Pacific and Indian Oceans.

- **Ship repair- the military's presence provides a base load of work for a privatized ship repair facility.**
- **Transshipment - for companies wishing to capitalize on Guam's strategic location in Micronesia and the Pacific Rim;**
- **Tourism - especially passenger liner facilities for the growing tourist market from Japan, Korea and Taiwan;**
- **Fisheries - to foster an abundance of purse seiner and long liner traffic in of the lucrative tuna trade; and**
- **Manufacturing - to diversify the local economic base.**

Finally, the local government is fully committed to ensuring the viability of businesses and welcomes foreign investment. A public-private partnership to develop Apra Harbor into a major seaport hub will assure profitability while allowing the Government of Guam to achieve its developmental, employment and modernization goals.

LAND INFORMATION SYSTEM

The Guam Economic Development Authority maintains an inventory of government and private lands that are available for development. Interested investors may obtain additional information by contacting GEDA by telephone at (671) 647-4332; by facsimile at (671) 649-4146; by email at <help@geda.guam.net>.

NEW OPPORTUNITIES FOR INSURANCE INDUSTRY

New laws have been passed to encourage the location of insurance underwriters on Guam and the formation of Guam-based trusts, to further expand the finance and investment sectors of the Guam economy towards making Guam a center for financial investment.

Spurred by increasing inquiries from underwriters throughout the world about Guam's potential as an insurance center, our government and private sectors joined forces to actively pursue incentives for this industry. Under Public Laws 23-109 and 24-266, insurance issuers -- reinsurers, commercial insurers, or captive insurers - whose headquarters are located in Guam, may enjoy the following benefits:

- **100% abatement of gross receipts taxes on insurance premiums and other revenues;**
- **Rebate of all income taxes resulting from the operation of an insurance underwriting entity.**
- **100% rebate of income tax withheld from shareholders on dividends from the insurance underwriting business.**

These incentives are available through the Qualifying Certificate Program of the Guam Economic Development Authority. Beneficiaries enjoy abatements and/or rebates for a period of twenty years, which may be extended for an additional twenty years if in good standing under the laws of Guam and under the rules and regulations of the Authority.

Just as Bermuda has become a financial capitol in the Atlantic over the last fifteen years with its insurance industry employing more than 17,000 and generating more than $18 billion per year,

Guam is now poised to serve as the financial and insurance hub of the Pacific for companies seeking a headquarters where they can be free of local taxes on worldwide income.

A prosperous international insurance market on Guam will also drive additional growth which broadens the island's economic base. Support industries like accounting, legal and courier services, office supply, and telecommunications are just a few business sectors which grow in connection with insurance. In addition, the deposit of collected premiums in local banks will significantly broaden the availability of capital, and can incite additional investment through convenient, local financing in areas such as hotels, residential homes, and commercial office space.

For the keen insurance investor, Guam offers the opportunity to operate agressively in worldwide markets without local taxes, while enjoying the advantages of U.S. soil, location in a modern island paradise community, state-of-the-art communications, and access to American courts, schools, and health care.

Guam Variety News and Views. Dec. 20, 1000. **Guam Waterworks Authority Seeking Private Partner.**
The Guam Waterworks Authority is seeking a private partner to upgrade its meter management system, sewer connections, and other initiatives. About $73 million of the $80 million needed would be for capital improvement projects. For further information, interested parties may contact GWA's Public Information Officer at pqlujan@mail.gov.gu.

Sports Tourism

Sports tourism is the fastest growing segment of the tourism industry.

AquaCulture

GovGuam initiated its support for aquaculture in the early 1970's. First commercial operation produced freshwater eels for export to Japan in the 70's and into 80's. Local aquaculture provided bait for tuna purse seiner fleets in the 80' and into the 90's.

Film Industry

U.S. & International Film markets are looking for new "unshot" locations to shoot motion pictures, TV shows or commercials, and still production events. Additionally, in light of global security issues, production companies are looking for scenic locations safe for visiting crews, and feature supporting service infrastructure and business friendly environments. Directors, specifically, are looking for locations that allow for shooting a variety of scenes in one location.

Kottura

KOTTURA has a threefold project focus; the first being Economic Development, the second is Cultural Preservation and the third being Artistic Accessibility. The KOTTURA proposal will be the first project of its kind for Guam and will be a flagship for The Guam Economic Development Authority as part of the Authority's strategy for continued economic development and economic diversity. Guam's downtown area will be a cultural destination not only for our community but for the millions of visitors who come to Guam seeking family friendly and educational attractions, specifically for information about our unique heritage and history.

EMERGING INDUSTRIES/OPPORTUNITIES

Arbitration & Mediation

Neutral location for U.S. companies to conduct arbitration with Asian businesses
Guam law provides for mediation and arbitration of contractual disputes that are enforceable in over 134 countries including Chine and other Asian nations.

Regional Distribution Center

Avoid delays in current distribution system
Utilizing bonded warehousing on Guam as a consolidation and customs clearance center

Regional Recycling Center

A hub for collection and transshipment of recyclable materials in the region

Captive Insurance

Captive Insurance with focus on Asian captives

Professional Education & Certification

Convenient location for US companies to credential Asian professional hires

Film, Video, Commercials

Regional venue for television and commercial film production for Asian producers

Ancestral Lands

GEDA under a property management agree with Ancestral Lands Commission has over 600 acres of public land available for development to support new industries

INVESTMENT AND TAX INCENTIVES

TAX INCENTIVES

The Government of Guam, through the Guam Economic Development Authority, is authorized by law to allow tax rebates to qualified investors. Qualifying Certificates for tax incentives are granted on the basis of investment commitment as well as the potential for creating new employment and expanding the base of the island's industry. These incentives are aimed primarily at manufacturers,insurance companies, commercial fishing companies, corporate headquarters, specialized medical facilities, high technology, agricultural and tourism development firms.

Qualified firms may be granted up to 100% income tax rebates for a maximum of 20 years; up to 100% abatement on real property tax for a maximum of 10 years; up to 75% rebate on corporate dividend tax for a maximum of 5 years; and abatement on gross receipts tax on petroleum and alcoholic beverages made in Guam for a maximum of 10 years.

Public Laws 23-135 and 24-266 allow developers of qualified hotels and tourist facilities to provide funds needed to "jump start" the construction of affordable housing on Guam, in exchange for enlarged tax benefits.

These two laws also provide a two-year period (extendible for another two years at the discretion of the GEDA Board) whereby eligible developers of hotels and tourist facilities may apply for these benefits under GEDA's Qualifying Certificate program. These expanded benefits include:

- **Exemption of Gross Receipts Taxes for suppliers of building materials & supplies, contractors for labor/supervision furnished for a qualified project.**
- **Exemption of Use Tax by the owner of the hotel/tourist facilities**
- **Rebate of Rental Income, up to 50% for the first 5 years and up to 25% for the next 5 years, to the lessor of land, buildings, machinery/equipment to QC holder for hotel/tourist facilities.**
- **Rebate of Capital Gains, up to 50%, to the seller of land and other real property to hotel/tourist facility of affordable housing developer.**

Other tax incentives qualified firms may take advantage of are:

- **Firms licensed to do business on Guam pay a territorial income tax based on a tax code that mirrors the U.S. Internal Revenue Service Code; however, they do not pay federal income taxes;**
- **Tax aspects of off-shore lending, whereby interest earned by a bank through the operation of an off-shore lending facility in Guam is not treated as a Guam source income for tax purposes.**

FINANCIAL INCENTIVES

FOREIGN SALES CORPORATION

Guam became the first eligible jurisdiction to provide financial incentives for the establishment of Foreign Sales Corporation, (FSC), through a Guam law known as the Export Incentive Act. FSCs are foreign incorporated subsidiaries of U.S. parent corporations engaged in export transactions which qualify them for partial U.S. tax exemptions, provided they maintain certain processes.

FSCs can be formed by manufacturers or export groups, such as export trading companies, and other non-manufacturers. An FSC can function as a principal, buying and selling for its own account, or as a commission agent. It can be related to a manufacturing parent company or an independent merchant or broker.

FINANCIAL ASSISTANCE PROGRAMS

GEDA administers four loan programs to assist local businesses with financing for startup and expansion. The Guam Development Fund Act (GDFA) provides financing in areas of agriculture, aquaculture, manufacturing, tourism, commercial support industries and any other industry that GEDA's board of directors determines will improve the island's economy. The Agriculutural

Development Fund offers low interest loans to bonafide commercial farmers and agricultural related businesses. The Chamorro Heritage Foundation Program provides loans or grants for activities that preserve, develop and enhance the Chamorro culture and heritage of the indigenous people of Guam. The Micro Enterprise Development Program (MDP) provides financial assistance to establish, stabilize and expand micro-enterprises, with funds from the U.S. Department of Housing and Urban Development Community Development Block Grant sponsored by the Guam Housing and Urban Renewal Authority.

For loans under the GDFA, applicants must demonstrate that they have sought and were declined financial assistance under reasonable terms and conditions from at least three private lenders on island. Following are other prerequisites applicants must meet: 1) If a sole proprietorship, the owner must be a resident of Guam and either a U.S. citizen or permanent resident alien; 2) If a partnership or corporation, the entity must be registered with the Government of Guam's Department of Revenue and Taxation; 3) All applicants must be licensed to do business on Guam.

FOREIGN SALES CORPORATION TAX INCENTIVES

§60100. Legislative Intent.
§60101. Definitions.
§60102. Tax exemption.
§60103. Special Qualifying Certificates.
§60104. License Requirement.

§60100. Legislative Intent. The Legislature finds that it is in the best interest of the territory of Guam to offer inducements to attract United States companies which are engaged in export trade to establish Foreign Sales Corporations in Guam and that special tax incentives are necessary for this purpose.

SOURCE: Added by P.L. 17-63.

§60101. Definitions. For the purposes of this Chapter:
(a) The term *FSC* means a Guam domestic corporation which is:
(1) A *FSC* as defined in §922(a) of the Internal Revenue Code as the same may be amended from time to time, and
(2) the holder of a valid Guam *FSC* license duly issued pursuant to 11 GCA Chapter 78.
(b) The term *foreign trade income* means income which is both:
(1) *foreign trade income* as defined in §923(b) of the Internal Revenue Code, as the same may be amended from time to time, and
(2) gross income of a FSC attributable to non-Guam trading gross receipts.
(c) the term *non-Guam trading gross receipts* means the gross receipts of any FSC which are:
(1) from the sale, exchange, or other disposition of non-Guam property for direct use, consumption or disposition outside the territory of Guam, or
(2) from the lease or rental of non-Guam property for use by the lessee outside the territory of Guam, or
(3) for services which are related and subsidiary to
(i) any sale, exchange, or other disposition of non-Guam property by such corporation, or
(ii) any lease or rental of non-Guam property described in item (2) of this Subsection by such corporation,
(4) for engineering or architectural services for construction projects located (or proposed for location) outside the territory of Guam, or
(5) for the performance of managerial services for an unrelated FSC in furtherance of the production of non-Guam trading gross receipts described in items (1), (2), or (3) of this Subsection, provided that this item (5) shall not apply to a FSC for any taxable year unless at

least fifty percent (50%) of its gross receipts for such taxable year are derived from activities described in items (1), (2), or (3) of this Subsection.
(d) The term *non-Guam property* means property which is
(1) export property as defined in §927(a) of the Internal Revenue Code as the same may be amended from time to time, and
(2) held primarily for sale, lease, or rental, in the ordinary course of trade or business, by, or to, a FSC, for direct use, consumption, or disposition outside the territory of Guam.
(e) The term *Corporation* means the Guam Economic Development Authority.
(f) The term *investment income* means investment income as defined §927(c) of the Internal Revenue Code as the same may be amended from time to time, but only to the extent such income
(1) is derived from investment of foreign trade income or
(2) is effectively connected with the trade or business conducted by the FSC which produces the foreign trade income.
(g) the term *carrying charges* means carrying charges as defined in §927(d)(1) of the Internal Revenue Code as the same may be amended from time to time but only to the extent such charges
(1) are related to or derived in connection with the sale or lease of non-Guam property as defined in 12 GCA §60101(d) or
(2) are effectively connected with the trade or business of the FSC which produces foreign trade income.

SOURCE: Added by P.L. 17-63; Subsection (a)(1) amended by P.L. 17-75; Subsection (b)(1) amended by P.L. 17-75; Subsection (d)(1) amended by P.L. 17-75; Subsection (f) added by P.L. 17-75; Subsection (g) added by P.L. 17-75.

§60102. Tax exemptions. (a) For the purpose of the taxes imposed upon income pursuant of the Guam Territorial Income Tax (as established and defined in 48 U.S.C. §1424(i) gross income of a FSC does not include any foreign trade income of such FSC.
(b) For the purpose of the taxes imposed upon income pursuant to the Guam Territorial Income Tax (as established and defined in 48 U.S.C. §1424(i) gross income of a FSC does not include any investment income or carrying charges of such FSC.
(c) for the purposes of the taxes imposed upon income pursuant to the Guam Territorial Income Tax (as established and defined in 48 U.S.C. §1424(i)), gross income of an FSC does not include any gross income derived from sources without Guam, determined under Section 862 of the Guam Territorial Income Tax (without regard to Section 865 of the Guam Territorial Income Tax).

SOURCE: Added by P.L. 17-63, amended by P.L. 17-75. Subsection (c) added by P.L. 22-55:1(d) (12/2/93).

§60103. Special Qualifying Certificates. (a) To the extent any foreign trade income, carrying charges, investment income, or gross income derived from sources without Guam as determined under Subsection (c) of §6102 of Title 12, Guam Code Annotated, at anytime now hereafter becomes includable without the gross income of a FSC for the purposes of the Guam Territorial Income Tax, a rebate of corporation income tax payable to the government of Guam in any single taxable year is hereby established and declared for FSCs. Upon application by an FSC after it has been issued a Guam FSC license pursuant to 11 GCA Chapter 78, a special qualifying Certificate shall be issued for a period expiring December 31, 2026 for the rebate of all income taxes applicable to corporate earnings on foreign trade income, carrying charges and investment income as defined in this Chapter and any gross income from sources without Guam as determined under Subsection (c) of 12 GCA §60102, occurring on and subsequent to the date of the issuance of the Special Qualifying Certificate and prior to the expiration of the Certificate.
(b) A FSC desiring to apply for a Special Qualifying Certificate shall make application by filing a certified copy of its Guam FSC license with the Corporation and furnishing the Corporation with

copies of all documents which were required to be furnished to obtain the Guam FSC license pursuant of 11 GCA Chapter 78. The corporation, upon ascertaining that the material furnished by the applicant is in proper order, shall thereupon promptly forward its recommendation for issuance of the Special Qualifying Certificate to the Governor of Guam who shall approve the application.

(c) A true copy of the Special Qualifying Certificate shall be attached to each corporate tax return of the FSC and the amount of tax due prior to the rebate shall be deposited with the Government at the time of filing of each income tax return. Taxes deposited by a FSC shall not be placed in the General Fund or commingled with other funds, but shall be deposited by the Director of Revenue and Taxation in special purpose trust accounts in one or more FDIC insured banks with offices within the territory of Guam and shall be withdrawn from such accounts only for the purpose of (i) making rebates as provided herein or (ii) payment into the General Fund after a final determination, including a judicial determination if requested by the FSC taxpayer, that taxes are validly due and payable and that the FSC is not entitled to any rebate.

Upon filing by a FSC of a tax return, the Director of Revenue and Taxation shall immediately thereafter cause the return to be reviewed, and, if the rebate appears to be in order shall cause the amount of tax deposited by the FSC to be returned to the FSC within fifteen (15) days from the date of deposit. If for any reason the amount to be rebated is not returned to the FSC within fifteen (15) days from the date of a deposit, the unreturned amount shall bear interest at the rate determined under §6611 of the Guam Territorial Income Tax law from the date of deposit until the date of return to the FSC of the money due to it. In the event of any failure to make the rebate provided for herein within thirty (30) days from the date of deposit by a FSC of the taxes due prior to rebate, the government of Guam consents to suit and consents to a decree of specific performance being entered against it for payments found to be lawfully due. The fifteen day review by the Director of Revenue and Taxation of a tax return of a FSC shall not constitute an audit or final determination by the Director of taxes due, but the rebate provided for herein shall be made notwithstanding that an audit or final determination of taxes due has not been completed with the fifteen day period. Amounts rebated to a FSC as provided herein shall not constitute income to such FSC and shall not be included within the gross income of a FSC for tax purposes.
(d) the provisions of 12 GCA Chapter 58 shall not apply to any FSC which holds a Special Qualifying Certificate except as otherwise specifically set forth in this Subsection. 12 GCA Sections 58102, 58104, 58106 (except for item 5, thereof), 58107 (except for the first paragraph thereof), 58109, 58122 and 58123 shall apply to such FSCs. Any FSC holding a Special Qualifying Certificate issued pursuant to this Chapter shall also be entitled to obtain an ordinary Qualifying Certificate issued pursuant to 12 GCA Chapter 58 from the corporation as to any activities of the FSC which result or are intended to result in the earning by the FSC of any income other than foreign trade income, carrying charges or investment income; provided any FSC desiring a regular Qualifying Certificate shall meet such requirements as are required of any other applicant for a regular Qualifying Certificate. It is the intent of the Legislature that no portion of the rebates of income tax made under this Section shall be subject to income taxation.

SOURCE: Added by P.L. 17-63, Subsection (a) amended by P.L. 17-75; Subsection (d) amended by P.L. 17-75. Subsection (a) amended by P.L. 22-55:1(f) (12/2/93).

§60104. License Requirement. It shall be a condition of the tax exemptions provided for in §60102 of this Chapter and of the Special Qualifying Certificate provided for in §60103 of this Chapter that a FSC shall at all times maintain a valid Guam FSC license in good standing pursuant to the provisions of 11 GCA Chapter 78.
SOURCE: Added by P.L. 17-63; amended by P.L. 17-75.

TRADE INCENTIVES

Headnote 3(A)

The General Headnote 3(a) program of the Tariff Schedules of the United States (TSUS) allows duty-free entry into the U.S. Customs Territory for those items manufactured or assembled in Guam that meet certain requirements that enable Guam to be considered the "country of origin." Manufacturers may import foreign raw materials or component parts, to which at least 30% (in some cases, 50%) of the value of the finished product must be added on Guam. These items must undergo a "substantial transformation" in order to benefit from the duty free provision of this program. It is advisable for an exporter to obtain a binding ruling as to whether the specific article meets the criteria for a duty-free (in certain cases, quota free) entry in the U.S. Customs Territory, by writing to the director, classification and value division, U.S. Customs Service, 1301 Constitution Avenue, N.W., Washington, D.C. 20229..

Generalized System of Preferences

Another trade incentive program allows products manufactured in Guam to be imported by participating nations at a reduced tariff rate. Guam is the beneficiary of the following countries: Japan, Australia and the European Common Market nations. Requirements of each participant vary, so interested exporters should contact the appropriate trade office of the particular country of destination.

INSURANCE INDUSTRY INCENTIVES

Insurance issuers -- whether reinsurers, commercial insurers or captive insurers -- whose headquarters are located in Guam, may enjoy the following benefits:

- **A 100% abatement of gross receipts tax on insurance premiums and other revenues.**
- **Rebate of up to 100% of income taxes resulting from the operation of an insurance underwriting entity.**
- **100% rebate of income tax withheld from shareholders of an insurance underwriting business on the dividends from such business.**

Similar benefits are now available for Guam-based Trusts under Public Law 24-266.

These incentives are made available through the Qualifying Certificate program of the Guam Economic Development Authority. Beneficiaries of the qualifying certificate may enjoy the abatements or rebates for a period of 20 years, which may be renewed for additional periods of 20 years so long as they remain in good standing under the laws of Guam and under the rules and regulations of the Authority.

OTHER INCENTIVES

GUAM PRODUCT SEAL

To help promote products made on Guam for the tourism industry and to enhance export potential, Public Law 18-42 created the Guam Product Seal to identify products manufactured on Guam. To be eligible, a manufacturer must:

- Possess a valid Guam business license

◈Substantially transform the material(s) so that the final product is converted into a different and distinguishable commercial use or character when completed

◈Must add value of at least 50 percent of the production cost on Guam

OFFSHORE SECTOR

INSURANCE INDUSTRY

Guam requests and welcomes any expressions of interest from your company about the possibility of incorporating on our island. In addition to many investment incentives Guam offers, your company also can enjoy the benefits of U.S. law, advanced telecommunications and computerized networks, world-class ports of call, and a highly developed business infrastructure. A quick glance at our island and proximity map shows you the diversity of its attributes and central location to major markets. We look forward to the opportunity to provide you assistance with any special needs you may have. Please contact the Guam Economic Development Authority at (671) 647-4332, fax at (671)649-4146, or e-mail at **help@geda.guam.net**.

Guam USA, the closest United States area to Asia, has established itself as the fastest growing and most stable island in Micronesia.

Spurred by increasing inquiries from underwriters throughout the world about Guam's potential as an insurance center, the Government of Guam and private sector joined forces to actively pursue incentives for this industry. Under this new law, insurance issuers (whether reinsurers, commercial insurers, or captive insurers) who incorporate in Guam, may enjoy the following benefits:

100% abatement of gross receipts taxes on insurance premiums and other revenues.
Rebates on all income taxes resulting from the operation of an insurance underwriting entity.
100% rebate of income tax withheld from shareholders of an insurance underwriting business on the dividends from such business.

These incentives are available through the Qualifying Certificate program of the Guam Economic Development Authority. Beneficiaries enjoy abatements and/or rebates for a period of twenty years and may apply for an extension of the certificate for an additional twenty years if the entity remains in good standing under the laws of Guam and the rules and regulations of the Authority.

The supporting captive insurance infrastructure located in Guam, includes more than 16 international and local banks, subsidiaries of "Big Eight" accounting firms, two international insurance fronting companies, a strong network of local insurance agents and brokers, and a substantive number of legal firms experienced in doing business with Asia. Most importantly, the Department of Revenue & Taxation which oversees the licensing and regulating of captives, is structured to provide a comprehensive review of all applications and to assist with the individual needs and objectives of established captive companies.

To inquire further about Guam as a captive insurance domicile, and its captive insurance law, please contact the Department of Revenue & Taxation, Insurance Branch, via telephone (671) 475-1817 or facsimile (671) 472-2643, or write to Post Office Box 23607, GMF, Barrigada, Guam USA 96921. Please send to the attention of theInsurance Commissioner, Mr. Joey Duenas.

To inquire further of the tax benefits available under the Qualifying Certificate program, please contact the Guam Economic Development Authority (GEDA), Industry Development Division via telephone (671) 647-4332, facsimile (671) 649-4146, e-mail at help@geda.guam.net , or write GEDA at ITC Building, Suite 511, 590 South Marine Drive, Tamuning, Guam 96911. Please send to the attention of the Administrator, Mr. Edward Untalan.

GUAM AS YOUR DOMICILE

WHAT IS A CAPTIVE?

Captive insurance refers to a subsidiary corporation established to provide insurance to the parent company and its affiliates not primarily engaged in the business of insurance. A captive may be a single-parent shareholder (pure captive), or a group of shareholders with similar captive risks (group captives). As the name implies, all or a significant portion of the risks written are "captive," related in some way to the risks of shareholders, or third-party risks which the shareholders control.

This approach provides an option for many corporations and groups who wish to take financial control and manage risks by underwriting their own insurance rather than paying premiums to third-party insurers. A captive may underwrite U.S. risks, foreign risks, or both. The coverage may include workers' compensation, property, liability, employee benefits or malpractice.

WHY FORM A CAPTIVE?

There are numerous advantages to forming a captive, however a company should conduct a feasibility study to determine whether a captive is the best means for the company to achieve its risk management objectives and other goals.

Captives are formed to provide necessary coverage at acceptable prices and for various good economic reasons that include the following:

- Tailored coverage to a company's specific needs
- Reduction of operating costs
- Improved cash flow
- Accumulated investment income to fund losses
- Increased coverage and capacity for risks uninsurable in conventional markets
- Direct access to wholesale reinsurance markets

GUAM'S CAPTIVE INCENTIVES

In a collective effort between the public and private sector, Guam's legal and regulatory framework was established to provide for a stable, yet flexible environment for captive companies. Coupled with the presence of most international and national legal and accounting firms and insurance brokers, Guam is positioned to be the jurisdiction in the Pacific Rim to offer the greatest value and the most appealing environment for those considering the opportunities a captive has to offer.

TAX INCENTIVES

Public Law 23-109 authorizes the Guam Economic Development Authority (GEDA) to offer tax incentives to the insurance industry through its Qualifying Certificate program. A qualifying certificate is a contract issued by the Governor of Guam on the recommendation of GEDA and grants abatements and rebates of all Guam taxes for periods not to exceed twenty (20) years; provided, that the entity remains in good standing under the laws of Guam and GEDA's rules and regulations. Beneficiaries may apply for an extension of the certificate for an additional twenty (20) years.

To apply for a QC, a Domestic Insurer must file certified copies of the following with GEDA:

- Certificate of Authority or Insurance License issued by the Guam Insurance Commissioner
- Application to the Insurance Commissioner for a Certificate or License
- Complete and verified QC application form (GEDA Form QC-1I)
- Complete and verified affidavit of compliance (GEDA Form QC-2I)
- Insurance Commissioner's certificate of compliance

Current Summary of Fees for Qualifying Certificate Program:

Application Fee:	**$ 750**
Annual Surveillance Fee:	**$1000**

The incentives are available through the Qualifying Certificate Program of the Guam Economic Development Authority.

BILL 386 - PASSED INTO LAW OCTOBER 9, 1997

Guam's captive insurance law was created through the enactment of 22 Guam Code Annotated, Chapter 23 Captive Insurance Companies. This law was amended in 1997 in order to make easier the formation of a captive in Guam and to create the environment conducive to captive companies. The major provisions of the Amended Captive Insurance Law are as follows:

- The law redefines captive insurance and affiliated companies.
- No captive insurance company may directly insure any risks arising in Guam.
- Pure captives are required a minimum of $50,000 capital and $100,000 of surplus.
- Group captive companies incorporated as a stock insurer are required $100,000 capital and $150,000 surplus.
- Incorporated industrial insured captives as a stock insurer are required $150,000 capital and $200,000 surplus.
- Incorporated industrial insured captives as a mutual insurer are required $200,000 surplus.
- Capital must be in the form of cash deposited in a member bank of the Federal Reserve System licensed to do business in Guam and approved by the Commissioner.
- Surplus may be in the form of cash or an irrevocable letter of credit (LOC). The form of the LOC, or any other form of surplus, must be approved by the Insurance Commissioner.
- All information pertaining to Guam captive insurance companies are deemed proprietorial and confidential.

BENEFITS FOR CHOOSING GUAM AS A DOMICILE

- Geographic location provides a secure U.S. gateway access to international markets
- 100% tax rebates for commercial, captive and reinsurers
- Established financial services community
- Guam does not require an annual board of directors meeting in the domicile

- ◆There is no requirement for proof of necessity
- ◆Insurance risks are generally allowed (writing direct Guam risks is prohibited)
- ◆Reinsurance business is allowed in Guam
- ◆Start up costs include a minimal application fee of $200 and a $2500 licensing fee
- ◆Foreign tax credit eligibility in certain cases for U.S. companies
- ◆Details of captive insurance companies on Guam are kept confidential

THE LICENSING PROCESS

The initial step in forming a captive in Guam involves an introductory meeting of the applicant and a representative of the Insurance Branch to discuss the captive insurance application process.

Once the application has been completed entirely as instructed by the Insurance Branch, it can then be submitted. The application will then be forwarded to an independent risk consultant for review, and within 28 calendar days, the applicant will receive notification from the Insurance Commissioner. Once the application has been approved and the company has been incorporated and funded, the applicant has 30 days following approval to submit the application fee to the Insurance Branch.

It is strongly suggested that companies seeking to form captives in Guam solicit professional assistance of risk consultants, and supporting professionals who are knowledgeable and familiar with Guam's captive insurance law and the application process in order to facilitate a successful application.

REGULATORY REQUIREMENTS

After receiving a certificate of authority from the Insurance Commissioner, the following must be complied with on a yearly basis:

- ◆Principal place of business must be established in Guam.
- ◆An annual report of financial condition and an audited annual financial statement by a Guam approved actuary, must be submitted on or before March 1 of each year.
- ◆Captive companies must be examined by the Insurance Commissioner every three years.

SUMMARY OF FEES

Current incorporation and annual fees are as follows:

Application Fee	$2500
Incorporation Fee	$ 200
Independent Review Fee	$3500+ (Based on complexity of application)
Annual License Fees	$2500

CAPTIVE INSURANCE

The Guam Captive Insurance Association Corporation (GCIA) was formally organized in 1997. GCIA was formed to support, promote, foster, and market Guam as an attractive and competitive captive insurance domicile; to assist and advise the Insurance Commissioner regarding matters affecting captive insurance companies in Guam; and to support Guam's captive insurance industry with respect to legislative, regulatory and other matters which affect formation or operation of captive insurance companies.

MEMBERSHIP

Membership in GCIA is open to all captive insurance companies licensed in Guam and to all individuals and entities with a bona fide interest consistent with the positive promotion, development and maintenance of captive insurance in Guam. Annual dues are $500 per Corporate member and are not prorated. Two current members of GCIA are needed to sponsor prospective members.

In addition to Guam's Insurance Commissioner (an ex officio member), plus captives licensed in Guam, GCIA members include captive managers, brokers, financial institutions, accounting firms, legal firms, actuary/risk consultants, insurance companies, and claims administrators, all of whom are either directly involved in captives and/or support the development of a quality captive environment in Guam.

View the current membership listing for the Guam Captive Insurance Association: GCIA members. (Adobe Acrobat Reader file)

Obtain the GCIA Application form: GCIA Application.pdf (Adobe Acrobat Reader file)

MEMBERSHIP BENEFITS

- Opportunity to participate in Guam/GCIA promotional events
- Organization/Name listing in captive insurance literature for prospective captive companies
- Annual update of captive insurers
- Opportunity to participate in GICA's recommendations to the Guam Legislature and other regulatory bodies
- Participation in educational workshops
- Notices of GCIA meetings
- Each member will have one vote in GCIA

ASSOCIATION COMMITTEES

Membership/Education Committee:

Members in this Committee are responsible for matters relating to membership requirements, fees, and ongoing education.

Legislation/Tax/Accounting Committee:

This Committee shall propose and/or review legislative, regulatory, and administrative bills, proposals, and other initiatives which affect the formation and maintenance of captive insurance companies in Guam, and to make recommendations to the GCIA Board regarding same. When appropriate and necessary, the committee shall assist in the drafting of legislative, regulatory and other administrative initiatives which would improve the climate for the formation and maintenance of captives domiciled in Guam.

Marketing Committee:

Members in this Committee are responsible for matters relating to marketing Guam as a captive domicile.

Conference Committee:

This Committee is responsible for planning, organizing, and overseeing an annual captive conference to be held in Guam and in-part sponsored by the corporation.

GUAM VISITORS[6]

The increase in Japanese visitors to Guam this year could probably be attributed to price reductions at Guam hotels and the slightly stronger yen. According to the GVB study, Japanese visitors surveyed reported an average length of stay of 3.3 nights, similar to the prior fiscal year. Remaining at the head of the list of attractions they would like to see on Guam is "theme park" at 40%, followed by "archaeological site visit", and "village fiesta". Average local expenditure was $530, as compared with $450 last July.

The average stay of American visitors to Guam was about two weeks, with total local expenditures averaging $2,000, about the same level as last year. The attractions they would most like to see are "festival highlighting Guam's culture" as expressed by 50% of the respondents, followed by a "Tumon Bay Boardwalk" and a "village fiesta". "Nature hiking trails" and "archeological sites" follow closely behind.

Hong Kong Exit Survey, Guam Visitors Bureau, July 2000. **A Look at Visitors from Hong Kong to Guam**
The average length of stay of visitors from Hong Kong was 4.45 nights, as compared with 3.34 in Fiscal Year 99. Among the choices of desired attractions, these visitors were most interested in seeing a "Guam cultural festival" and a "theme park". Average local expenditure was $546, which is slightly higher than $534 in the previous study.

Preliminary statistics from the Guam Visitors Bureau showing 111,302 visitors coming to Guam during the last month of the year indicate a 10.2% increase over December 1999. 85,308 were from Japan, representing a 5.2% increase from the same period last year, and 11,305 from Korea, reflecting an increase of 78.8%. For CY2000, Guam welcomed 1,048,813 visitors, registering a 9.5% increase from CY1999.

The Military Sealift Command has awarded a contract to Guam Shipyard for the repair of the USNS San Jose, scheduled to commence in mid-February. This and other work will require the Shipyard to employ approximately 250 people. Recent contracts successfully completed by the shipyard include major dry docking overhauls of the USNS Flint and the USNS Niagara Falls as well as smaller repair tasks for the USS Frank Cable home ported in Guam. In October 2000, Guam Shipyard signed a Master Ship Repair Agreement with the U.S. Navy. This provides re-certification of the shipyard management and employees and also licenses the shipyard to repair U.S. Navy ships.

Guam professionals or those aspiring to upgrade their knowledge now have a new option to prepare for industry specialist and management positions. **Westpac Institute of Management (WIM)** opened its doors on Guam to provide Executive Education and Seminars and Workshops directed toward industry diploma, certificate and licensing. The institute also offers graduate

[6] *Japanese Exit Survey*, Guam Visitors Bureau, July 2000. **A Look at Japanese Visitors to Guam**

programs in business management and entrepreneurship in conjunction with universities on Guam and off-island. WIM has been authorized by the American Banker's Association and the American Institute of Banking to provide courses in banking, real estate and finance. Courses in computer, English and Japanese are also available.

Guam travelers to the U.S. mainland or Hawaii now have the option to receive and make calls on their wireless digital phones, as a result of the PCS roaming service offered by one of the five major telecommunication services providers on island in partnership with several PCS providers throughout the United States. Likewise, CDMA (Code Division Multiple Access) digital PCS subscribers from the U.S. mainland can travel to Guam and keep in touch while using their PCS phones through the company's all digital network.

TRAVEL TO GUAM

Guam is a tropical paradise, given its location, climate, and scenic beauty! It is home to elegant world class hotels, Asian PGA golf resorts, and beautiful beaches. Situated on a strip of white sand beaches known as Tumon Bay, fine business hotels and family accommodations include the Guam Hilton Hotel, Westin Resort Guam, Hyatt Regency Guam, Hotel Okura, Hotel Nikko Guam, Outrigger Hotel and the Ladera Tower - Aston International.

Guam is a melting pot of Chamorro, Micronesian, American, and Asian cultures. Petroglyph (Cave Paintings) and Latte Stones (pillars which supported ancient structures and houses) provide insight into the lives of the Chamorro people in their earliest times. Spanish ruins and World War II memorials are reminders of more recent history.

Guam is also home to a haven of a fantastic diversity of restaurants with worldwide cuisines as Niji, Kurumaya, Planet Hollywood, Hard Rock Cafe, Friday's, Capricciosa, Creations, Joinus, Sam Choy's, Tony Roma Ribs and Outback Steakhouse.

The island's duty-free status means that name brand merchandise are often less expensive than its country of origin. The variety of retail shops on Guam can satisfy any shopper - from Tiffany's, Chanel, to K-Mart. In addition to outlet shops and malls, the island also offers shoppers with the I Sengsong Chamorro Village, a venue to purchase local handicrafts.

There are five galleon shipwrecks below the waters around Guam. The Neustra Senora del Pilar is purported to be one of the 10 richest wrecks in the world. There are scuba experiences for the uninitiated and diving adventures to World War II shipwrecks for those with advance skills. Tokai Maru and SMS Comoran, Guam's favorite twin wreck dives provide a unique juxtaposition of World Wars I and II. Actually touching underwater, two ships from two different wars lie at Pier 1 in Apra Harbor. The SMS Cormoran is a 95-metre 320-foot auxiliary cruiser, built in China and part of the Russian fleet. Taken by Germany, it was put into service in WWI. Purposely blown up to avoid capture, it was the first ship sunk by the U.S. entering WWI in 1917. Today, the Cormoran lies on its starboard side between 21-36 metres / 70-120 feet with spacious holds and meandering passageways. Home to clouds of fish and morays, it provides an exciting exploration of a rare WWI artifact.

The Tokai Maru, a 150-metre / 500-foot 8,300-ton Japanese passenger-cargo ship, lies just to the side of the Cormoran, beginning in about 15 metres /50 feet of water. Sunk by a torpedo from the submarine Flying Fish in WWII, lying on its port side is clean of overgrowth and easy to explore in a single dive. Of special interest are the marble baths near the bridge.

The Kitsugawa Maru a 1,900-ton freighter also sunk in 1944 was hit by the submarine Seahorse, but managed to sail to Apra Harbor before it was hit by Dauntless dive bombers. It rests permanently in about 160 feet of water.

Jet skiing, trips to watch wild pods of spinner dolphins, fishing and trawling , river cruises, ocean dinner cruises, underwater observatories, ocean parasailing, helitours, ecotours, and snorkling are normal water activities. There are also amusement Parks as Underwater World, Stephen Spielberg's GameWorld, Tarza and Onward's Water Parks. There are more than 1200 species of fish in Micronesia and Guam. Some tourists plan their visits to coincide with Cultural Fairs.

PRACTICAL INFORMATION ABOUT GUAM

POSTAL SERVICE

Postage stamps are readily available at the U.S. Post Offices, hotels, some stores and vending machines. Mail freight also is supported by DHL, UPS, DHX, EMERY, FEDEX.

ELECTRICITY

All normal wall outlets are 120 volts, 60 cycles with U.S. plug patterns.

COMMUNICATIONS

Cable, telex, direct dial phone service, and Internet connectivity via T1 lines, dsl or cable modems are available to all overseas points. Local phone service is provided by the Guam Telephone Authority with over 71,000 subscribers. The telephone network features digital switching and redundant fiber inter-office facilities as well as cellular service. The telephone switching protocal called Feature Group D places Guam in World Zone I which includes the continental United States, Alaska, Hawaii that are reached by dialing 1+ the area code + number. Because Guam is considered domestic by the FCC, domestic rates and access to toll-free numbers (i.e. 800, 877, 888) are similar to those in the U.S.

Guam is a telecommunications trans-Pacific hub for Sprint, MCI, GTE, IT&E and AT&T linking the US and Asia. It falls within an area covered by several Asian communications satellites and is within two time zones of almost all East Asian countries. Integrated Switching digital Network (ISDN), dsl, cable modem connections for Internet access locally as well as Internet ds3 lines to the States are solidly established.

TRANSPORTATION

There are several airlines serving Guam to most major international, continental, and Pacific destinations. These are ANA, Gulf Air, JAL, Northwest, Continental, Thai Air, Qantas, Philippine Air, and Nauru Air. A public bus transportation system began operation in 1982. Tour excursions, taxicabs, and car rentals are available.

RADIO AND TELEVISION

The radio stations operating on Guam are Adventist world Radio, Catholic Education Radio, Hit Radio 100-KOKU, KOLG Light 91 FM, KPRG Public Radio, KSDA FM JOY 92, KTWG 801 am, K-Stereo 95.5 FM, KUAM 610AM, Newstalk K-57, Power 98FM, and Trans World Radio.

The television broadcasting companies are KGTF Public TV, Kuam TV8, KTGM-TV14 and Marianas Cable TV (about 100 channels of programming).

BANKING INSTITUTIONS

The financial institutions operating on Guam are: Allied Bank, American Savings & Loan, Asahi Bank, Bank of Guam, Bank of Hawaii, Bank of the Orient, Century Bank, Citibank N A, Citizens Security Bank Inc, Finance Factors Ltd, First commercial Bank, First Hawaiian Bank, Hongkong Bank, First Savings & Loan of America, Guam Savings & Loan, Metropolitan Bank and Trust Co, NAVMAR Federal Credit Union, Oceanic Bank, Pacific Islands Dev Bank, Union Bank, Hawaiian Trust Company Ltd.

CUSTOMS

Guam, also called Guahan {meaning "we have"}, is a duty free port and is outside the United States Customs Zone. All luggage containers are inspected upon arrival by customs officials. Importation of plants, fruits, and animals are restricted without proper documentation from the point of origin. Narcotics and deadly weapons are also prohibited.

DOCUMENTATION

American citizens do not need a passport to enter Guam, although some itineraries may pass through ports that require them, so it is a good idea to carry yours on your visit to Guam. Citizens of other countries require a passport and a U.S. visa.

MONEY EXCHANGE

Guam uses the American dollar. Banks, hotels, and money exchange firms change foreign currency equivalent to U.S. dollars.

The Betelnut also called *Pugua or Mama'on* by Guamanians are 'palm nuts' from the areca tree. The scientific name for the tree is 'Areca catechu' and resembles a thin coconut palm tree. These hard nuts are chewed casually like chewing gum by islanders and is a permanent feature of the cultures of the Pacificinto Honolulu or the States: Food and Drug Administration in 2000 lifted the ban on bringing betel nuts into the U.S. Mainland. FDA Import Bulletin #23-814 declares that betel nuts are no longer prohibited or considered contraband provided the nuts are in compliance with existing USDA rules which require the husks to be removed and the nuts to be cracked or cut. Pepperleaves (pupulu) are not allowed. Betel nuts products entering the U.S. may be handcarried or mailed for personal consumption in amounts not exceeding five pounds.

MOVING TO GUAM AND BRINGING YOUR PETS FOR AN EXTENDED STAY? Click this line for information on quarantine and government agency contacts.

RELATED LINKS ABOUT THE ISLE OF GUAM IN THE MARIANAS ARCHIPELEGO

RECREATION

Guam is a virtual tropical playground with recreational activities to suit every taste. In addition to a variety of international cuisines offered at local eateries and numerous formal dining establishments, Guam's dazzling hotel district features regular exhibitions, shows, concerts, carnivals and special events.

Each of Guam's villages hold a traditional "fiesta" celebration each year in honor of their patron saints. Fiestas are open to all, and feature outdoor feasts, music, dancing, and a chance to visit with friends and family.

For individual and family recreation, a long list of "things to do" can quickly fill an active social and recreational calendar:

- **parasailing**
- **helicopter tours**
- **jet skiing**
- **snorkeling and diving**
- **golfing**
- **gun shooting and horse back riding**
- **dog racing**

- **dinner shows**
- **shopping**
- **jungle hiking**
- **submarine tours**
- **sight seeing**
- **dinner cruises**
- **deep sea fishing**

In addition, many sports leagues play year-round throughout the island and offer team sports for all ages in softball, baseball, basketball, football, soccer, tennis, swimming, canoeing, kayaking and more

SUPPLEMENTS

GUAM WEBSITES

Official Guam Website
ns.gov.gu
Provides information about Guam; entry requirements; practical information about postal service, electricity, utilities, transportation and banking institutions; links to congressional representative, University of Guam, Justice Network and other information.

Government of Guam Official Departments
ns.gov.gu/government.html
Contains links to Guam government agencies.

Attorney General
www.guamattorneygeneral.com/
Includes attorney general opinions, press releases and public service announcements. Provides a browsable, PDF version of the Guam Code Annotated. Includes background on the code; link to public laws enacted by the Legislature. Also provides Guam Organic Code, Administrative Rules, Procurement Regulations. Codes, rules and regulations all are linked from the attorney general's home page.

Board of Registration for Professional Engineers, Architects and Land Surveyors
www.guam-peals.org/
Provides exam information and schedule; professional code; rules and regulations; code of ethics; information bulletins; and contact information. Includes searchable roster of registrants; board meeting notices; forms; board and staff directions.

Chamber of Commerce
www.guamchamber.com.gu
Provides information about business relocation support and services; business licensing; investment incentives. Can order business relocation packet and publications online. Includes visitor guide.

Department of Labor
www.labor.gov.gu/
Includes Bureau of Labor Statistics and Occupational Safety and Health Administration; information on worker's compensation and fair employment practices.

Department of Revenue and Taxation
www.admin.gov.gu/revtax/index.html
Includes text of the code sections that apply to business licensing, registration and taxation; employee handbook.

Economic Development Authority
www.investguam.com
Provides information about development and investment opportunities in Guam.

Environmental Protection Agency
www.guamepa.govguam.net/
Provides information on environmental programs on Guam, permits; environmental regulations.

General Services Agency
www.admin.gov.gu/doa/gsa.htm

Provides information on doing business with Guam.

Port Authority
www.netpci.com/~pag4/
Describes facilities and services; provides port rules and regulations; posts RFPs.

STRATEGIC STATISTICS

GENERAL INFORMATION

Location	13N Lat,144E Long
Geography	
Total land area	Approx 209 sq mi/541.3 sq km
Length/width	30 mi(48.3km)/4-12 mi(6.4-19.3km)
Shoreline length	116.5 mi/187.5 km
Coral reef length	80 mi/128.7 km
parklands	1,927.6 acres/780.1 hectares
Climate	
Avg day/night time temperature	85F/65-75F
Coolest/warmest months	Jan-Feb(83.4F)/Jun(86.9F)
Wettest months	Jul-Oct(13.1 in. rain fall)
Humidity	Average between 72% and 86%
Annual rainfall	80 to 110 inches
Official languages	Chamorro and English
Political status:	
....	Unincorporated U.S. Territory
Head of Government	Governor Carl T.C Gutierrez

GROWTH

Population	Unit	% Rate		Est. 1990			
Total population	No.		140,635		-156,302		
Resident population	No.	133,152		2.31	145,881		
Military total pop	No.		24,101		- 15,950		
Dependents	No.		12,149		-8,034		
Pop. density	Sq.mi.		637.1		- 698.0		
Natural Increase							
Per 1000 pop.	Rate.		24.73		-26.04		
Males per 100 females	Ratio.		114.0		-116.0		
Households	No.		31,373		2.36	34,448	
Persons per household	No.		3.97		-3.93		
Families	No.		27,313		2.29	29,902	
persons per family	No.	4.26		-4.21			
Married couple families	No.		21,342		1.45	22,611	
Female householder families	No.		3,824		4.70	4,596	
Median age	Yr.		25.0		1.19	26.2	
Age Distribution of Persons							
15 yrs old & under	Pct.		30.0	0.78	28.2		
16-64 yrs old	Pct.		66.		2.91		67.6

65 yrs old & over		Pct.		3.9		5.77		4.5
Dependency (young & old)								
Per 100 persons		Ratio.		51.4		-48.2		
Women 15-44 yrs old		No.	31,649		1.96		34,748	
Women in labor force	Pct.		59.5		4.79		64.2	
Physicians								
per 1000 total pop		Rate.		1.23			-.27	
Hospital beds								
Per 1000 total pop		Rate.		1.08			-1.23	
Ethnic Composition								
Chamorro		Pct.		43.3	1.88		42.6	
Filipino		Pct.		22.6	2.96		23.1	
Caucasian		Pct.		14.4	n/a		n/a	
Micronesian		Pct.		4.9	11.3		6.9	
Educational Attainment (25 yrs old & over)								
H/S grads & higher	Pct.		73.3	2.84		71.2		
College grads		Pct.		17.5	3.54		17.4	
Eligible voters, total		No.		68,960			-78,442	
Registered voters		No.		45,168			- 50,365	
Percent of eligibles		Pct.		65.5			-64.2	
Voter turnout		Pct.		86.5			- 89.3	

HOUSING

Total housing units		No.	35,223		2.23	38,473
Occupied units		No.	31,373		2.36	34,448
Owner-occupied	Pct.	45.6		2.24	45.4	
Renter-occupied	Pct.	54.4		2.47	54.6	
Vacant units for rents	No.	1,473		0.90	1,527	

Employment		Unit		1990	1993	1994		
Establishments, total	No.		2,224		2,741		n/a	
Private sector,	No. of employees							
Less than 5		Pct.		38.7		39.6		n/a
5 to 49		Pct.		50.9		49.8	n/a	
50 and over		Pct.		6.4		7.2		n/a
Payroll employment	No.		56,129		68,464		65,800	
Males per 100 fems	Ratio.		146.5	142.5		n/a		
U.S. Citizens		Pct.		75.3		72.6	n/a	
Perm resident aliens	Pct.		14.5		14.6	n/a		
Non-immigrant aliens	Pct.		7.2		8.4		n/a	
Private sector		No.		37,852		46,791		44,460
Trade(Whsle & Rtl)	Pct.		20.1		21.1		20.2	
Services(Ldge/Food)	Pct.		18.0		19.4		19.5	
Construction		Pct.		15.3		14.6		13.2
Public sector		No.		18,277		21,673		21,340
Gov't of Guam		Pct.		61.7	64.3		64.9	
Federal Gov't		Pct.		38.3	35.7		35.1	
Average hourly earnings								
Private sector		Dol.		7.60		8.95		8.95
GovGuam		Dol.		13.79		16.24		16.06

Law Enforcement	Unit	1990	1993	1994
Registered vehicles	No.	100,796	115,030	n/a
Driver's lic. issued	No.	32,445	40,095	n/a
Traffic accidents	No.	9,181	8,250	9,190
Fatalities	No.	34	39	12
Alcohol related	No.	357	305	456
DUI arrests	No.	896	914	933
Citations issued	No.	65,273	37,796	28,510
Daily avg	No.	179	101	78
Total UCR offenses	No.	5,000	5,788	7,909
Violent crimes	No.	378	400	474
Alcohol/Drug related	Pct.	68.2	72.3	78.1
Per 1000 pop	Rate.	2.84	2.81	3.25
Property crimes	No.	4,622	5,388	7,435
Alcohol/Drug related	Pct.	31.1	35.4	45.7
Per 1000 pop	Rate.	34.71	37.79	50.97
Officers per 1000 pop	Rate.	2.5	2.6	2.3

FINANCE, BUSINESS AND TRADE

Bank deposits, total	$Mil.	1,277	1,378	1,335
Time & Savings	Pct.	60.5	59.4	59.4
Bank loans, total	$Mil.	1,271	2,358	2,369
Commercial loans	Pct.	50.0	50.0	50.3
Construction, value	$Mil.	492.0	431.1	614.3
Building permits	No.	2,626	3,244	2,397
Average value	$Thous.	187.4	132.9	256.3
Gross bus. recpts	$Thous.	4,109.	4 4,728.2	n/a
License revenues	$Thous.	619.6	841.4	575.2
License issued	No.	15,756	22,992	18,361
Surface cargo	Mil Rev Tons	1,532.5	1,305.2	1,896.4
Imports	Pct.	70.4	74.0	62.4
Exports	Pct.	11.5	10.2	11.2
Transhipmt	Pct.	18.1	15.8	26.4
Air cargo	Metric Tons	44,449	42,774	48,415
Cargo	Pct.	86.3	81.2	84.6
Mail	Pct.	3.7	18.8	15.4

Tourism	Unit	1990	1993	1994
Visitor/Tourists	Thous.	780.4	784.0	1,086.7
Arrivals, air	Thous.	769.9	775.1	1 ,076.4
Arrovals, sea	No.	10,528	8,903	10,283
Japan visitors	Pct.	82.8	70.9	71.8
Hotel rooms available	No.	4,955	6,616	6,873
Hotel occupancy taxes	$Mil.	14.3	14.6	13.7
Hotel occupancy rate	Pct.	89.0	58.0	71.1
Golf courses	No.	5	8	7

Transportation	Unit	1990	1993	1994

Air passengers	Thous.	1,936	2,365	2,150
Arrivals	Thous.	943	1,178	1,073
Departures	Thous.	993	1,187	1,077
Transit passengers	Thous.	227	316	258
Acft takeoff & landings	No.	20,592	33,522	33,182
Port ship callings	No.	3,073	2,511	2,873
Airline flights	No.	163	196	233
Revenue pax seats	No.	35,657	44,257	48,535

GIP/PI	Unit	1990	1993	1994
Gross Island Product	$Mil.	2,312	2,917	3,003
Personal Income	$Mil.	1,680	2,247	2,325

Income	Unit	1990	1993	1994

HOUSEHOLD & PER CAPITA INCOMES

Per capita	Dol.	9,885	10,834	n/a
Mean income earners	Dol.	18,452	13,097	n/a
Mean household income	Dol.	36,772	44,369	n/a
Avg earners/household	No.	1.99	1.88	n/a
Adjusted Gross Income				
AGI per capita	Dol.	11,151	n/a	n/a
AGI per income filer	No.	25,547	n/a	n/a
Exemptions per filer	No.	2.3	n/a	n/a

FEDERAL GOVERNMENT

Expenditure, total	$Mil.	625.0	953.0	n/a
Wages & salaries	$Mil.	357.0	472.0	n/a
Procurement	$Mil.	69.0	166.0	n/a
Direct payments	$Mil.	80.0	137.0	n/a
Federal grants	$Mil.	116.0	161.0	n/a
Other programs	$Mil.	3.0	17.0	n/a

Local Government	Unit	1990	1993	1994

LAND MANAGEMENT

Land, total	Thous. acres	135.7	135.7	135.7
Private	Pct.	48.51	48.51	48.51
Local gov't	Pct.	18.69	18.75	18.75
Federal gov't	Pct.	32.80	32.74	32.74
Land & Building Parcels	No.	43,812	n/a	47,976
Aggregate value	$Bil.	3.66	4.26	4.92
GovGuam Retirement Fund				
Active members	No.	10,764	12,797	13,170
Pensioners	No.	3,038	3,794	4,152
Guam Airport Authority(GAA)				
Revenues	$Mil.	17.6	19.9	23.9
Capital & Liability	$Mil.	83.8	323.1	333.6

Port Authority Guam(PAG)					
Revenues	$Mil.		14.8	24.9	26.0
Capital & Liability	$Mil.		60.1	59.1	60.5
Owned-Utilities					
Guam Power Authority(GPA)					
Revenues	$Mil.		68.5	133.5	144.9
Customers	No.		32,353	37,532	38,004
KWH sales	$Mil.		761.3	1,433.7	1,578.4
Island Power system	MW's	284	367	407	
Capital & Liability	$Mil.		172.0	336.3	445.5
Guam Telephone Authority(GTA)					
Revenues	$Mil.		27.6	39.2	38.3
Customers	No.		38,029	59,554	62,296
Capital & Liability	$Mil.		96.0	176.7	176.7
Public Utility Agency of Guam(PUAG)					
Water: Revenues	$Mil.	7.1	8.8	9.1	
Customers	No.		27,917	32,401	32,962
Consumption	MGD.		15.9	18.9	19.5
Sewage: Revenues	$Mil.		3.1	4.2	4.3
Customers	No.		17,602	18,834	17,670
Discharges	MGD.		10.4	12.8	12.8
Capital & Liability	$Mil.		102.0	155.2	166.3

REVENUES AND EXPENDITURES

Revenues, total	$Mil.		547.4	707.6	679.5
Taxes	$Mil.		413.0	496.0	471.1
Income tax	$Mil.		261.6	303.8	277.9
Section 30	$Mil.		42.0	81.2	54.9
Gross Receipts	$Mil.		110.2	147.7	151.2
Real Property	$Mil.		7.8	9.0	0.0
Other taxes	$Mil.		7.6	6.2	5.9
License fee & permits	$Mil.	10.0	11.2	11.6	
UMP	$Mil.		17.1	10.2	20.3
Federal contributers	$Mil.	93.9	180.3	164.7	
Other revenues	$Mil.		13.4	9.9	11.8
Expenditures, total	$Mil.		363.1	593.0	621.6
Gen Government	$Mil.	56.4	66.6	61.6	
PLP	$Mil.		54.6	84.7	80.3
Public health	$Mil.		27.4	25.5	29.4
Community services	$Mil.	25.7	22.6	21.5	
Recreation	$Mil.		5.4	7.1	7.3
ICR	$Mil.		11.4	19.4	19.3
Transportation	$Mil.		15.8	12.9	8.7
Education	$Mil.		125.7	209.7	194.5
Environment protect	$Mil.	5.9	10.7	8.6	
Economic development	$Mil.		12.4	13.2	15.1
Transfer to pers	$Mil.		0.08	52.6	67.4
Capital project	$Mil.		17.7	48.5	75.8
Interests	$Mil.		3.5	8.9	10.5
Principal	$Mil.		1.0	10.7	21.6

Data Origin: Bureau of Planning 1996 Government of Guam

POPULATION FIGURES AS OF JULY 1, 2001 PACIFIC DAILY NEWS:

Village	Mayor	Population	Housing units	Zip
Hagatna	Felix F. Ungacta 671 477-8045/7	1,100	416	96910
Agana Heights	Paul McDonald 671 472-8285/6393	3,940	1,008	96910
Agat	Johnny Reyes 671 565-2524/4335	5,656	1,300	96915
Asan/Maina	Vicente San Nicolas 671 472-6581/2726	2,090	619	96910
Barrigada	Peter Aguon 671734-3737/5716	8,652	2,143	96913
Chalan Pago/Ordot	Vicente Aguon 671 477-1333/472-8302	5,923	1,047	96910
Dededo	Scott Duenas 632-5203/5019	42,980	7,538	96929
Inarajan	Franklin Taitague 828-8185/2542	3,052	556	96915
Mangilao & UOG	Nonito Blas 671 734-2163/5731	13,313	2,714	96913
Merizo	Rita Tainatongo 671 828-8312/8772	2,163	468	96915
Mongmong-Toto-Maite	Andrew Villagomez 671 477-9090/6758	5,845	1,730	96910
Piti	Isabel Haggard 671 472-1232/3	1,666	557	96915
Santa Rita	Joseph Wesley 671 565-2514/4337	7,500	2,344	96915
Sinajana	Daniel Sablan 477-3323/472-6707	2,853	713	96910
Talofofo	Anthony Leon Guerrero 671 789-1421/3262	3,215	546	96915
Tamuning/Tumon	Concepcion Duenas 671 646-5211/8646	18,012	6,291	96913
Umatac	Tony Quinata 671 828-2940/8258	887	188	96915

Yigo	Robert Lizama 671 653-9446/5248	19,474	3,738	96929
Yona	Jose Terlaje 671 789-1525/4798	6,484	1,361	96915
Guam	total	154,805	16% increase	-

Birth rate: 25.66 births/1,000 population (1994 est.)
Death rate: 3.86 deaths/1,000 population (1994 est.)
Net migration rate: 3 migrant(s)/1,000 population (1994 est.)
Infant mortality rate: 15.17 deaths/1,000 live births (1994 est.)
Life expectancy at birth:
total population: 74.29 years
male: 72.42 years
female: 76.13 years (1994 est.)
Total fertility rate: 2.39 children born/woman (1994 est.)

Senator (party)	Committee	Votes	Phone	Fax
Aguon, Frank Blas Jr (d)	-	27,752	479-4486	479-4827
Bermudes, Eulogio "Eloy" C (d)	-	19,002	472-3513/4	472-3511
Blaz, Anthony C. (r)	-	19,084	472-3557/8	472-3562
Brown, Joanne M S (r)	-	20,655	472-3450/1	472-4090
Calvo, Eduardo "Eddie" (r)	-	27,187	472-4040	472-4100
Camacho, Marcel G. (r)	-	21,596	479-8261-4	472-8223
Forbes, Mark (r)	-	22,629	472-3512/3407/3408	477-5036
Kasperbauer, Larry F.(r)	Vice Speaker	22,425	475-5437	475-2000
Lamorena, Alberto C. V(r)	-	22,181	472-3594/5	472-3588
Leon Guerrero, Carlotta A (r)	-	22,056	472-3416-8	477-1323
Moylan, Kaleo S (r)	-	23,721	472-3342/3	472-3440
Pangelinan, Vicente "Ben" (d)	-	23,316	472-3552-5	472-3556
Salas, John C.(r)	-	19,924	472-3431/2	472-3433
Sanchez, Simon A II(d)	-	23,938	649-5433	647-3234-6
Unpingco, Tony R.(r)	speaker	22,729	472-3455-7	472-3400

TOURISTS	1994	1995
Air Arrivals	1,076,437	1,350,476

Sea Arrivals	10,283	11,354
TOTALS	1,086,720	1,361,830
Japan Tourists	773,349	996,830
Kanto (Tokyo)	349,679	355,422
Chubu(Nagoya)	169,400	214,079
Kinki(Osaka)	94,954	216,450
Tohoku	43,843	53,030
Kyushu	46,686	60,915
Chugoku	26,217	39,448
Hokkaido	24,719	25,798
Shikoku	14,374	26,952
Other Japan	319	0
Okinawa/Miya	3,158	4,125
U.S./Hawaii	66,847	56,626
Philippines	6,811	4,533
Taiwan	38,791	31,816
Korea	118,538	186,264
CNMI	29,635	32,767
Micronesia	26,343	24,349
Other	16,123	17,664
Hotel Occupancy Tax collected	$13,695,652	$20,981,592

IMPORTANT ADDRESSES:

Agency for Human Resource Development AHRD / 304 C Street / Tiyan, Guam 96910 / (671)-475-0750/51

Chamorro Land Trust Commission / 901 Central Ave. / Tiyan, Guam 96910 / (671)-475-4251/52

Chamorro Language Commission / 101-103 H. St. / Tiyan, Guam 96910 / (671)-475-0221/26

Guam Dept of Agriculture / 192 Dairy Road / Mangilao, Guam 96923 / (671)-734-3942 /3

Dept of Commerce / 102-104 M St. / Tiyan, Guam 96910 / (671)-475-0321

Dept of Customs & Quarantine / 101 O St. / Tiyan, Guam 96910 / (671)-475-6202/04

Dept of Education / Bldg. 13-14, 24, 25 Seagull Ave. / Tiyan, Guam 96910 / (671)-475-0546/49/55

Dept of Labor / 504 D. St. / Tiyan, Guam 96910 / (671)-475-0101

Dept of Military Affairs / Bldg. 13-20 Mariner Ave / Tiyan, Guam 96910 / (671)-475-0803

Dept of Parks & Recreation / Bldg. 13-8 Seagull Ave. / Tiyan, Guam 96910 / (671)-475-6250

Department of Public Health and Social Services / Bureau of Management Support BMS / Bldg. 13-13 Seagull Ave. / Tiyan, Guam 96910 / (671)-475-2670

Division of Senior Citizens / 101/103 K. St. / Tiyan, Guam 96910 / (671)-472-0263

Dept of Revenue & Taxation / Bldg. 13-1, 2, 3 Mariner Ave. / Tiyan, Guam 96910 / (671)-475-5000

Dept of Vocational Rehabilitation / 1313/1315 Central Ave. / Tiyan, Guam 96910 / (671)-475-4646/47

Guam Energy Office / 1502 E. Sunset Blvd. / Tiyan, Guam 96910 / (671)-477-0557/0538

Guam Environmental Protection Agency / 102/104 N St. / Tiyan, Guam 96910 / (671)-472-8863/5703

Guam Finance Commission / 101/103 F St. / Tiyan, Guam 96910 / (671)-475-9422/9218

Guam Fire Department / Bldg. 1301 Central Ave. / Tiyan, Guam 96910 / (671)-472-3304/5

Guam Housing Corporation / 827 E. Sunset Blvd / Tiyan, Guam 96910 / (671)-475-4953/54

Guam Police Department / Bldgs. 1300/1301 Central Ave. / Tiyan, Guam 96910 / (671)-475-8473

Guam State Council on Vocational Education / 107 M St. / Tiyan, Guam 96910 / (671)-475-9325/9436

Guam Visitors Bureau P.O. Box 3520 Agana, Guam 96910 Telephone: (671)-646-5278 or (671)-646-5279 FAX: (671)-646-8861 TELEX: (671)-721-6432

Office of the Public Auditor / 1208 E. Sunset Blvd / Tiyan, Guam 96910 / (671)-475-0393

Tiyan Reuse Authority / Bldg. 13-33 Seagull Ave / Tiyan, Guam 96910 / (671)-475-9108/18

Territorial Planning Council / 101/103 N St. / Tiyan, Guam 96910 / (671)-472-9770/71

Veterans Affairs Office / 105 M St / Tiyan, Guam 96910 / (671)-475-4222/3

U.S. Passport Office / 107 B St. / Tiyan, Guam 96910 / (671)-477-8974/1404

-=-=-=-=-=-=-=-=-=-=-=-=-=-=-=-=-=-=-=

CONSULATES ON GUAM

Consulate general of Japan.........	(671)-646-1290
Korea Consulate Office.............	(671)-472-6488
CNMI Marianas/Guam Laison..........	(671)-646-9182
Coordination Counsel for North America	
Republic of China & Taiwan.........	(671)-472-5865
Consulate General of Palau.........	(671)-646-9281
Philippine Consulate General.......	(671)-646-7965
Federate States of Micronesia......	(671)-646-9154

NEW! WORLD OFFSHORE TAX GUIDES

Price: $149.95 each

1.	Andorra Offshore Tax Guide
2.	Anguilla Offshore Tax Guide
3.	Bahamas Offshore Tax Guide
4.	Barbados Offshore Tax Guide
5.	Belize Offshore Tax Guide
6.	Bermuda Offshore Tax Guide
7.	British Virgin Islands Offshore Tax Guide
8.	Cayman Islands Offshore Tax Guide
9.	Cook Islands Offshore Tax Guide
10.	Costa Rica Offshore Tax Guide
11.	Cyprus Offshore Tax Guide
12.	Dubai Offshore Tax Guide
13.	Gibraltar Offshore Tax Guide
14.	Grenada Offshore Tax Guide
15.	Guernsey Offshore Tax Guide
16.	Hong Kong Offshore Tax Guide
17.	Ireland Offshore Tax Guide
18.	Isle of Man Offshore Tax Guide
19.	Jersey Offshore Tax Guide
20.	Labuan Offshore Tax Guide
21.	Liechtenstein Offshore Tax Guide
22.	Luxembourg Offshore Tax Guide
23.	Madeira Offshore Tax Guide
24.	Malta Offshore Tax Guide
25.	Mauritius Offshore Business and Investment Opportunities Handbook
26.	Mauritius Offshore Tax Guide
27.	Monaco Offshore Tax Guide
28.	Nauru Offshore Tax Guide
29.	Netherlands Antilles Offshore Tax Guide
30.	Panama Offshore Tax Guide
31.	Seychelles Offshore Tax Guide
32.	Switzerland Offshore Tax Guide
33.	Turks & Caicos Islands Offshore Tax Guide
34.	Vanuatu Offshore Tax Guide

To order and for additional analytical and marketing information, please contacrt
International Business Publications, USA at:
P.O. Box 15343, Washington, DC 20003, USA. Phone: (202) 546-2103. Fax: (202) 546-3275.
World Business Info Catalog: http://www.ibous.com. E-mail: ibpusa@comcast.net

WORLD HOW TO INVEST, START AND RUN PROFITABLE BUSINESS LIBRARY

Strategic political, geographic, economic, business information, contacts and important developments

Price: $99.95 each

COMPLETE FULL TITLE	ISBN
How to Invest, Start and Run Profitable Business in Afghanistan Guide - Practical Information, Opportunities, Contacts	978-1-4330-8269-6
How to Invest, Start and Run Profitable Business in Aland Guide - Practical Information, Opportunities, Contacts	978-1-4330-8270-2
How to Invest, Start and Run Profitable Business in Albania Guide - Practical Information, Opportunities, Contacts	978-1-4330-8271-9
How to Invest, Start and Run Profitable Business in Algeria Guide - Practical Information, Opportunities, Contacts	978-1-4330-8272-6
How to Invest, Start and Run Profitable Business in Andorra Guide - Practical Information, Opportunities, Contacts	978-1-4330-8273-3
How to Invest, Start and Run Profitable Business in Angola Guide - Practical Information, Opportunities, Contacts	978-1-4330-8275-7
How to Invest, Start and Run Profitable Business in Anguilla Guide - Practical Information, Opportunities, Contacts	978-1-4330-8276-4
How to Invest, Start and Run Profitable Business in Antigua and Barbuda Guide - Practical Information, Opportunities, Contacts	978-1-4330-8277-1
How to Invest, Start and Run Profitable Business in Antilles (Netherlands) Guide - Practical Information, Opportunities, Contacts	978-1-4330-8278-8
How to Invest, Start and Run Profitable Business in Argentina Guide - Practical Information, Opportunities, Contacts	978-1-4330-8279-5
How to Invest, Start and Run Profitable Business in Armenia Guide - Practical Information, Opportunities, Contacts	978-1-4330-8280-1
How to Invest, Start and Run Profitable Business in Aruba Guide - Practical Information, Opportunities, Contacts	978-1-4330-8281-8
How to Invest, Start and Run Profitable Business in Australia Guide - Practical Information, Opportunities, Contacts	978-1-4330-8282-5
How to Invest, Start and Run Profitable Business in Austria Guide - Practical Information, Opportunities, Contacts	978-1-4330-8283-2
How to Invest, Start and Run Profitable Business in Azerbaijan Guide - Practical Information, Opportunities, Contacts	978-1-4330-8284-9
How to Invest, Start and Run Profitable Business in Bahamas Guide - Practical Information, Opportunities, Contacts	978-1-4330-8285-6
How to Invest, Start and Run Profitable Business in Bahrain Guide - Practical Information, Opportunities, Contacts	978-1-4330-8286-3
How to Invest, Start and Run Profitable Business in Bangladesh Guide - Practical Information, Opportunities, Contacts	978-1-4330-8287-0
How to Invest, Start and Run Profitable Business in Barbados Guide - Practical Information, Opportunities, Contacts	978-1-4330-8288-7
How to Invest, Start and Run Profitable Business in Belarus Guide - Practical Information, Opportunities, Contacts	978-1-4330-8289-4

COMPLETE FULL TITLE	ISBN
How to Invest, Start and Run Profitable Business in Belgium Guide - Practical Information, Opportunities, Contacts	978-1-4330-8290-0
How to Invest, Start and Run Profitable Business in Belize Guide - Practical Information, Opportunities, Contacts	978-1-4330-8291-7
How to Invest, Start and Run Profitable Business in Benin Guide - Practical Information, Opportunities, Contacts	978-1-4330-8292-4
How to Invest, Start and Run Profitable Business in Bermuda Guide - Practical Information, Opportunities, Contacts	978-1-4330-8293-1
How to Invest, Start and Run Profitable Business in Bhutan Guide - Practical Information, Opportunities, Contacts	978-1-4330-8294-8
How to Invest, Start and Run Profitable Business in Bolivia Guide - Practical Information, Opportunities, Contacts	978-1-4330-8295-5
How to Invest, Start and Run Profitable Business in Bosnia and Herzegovina Guide - Practical Information, Opportunities, Contacts	978-1-4330-8296-2
How to Invest, Start and Run Profitable Business in Botswana Guide - Practical Information, Opportunities, Contacts	978-1-4330-8297-9
How to Invest, Start and Run Profitable Business in Brazil Guide - Practical Information, Opportunities, Contacts	978-1-4330-8298-6
How to Invest, Start and Run Profitable Business in Brunei Guide - Practical Information, Opportunities, Contacts	978-1-4330-8299-3
How to Invest, Start and Run Profitable Business in Bulgaria Guide - Practical Information, Opportunities, Contacts	978-1-4330-8300-6
How to Invest, Start and Run Profitable Business in Burkina Faso Guide - Practical Information, Opportunities, Contacts	978-1-4330-8301-3
How to Invest, Start and Run Profitable Business in Burundi Guide - Practical Information, Opportunities, Contacts	978-1-4330-8302-0
How to Invest, Start and Run Profitable Business in Cambodia Guide - Practical Information, Opportunities, Contacts	978-1-4330-8303-7
How to Invest, Start and Run Profitable Business in Cameroon Guide - Practical Information, Opportunities, Contacts	978-1-4330-8304-4
How to Invest, Start and Run Profitable Business in Canada Guide - Practical Information, Opportunities, Contacts	978-1-4330-8305-1
How to Invest, Start and Run Profitable Business in Cape Verde Guide - Practical Information, Opportunities, Contacts	978-1-4330-8306-8
How to Invest, Start and Run Profitable Business in Cayman Islands Guide - Practical Information, Opportunities, Contacts	978-1-4330-8307-5
How to Invest, Start and Run Profitable Business in Central African Republic Guide - Practical Information, Opportunities, Contacts	978-1-4330-8308-2
How to Invest, Start and Run Profitable Business in Chad Guide - Practical Information, Opportunities, Contacts	978-1-4330-8309-9
How to Invest, Start and Run Profitable Business in Chile Guide - Practical Information, Opportunities, Contacts	978-1-4330-8310-5
How to Invest, Start and Run Profitable Business in China Guide - Practical Information, Opportunities, Contacts	978-1-4330-8311-2
How to Invest, Start and Run Profitable Business in Colombia Guide - Practical Information, Opportunities, Contacts	978-1-4330-8312-9
How to Invest, Start and Run Profitable Business in Comoros Guide - Practical Information, Opportunities, Contacts	978-1-4330-8313-6
How to Invest, Start and Run Profitable Business in Congo Guide - Practical Information, Opportunities, Contacts	978-1-4330-8314-3
How to Invest, Start and Run Profitable Business in Congo, Democratic Republic Guide - Practical Information, Opportunities, Contacts	978-1-4330-8315-0
How to Invest, Start and Run Profitable Business in Cook Islands Guide - Practical Information, Opportunities, Contacts	978-1-4330-8316-7
How to Invest, Start and Run Profitable Business in Costa Rica Guide - Practical Information, Opportunities, Contacts	978-1-4330-8317-4
How to Invest, Start and Run Profitable Business in Cote d'Ivoire Guide - Practical Information, Opportunities, Contacts	978-1-4330-8318-1
How to Invest, Start and Run Profitable Business in Croatia Guide - Practical Information, Opportunities, Contacts	978-1-4330-8319-8
How to Invest, Start and Run Profitable Business in Cuba Guide - Practical Information,	978-1-4330-8320-4

COMPLETE FULL TITLE	ISBN
Opportunities, Contacts	
How to Invest, Start and Run Profitable Business in Cyprus Guide - Practical Information, Opportunities, Contacts	978-1-4330-8321-1
How to Invest, Start and Run Profitable Business in Czech Republic Guide - Practical Information, Opportunities, Contacts	978-1-4330-8322-8
How to Invest, Start and Run Profitable Business in Denmark Guide - Practical Information, Opportunities, Contacts	978-1-4330-8323-5
How to Invest, Start and Run Profitable Business in Djibouti Guide - Practical Information, Opportunities, Contacts	978-1-4330-8324-2
How to Invest, Start and Run Profitable Business in Dominica Guide - Practical Information, Opportunities, Contacts	978-1-4330-8325-9
How to Invest, Start and Run Profitable Business in Dominican Republic Guide - Practical Information, Opportunities, Contacts	978-1-4330-8326-6
How to Invest, Start and Run Profitable Business in Ecuador Guide - Practical Information, Opportunities, Contacts	978-1-4330-8327-3
How to Invest, Start and Run Profitable Business in Egypt Guide - Practical Information, Opportunities, Contacts	978-1-4330-8328-0
How to Invest, Start and Run Profitable Business in El Salvador Guide - Practical Information, Opportunities, Contacts	978-1-4330-8329-7
How to Invest, Start and Run Profitable Business in Equatorial Guinea Guide - Practical Information, Opportunities, Contacts	978-1-4330-8330-3
How to Invest, Start and Run Profitable Business in Eritrea Guide - Practical Information, Opportunities, Contacts	978-1-4330-8331-0
How to Invest, Start and Run Profitable Business in Estonia Guide - Practical Information, Opportunities, Contacts	978-1-4330-8332-7
How to Invest, Start and Run Profitable Business in Ethiopia Guide - Practical Information, Opportunities, Contacts	978-1-4330-8333-4
How to Invest, Start and Run Profitable Business in Falkland Islands Guide - Practical Information, Opportunities, Contacts	978-1-4330-8334-1
How to Invest, Start and Run Profitable Business in Faroes Islands Guide - Practical Information, Opportunities, Contacts	978-1-4330-8335-8
How to Invest, Start and Run Profitable Business in Fiji Guide - Practical Information, Opportunities, Contacts	978-1-4330-8336-5
How to Invest, Start and Run Profitable Business in Finland Guide - Practical Information, Opportunities, Contacts	978-1-4330-8337-2
How to Invest, Start and Run Profitable Business in France Guide - Practical Information, Opportunities, Contacts	978-1-4330-8338-9
How to Invest, Start and Run Profitable Business in Gabon Guide - Practical Information, Opportunities, Contacts	978-1-4330-8339-6
How to Invest, Start and Run Profitable Business in Gambia Guide - Practical Information, Opportunities, Contacts	978-1-4330-8340-2
How to Invest, Start and Run Profitable Business in Georgia Republic Guide - Practical Information, Opportunities, Contacts	978-1-4330-8341-9
How to Invest, Start and Run Profitable Business in Germany Guide - Practical Information, Opportunities, Contacts	978-1-4330-8342-6
How to Invest, Start and Run Profitable Business in Ghana Guide - Practical Information, Opportunities, Contacts	978-1-4330-8343-3
How to Invest, Start and Run Profitable Business in Gibraltar Guide - Practical Information, Opportunities, Contacts	978-1-4330-8344-0
How to Invest, Start and Run Profitable Business in Greece Guide - Practical Information, Opportunities, Contacts	978-1-4330-8345-7
How to Invest, Start and Run Profitable Business in Greenland Guide - Practical Information, Opportunities, Contacts	978-1-4330-8346-4
How to Invest, Start and Run Profitable Business in Grenada Guide - Practical Information, Opportunities, Contacts	978-1-4330-8347-1
How to Invest, Start and Run Profitable Business in Guam Guide - Practical Information, Opportunities, Contacts	978-1-4330-8348-8
How to Invest, Start and Run Profitable Business in Guatemala Guide - Practical Information, Opportunities, Contacts	978-1-4330-8349-5
How to Invest, Start and Run Profitable Business in Guernsey Guide - Practical Information, Opportunities, Contacts	978-1-4330-8350-1

COMPLETE FULL TITLE	ISBN
How to Invest, Start and Run Profitable Business in Guinea Guide - Practical Information, Opportunities, Contacts	978-1-4330-8351-8
How to Invest, Start and Run Profitable Business in Guinea-Bissau Guide - Practical Information, Opportunities, Contacts	978-1-4330-8352-5
How to Invest, Start and Run Profitable Business in Guyana Guide - Practical Information, Opportunities, Contacts	978-1-4330-8353-2
How to Invest, Start and Run Profitable Business in Haiti Guide - Practical Information, Opportunities, Contacts	978-1-4330-8354-9
How to Invest, Start and Run Profitable Business in Honduras Guide - Practical Information, Opportunities, Contacts	978-1-4330-8355-6
How to Invest, Start and Run Profitable Business in Hungary Guide - Practical Information, Opportunities, Contacts	978-1-4330-8356-3
How to Invest, Start and Run Profitable Business in Iceland Guide - Practical Information, Opportunities, Contacts	978-1-4330-8357-0
How to Invest, Start and Run Profitable Business in India Guide - Practical Information, Opportunities, Contacts	978-1-4330-8358-7
How to Invest, Start and Run Profitable Business in Indonesia Guide - Practical Information, Opportunities, Contacts	978-1-4330-8359-4
How to Invest, Start and Run Profitable Business in Iran Guide - Practical Information, Opportunities, Contacts	978-1-4330-8360-0
How to Invest, Start and Run Profitable Business in Iraq Guide - Practical Information, Opportunities, Contacts	978-1-4330-8361-7
How to Invest, Start and Run Profitable Business in Ireland Guide - Practical Information, Opportunities, Contacts	978-1-4330-8362-4
How to Invest, Start and Run Profitable Business in Israel Guide - Practical Information, Opportunities, Contacts	978-1-4330-8363-1
How to Invest, Start and Run Profitable Business in Italy Guide - Practical Information, Opportunities, Contacts	978-1-4330-8364-8
How to Invest, Start and Run Profitable Business in Jamaica Guide - Practical Information, Opportunities, Contacts	978-1-4330-8365-5
How to Invest, Start and Run Profitable Business in Japan Guide - Practical Information, Opportunities, Contacts	978-1-4330-8366-2
How to Invest, Start and Run Profitable Business in Jersey Guide - Practical Information, Opportunities, Contacts	978-1-4330-8367-9
How to Invest, Start and Run Profitable Business in Jordan Guide - Practical Information, Opportunities, Contacts	978-1-4330-8368-6
How to Invest, Start and Run Profitable Business in Kazakhstan Guide - Practical Information, Opportunities, Contacts	978-1-4330-8369-3
How to Invest, Start and Run Profitable Business in Kenya Guide - Practical Information, Opportunities, Contacts	978-1-4330-8370-9
How to Invest, Start and Run Profitable Business in Kiribati Guide - Practical Information, Opportunities, Contacts	978-1-4330-8371-6
How to Invest, Start and Run Profitable Business in Korea, North Guide - Practical Information, Opportunities, Contacts	978-1-4330-8372-3
How to Invest, Start and Run Profitable Business in Korea, South Guide - Practical Information, Opportunities, Contacts	978-1-4330-8373-0
How to Invest, Start and Run Profitable Business in Kosovo Guide - Practical Information, Opportunities, Contacts	978-1-4330-8374-7
How to Invest, Start and Run Profitable Business in Kurdistan Guide - Practical Information, Opportunities, Contacts	978-1-4330-8375-4
How to Invest, Start and Run Profitable Business in Kuwait Guide - Practical Information, Opportunities, Contacts	978-1-4330-8376-1
How to Invest, Start and Run Profitable Business in Kyrgyzstan Guide - Practical Information, Opportunities, Contacts	978-1-4330-8377-8
How to Invest, Start and Run Profitable Business in Laos Guide - Practical Information, Opportunities, Contacts	978-1-4330-8378-5
How to Invest, Start and Run Profitable Business in Latvia Guide - Practical Information, Opportunities, Contacts	978-1-4330-8379-2
How to Invest, Start and Run Profitable Business in Lebanon Guide - Practical Information, Opportunities, Contacts	978-1-4330-8380-8
How to Invest, Start and Run Profitable Business in Lesotho Guide - Practical Information,	978-1-4330-8381-5

COMPLETE FULL TITLE	ISBN
Opportunities, Contacts	
How to Invest, Start and Run Profitable Business in Liberia Guide - Practical Information, Opportunities, Contacts	978-1-4330-8382-2
How to Invest, Start and Run Profitable Business in Libya Guide - Practical Information, Opportunities, Contacts	978-1-4330-8383-9
How to Invest, Start and Run Profitable Business in Liechtenstein Guide - Practical Information, Opportunities, Contacts	978-1-4330-8384-6
How to Invest, Start and Run Profitable Business in Lithuania Guide - Practical Information, Opportunities, Contacts	978-1-4330-8385-3
How to Invest, Start and Run Profitable Business in Luxembourg Guide - Practical Information, Opportunities, Contacts	978-1-4330-8386-0
How to Invest, Start and Run Profitable Business in Macao Guide - Practical Information, Opportunities, Contacts	978-1-4330-8387-7
How to Invest, Start and Run Profitable Business in Macedonia Guide - Practical Information, Opportunities, Contacts	978-1-4330-8388-4
How to Invest, Start and Run Profitable Business in Madagascar Guide - Practical Information, Opportunities, Contacts	978-1-4330-8389-1
How to Invest, Start and Run Profitable Business in Madeira Guide - Practical Information, Opportunities, Contacts	978-1-4330-8390-7
How to Invest, Start and Run Profitable Business in Malawi Guide - Practical Information, Opportunities, Contacts	978-1-4330-8391-4
How to Invest, Start and Run Profitable Business in Malaysia Guide - Practical Information, Opportunities, Contacts	978-1-4330-8392-1
How to Invest, Start and Run Profitable Business in Maldives Guide - Practical Information, Opportunities, Contacts	978-1-4330-8393-8
How to Invest, Start and Run Profitable Business in Mali Guide - Practical Information, Opportunities, Contacts	978-1-4330-8394-5
How to Invest, Start and Run Profitable Business in Malta Guide - Practical Information, Opportunities, Contacts	978-1-4330-8395-2
How to Invest, Start and Run Profitable Business in Man Guide - Practical Information, Opportunities, Contacts	978-1-4330-8396-9
How to Invest, Start and Run Profitable Business in Marshall Islands Guide - Practical Information, Opportunities, Contacts	978-1-4330-8397-6
How to Invest, Start and Run Profitable Business in Mauritania Guide - Practical Information, Opportunities, Contacts	978-1-4330-8398-3
How to Invest, Start and Run Profitable Business in Mauritius Guide - Practical Information, Opportunities, Contacts	978-1-4330-8399-0
How to Invest, Start and Run Profitable Business in Mayotte Guide - Practical Information, Opportunities, Contacts	978-1-4330-8400-3
How to Invest, Start and Run Profitable Business in Mexico Guide - Practical Information, Opportunities, Contacts	978-1-4330-8401-0
How to Invest, Start and Run Profitable Business in Micronesia Guide - Practical Information, Opportunities, Contacts	978-1-4330-8402-7
How to Invest, Start and Run Profitable Business in Moldova Guide - Practical Information, Opportunities, Contacts	978-1-4330-8403-4
How to Invest, Start and Run Profitable Business in Monaco Guide - Practical Information, Opportunities, Contacts	978-1-4330-8404-1
How to Invest, Start and Run Profitable Business in Mongolia Guide - Practical Information, Opportunities, Contacts	978-1-4330-8405-8
How to Invest, Start and Run Profitable Business in Monserrat Guide - Practical Information, Opportunities, Contacts	978-1-4330-8406-5
How to Invest, Start and Run Profitable Business in Morocco Guide - Practical Information, Opportunities, Contacts	978-1-4330-8407-2
How to Invest, Start and Run Profitable Business in Mozambique Guide - Practical Information, Opportunities, Contacts	978-1-4330-8408-9
How to Invest, Start and Run Profitable Business in Myanmar Guide - Practical Information, Opportunities, Contacts	978-1-4330-8409-6
How to Invest, Start and Run Profitable Business in Namibia Guide - Practical Information, Opportunities, Contacts	978-1-4330-8410-2
How to Invest, Start and Run Profitable Business in Nauru Guide - Practical Information, Opportunities, Contacts	978-1-4330-8411-9

COMPLETE FULL TITLE	ISBN
How to Invest, Start and Run Profitable Business in Nepal Guide - Practical Information, Opportunities, Contacts	978-1-4330-8412-6
How to Invest, Start and Run Profitable Business in Netherlands Guide - Practical Information, Opportunities, Contacts	978-1-4330-8413-3
How to Invest, Start and Run Profitable Business in New Caledonia Guide - Practical Information, Opportunities, Contacts	978-1-4330-8414-0
How to Invest, Start and Run Profitable Business in New Zealand Guide - Practical Information, Opportunities, Contacts	978-1-4330-8415-7
How to Invest, Start and Run Profitable Business in Nicaragua Guide - Practical Information, Opportunities, Contacts	978-1-4330-8416-4
How to Invest, Start and Run Profitable Business in Niger Guide - Practical Information, Opportunities, Contacts	978-1-4330-8417-1
How to Invest, Start and Run Profitable Business in Nigeria Guide - Practical Information, Opportunities, Contacts	978-1-4330-8418-8
How to Invest, Start and Run Profitable Business in Niue Guide - Practical Information, Opportunities, Contacts	978-1-4330-8419-5
How to Invest, Start and Run Profitable Business in Northern Mariana Islands Guide - Practical Information, Opportunities, Contacts	978-1-4330-8420-1
How to Invest, Start and Run Profitable Business in Norway Guide - Practical Information, Opportunities, Contacts	978-1-4330-8421-8
How to Invest, Start and Run Profitable Business in Oman Guide - Practical Information, Opportunities, Contacts	978-1-4330-8422-5
How to Invest, Start and Run Profitable Business in Pakistan Guide - Practical Information, Opportunities, Contacts	978-1-4330-8423-2
How to Invest, Start and Run Profitable Business in Palau Guide - Practical Information, Opportunities, Contacts	978-1-4330-8424-9
How to Invest, Start and Run Profitable Business in Palestine Guide - Practical Information, Opportunities, Contacts	978-1-4330-8425-6
How to Invest, Start and Run Profitable Business in Panama Guide - Practical Information, Opportunities, Contacts	978-1-4330-8426-3
How to Invest, Start and Run Profitable Business in Papua New Guinea Guide - Practical Information, Opportunities, Contacts	978-1-4330-8427-0
How to Invest, Start and Run Profitable Business in Paraguay Guide - Practical Information, Opportunities, Contacts	978-1-4330-8428-7
How to Invest, Start and Run Profitable Business in Peru Guide - Practical Information, Opportunities, Contacts	978-1-4330-8429-4
How to Invest, Start and Run Profitable Business in Philippines Guide - Practical Information, Opportunities, Contacts	978-1-4330-8430-0
How to Invest, Start and Run Profitable Business in Pitcairn Islands Guide - Practical Information, Opportunities, Contacts	978-1-4330-8431-7
How to Invest, Start and Run Profitable Business in Poland Guide - Practical Information, Opportunities, Contacts	978-1-4330-8432-4
How to Invest, Start and Run Profitable Business in Polynesia French Guide - Practical Information, Opportunities, Contacts	978-1-4330-8433-1
How to Invest, Start and Run Profitable Business in Portugal Guide - Practical Information, Opportunities, Contacts	978-1-4330-8434-8
How to Invest, Start and Run Profitable Business in Qatar Guide - Practical Information, Opportunities, Contacts	978-1-4330-8435-5
How to Invest, Start and Run Profitable Business in Romania Guide - Practical Information, Opportunities, Contacts	978-1-4330-8436-2
How to Invest, Start and Run Profitable Business in Russia Guide - Practical Information, Opportunities, Contacts	978-1-4330-8437-9
How to Invest, Start and Run Profitable Business in Rwanda Guide - Practical Information, Opportunities, Contacts	978-1-4330-8438-6
How to Invest, Start and Run Profitable Business in Saint Kitts and Nevis Guide - Practical Information, Opportunities, Contacts	978-1-4330-8439-3
How to Invest, Start and Run Profitable Business in Saint Lucia Guide - Practical Information, Opportunities, Contacts	978-1-4330-8440-9
How to Invest, Start and Run Profitable Business in Saint Vincent and The Grenadines Guide - Practical Information, Opportunities, Contacts	978-1-4330-8441-6
How to Invest, Start and Run Profitable Business in Samoa (American) A Guide - Practical	978-1-4330-8442-3

COMPLETE FULL TITLE	ISBN
Information, Opportunities, Contacts	
How to Invest, Start and Run Profitable Business in Samoa (Western) Guide - Practical Information, Opportunities, Contacts	978-1-4330-8443-0
How to Invest, Start and Run Profitable Business in San Marino Guide - Practical Information, Opportunities, Contacts	978-1-4330-8444-7
How to Invest, Start and Run Profitable Business in Sao Tome and Principe Guide - Practical Information, Opportunities, Contacts	978-1-4330-8445-4
How to Invest, Start and Run Profitable Business in Saudi Arabia Guide - Practical Information, Opportunities, Contacts	978-1-4330-8446-1
How to Invest, Start and Run Profitable Business in Scotland Guide - Practical Information, Opportunities, Contacts	978-1-4330-8447-8
How to Invest, Start and Run Profitable Business in Senegal Guide - Practical Information, Opportunities, Contacts	978-1-4330-8448-5
How to Invest, Start and Run Profitable Business in Serbia Guide - Practical Information, Opportunities, Contacts	978-1-4330-8449-2
How to Invest, Start and Run Profitable Business in Seychelles Guide - Practical Information, Opportunities, Contacts	978-1-4330-8450-8
How to Invest, Start and Run Profitable Business in Sierra Leone Guide - Practical Information, Opportunities, Contacts	978-1-4330-8451-5
How to Invest, Start and Run Profitable Business in Singapore Guide - Practical Information, Opportunities, Contacts	978-1-4330-8452-2
How to Invest, Start and Run Profitable Business in Slovakia Guide - Practical Information, Opportunities, Contacts	978-1-4330-8453-9
How to Invest, Start and Run Profitable Business in Slovenia Guide - Practical Information, Opportunities, Contacts	978-1-4330-8454-6
How to Invest, Start and Run Profitable Business in Solomon Islands Guide - Practical Information, Opportunities, Contacts	978-1-4330-8455-3
How to Invest, Start and Run Profitable Business in Somalia Guide - Practical Information, Opportunities, Contacts	978-1-4330-8456-0
How to Invest, Start and Run Profitable Business in South Africa Guide - Practical Information, Opportunities, Contacts	978-1-4330-8457-7
How to Invest, Start and Run Profitable Business in Spain Guide - Practical Information, Opportunities, Contacts	978-1-4330-8458-4
How to Invest, Start and Run Profitable Business in Sri Lanka Guide - Practical Information, Opportunities, Contacts	978-1-4330-8459-1
How to Invest, Start and Run Profitable Business in St. Helena Guide - Practical Information, Opportunities, Contacts	978-1-4330-8460-7
How to Invest, Start and Run Profitable Business in St. Pierre & Miguel Guide - Practical Information, Opportunities, Contacts	978-1-4330-8461-4
How to Invest, Start and Run Profitable Business in Sudan (North) Guide - Practical Information, Opportunities, Contacts	978-1-4330-8462-1
How to Invest, Start and Run Profitable Business in Suriname Guide - Practical Information, Opportunities, Contacts	978-1-4330-8463-8
How to Invest, Start and Run Profitable Business in Swaziland Guide - Practical Information, Opportunities, Contacts	978-1-4330-8464-5
How to Invest, Start and Run Profitable Business in Sweden Guide - Practical Information, Opportunities, Contacts	978-1-4330-8465-2
How to Invest, Start and Run Profitable Business in Switzerland Guide - Practical Information, Opportunities, Contacts	978-1-4330-8466-9
How to Invest, Start and Run Profitable Business in Syria Guide - Practical Information, Opportunities, Contacts	978-1-4330-8467-6
How to Invest, Start and Run Profitable Business in Taiwan Guide - Practical Information, Opportunities, Contacts	978-1-4330-8468-3
How to Invest, Start and Run Profitable Business in Tajikistan Guide - Practical Information, Opportunities, Contacts	978-1-4330-8469-0
How to Invest, Start and Run Profitable Business in Tanzania Guide - Practical Information, Opportunities, Contacts	978-1-4330-8470-6
How to Invest, Start and Run Profitable Business in Thailand Guide - Practical Information, Opportunities, Contacts	978-1-4330-8471-3
How to Invest, Start and Run Profitable Business in Togo Guide - Practical Information, Opportunities, Contacts	978-1-4330-8472-0

COMPLETE FULL TITLE	ISBN
How to Invest, Start and Run Profitable Business in Tonga Guide - Practical Information, Opportunities, Contacts	978-1-4330-8473-7
How to Invest, Start and Run Profitable Business in Trinidad and Tobago Guide - Practical Information, Opportunities, Contacts	978-1-4330-8474-4
How to Invest, Start and Run Profitable Business in Tunisia Guide - Practical Information, Opportunities, Contacts	978-1-4330-8475-1
How to Invest, Start and Run Profitable Business in Turkey Guide - Practical Information, Opportunities, Contacts	978-1-4330-8476-8
How to Invest, Start and Run Profitable Business in Turkmenistan Guide - Practical Information, Opportunities, Contacts	978-1-4330-8477-5
How to Invest, Start and Run Profitable Business in Turks & Caicos Guide - Practical Information, Opportunities, Contacts	978-1-4330-8478-2
How to Invest, Start and Run Profitable Business in Tuvalu Guide - Practical Information, Opportunities, Contacts	978-1-4330-8479-9
How to Invest, Start and Run Profitable Business in Uganda Guide - Practical Information, Opportunities, Contacts	978-1-4330-8480-5
How to Invest, Start and Run Profitable Business in Ukraine Guide - Practical Information, Opportunities, Contacts	978-1-4330-8481-2
How to Invest, Start and Run Profitable Business in the United Arab Emirates Guide - Practical Information, Opportunities, Contacts	978-1-4330-8482-9
How to Invest, Start and Run Profitable Business in United Kingdom Guide - Practical Information, Opportunities, Contacts	978-1-4330-8483-6
How to Invest, Start and Run Profitable Business in United States Guide - Practical Information, Opportunities, Contacts	978-1-4330-8484-3
How to Invest, Start and Run Profitable Business in Uruguay Guide - Practical Information, Opportunities, Contacts	978-1-4330-8485-0
How to Invest, Start and Run Profitable Business in Uzbekistan Guide - Practical Information, Opportunities, Contacts	978-1-4330-8486-7
How to Invest, Start and Run Profitable Business in Vanuatu Guide - Practical Information, Opportunities, Contacts	978-1-4330-8487-4
How to Invest, Start and Run Profitable Business in Vatican City Guide - Practical Information, Opportunities, Contacts	978-1-4330-8488-1
How to Invest, Start and Run Profitable Business in Venezuela Guide - Practical Information, Opportunities, Contacts	978-1-4330-8489-8
How to Invest, Start and Run Profitable Business in Vietnam Guide - Practical Information, Opportunities, Contacts	978-1-4330-8490-4
How to Invest, Start and Run Profitable Business in Virgin Islands, British Guide - Practical Information, Opportunities, Contacts	978-1-4330-8491-1
How to Invest, Start and Run Profitable Business in Wake Atoll Guide - Practical Information, Opportunities, Contacts	978-1-4330-8492-8
How to Invest, Start and Run Profitable Business in Wallis & Futuna Guide - Practical Information, Opportunities, Contacts	978-1-4330-8493-5
How to Invest, Start and Run Profitable Business in Western Sahara Guide - Practical Information, Opportunities, Contacts	978-1-4330-8494-2
How to Invest, Start and Run Profitable Business in Yemen Guide - Practical Information, Opportunities, Contacts	978-1-4330-8495-9
How to Invest, Start and Run Profitable Business in Zambia Guide - Practical Information, Opportunities, Contacts	978-1-4330-8496-6
How to Invest, Start and Run Profitable Business in Zimbabwe Guide - Practical Information, Opportunities, Contacts	978-1-4330-8497-3
How to Invest, Start and Run Profitable Business in Sudan (South) Guide - Practical Information, Opportunities, Contacts	978-1-4330-8498-0

To order and for additional analytical and marketing information, please contacts
International Business Publications, USA at:
P.O. Box 15343, Washington, DC 20003, USA. Phone: (202) 546-210 Fax: (202) 546-32
E-mail: ibpusa3@gmail.com

www.ingramcontent.com/pod-product-compliance
Ingram Content Group UK Ltd.
Pitfield, Milton Keynes, MK11 3LW, UK
UKHW051459290926
15471UKWH00008B/1297

9 781433 083488